THE UNITED STATES ARMY
AND RECONSTRUCTION

THE

UNITED STATES ARMY

AND

RECONSTRUCTION

1865-1877

★ ★ ★ ★ ★ ★ ★

by
James E. Sefton

LOUISIANA STATE UNIVERSITY PRESS
BATON ROUGE

Copyright © 1967 by
LOUISIANA STATE UNIVERSITY PRESS

Library of Congress Catalog Card Number: 67-21377
Manufactured in the United States of America by
Thos. J. Moran's Sons, Inc.
Designed by Jules B. McKee

To
My Mother
and
the Memory of
My Father

Preface

Some Thoughts Upon the Work of Others
and Upon the Sources

BOOKS and articles dealing with Reconstruction are legion, but none offer any satisfactory treatment of the Army's role in that troubled twelve-year period. We have heard about the "prostrate South" and about its great postwar social and economic problems, largely from the still useful works of William A. Dunning and his students. We have heard about the unfortunate and undeniable plight of the Negro and about the obvious need for some form of protection for the Negro's rights, from works of more recent vintage. And we have heard about the purely political aspects of Reconstruction, notably the struggle between President Johnson and Congress, from a long and still lengthening list of historians. But we have heard little about the role of the United States Army as an occupation force, except as a peripheral topic in works having a different focus. An investigation of the problems the Army faced in the South, as a military institution enforcing civil policy, in addition to being valuable as a study in military history, also throws new and different light on past and present interpretations of the political, constitutional, and social aspects of Reconstruction.

In recent years historians have showed renewed and sustained interest in Reconstruction. Their efforts, however, have been principally directed toward revising earlier appraisals of Andrew Johnson and the "Radical Republicans." Kenneth Stampp, David Donald, Eric McKitrick, John and LaWanda Cox, W. R. Brock, John Hope Franklin, and Harold M. Hyman have all recently produced significant works; but only the last two have showed much interest in the military aspect or offered significant conclusions with regard to the Army's role. Franklin, in supporting the contention that Radical Reconstruction was not really hard on the South, argues that the power and influence of the Army between 1867 and 1877 was small and that federal military activity was negligible. There is more to the basic question of whether Radical Reconstruction was hard on the South than just the matter of military power, but Franklin's position on the Army's influence is untenable. He bases his conclusion simply on the number of troops in the South at given times, which superficially may seem a sound analysis; in reality, however, power, influence, and activity are functions of much more than mere numbers.

Hyman, working in part with the late Benjamin P. Thomas, deals in greater detail than Franklin with the Army in the South, but his analysis also presents difficulties. The Hyman thesis is essentially that the struggle between Johnson and Congress should be viewed as a struggle for control of the Southern occupation forces. These forces were under executive leadership in mid-1865 but three years later, according to this interpretation, were essentially a legislative agency. Johnson is the shortsighted, obstinate President who alienates the Army by a too-lenient policy and by failure to support the Army's Southern activities; Stanton and Grant shield the soldiers from the ill effects of Johnson's actions and facilitate the Army's transfer from an executive to a legislative agency.

Hyman's case is weakened by doubtful interpretations of critical events during 1866–68. Actually, many of the Army's actions never received presidential review, and of those that did, most did not come before him in a form which necessitated definite action on his part. Consequently, whatever action Johnson took was often upon his own initiative. Because his action was both voluntary and discretionary, it is particularly important to realize that he did not often directly overrule a general's decision, and in several instances the fact that he did *not* do so is even more significant. On the other hand, there were occasions when Johnson supported the Army in conflicts with civil officials and approved sentences imposed by military commissions.

In contrast to the contention that Johnson precipitated most of the problems which plagued generals in the South, it can be demonstrated that Congress caused the Army fully as much difficulty as the President, if not more. The lawmakers refused acquiescence in the results of Johnson's plan in December, 1865. They then kept the Army in suspense as to the national policy on reconstruction by frittering away the entire year of 1866, passing only four significant laws bearing on the Southern question. Two of these which made the Army's task more difficult Johnson opposed (though not for that reason); the one which helped the Army he did not veto. By the spring of 1867 Congress finally formulated a "plan" of reconstruction, but in such vague terms that for several more months the Army was still not sure what powers it possessed. It is clear from recent research that some Congressmen objected to Johnson's plan because of their sincere and understandable concern that it did not require sufficient repentance from the South or ensure the inviolability of the Negro's civil and political rights. It is also clear that the composition of Congress, and other factors, partially account for the delay in formulating a replacement plan. But recognition of these things does not alter the *fact* that Congress' action of December, 1865, plus its inaction of the following months, taken together, left the Army in a quandary over national policy and thus compounded the Army's problems.

The idea that the Army changed from an executive to a legislative agency is not really as remarkable as it might seem. A clear Constitutional provision does, to be sure, make the Executive the Commander-in-Chief. However, that provision does not prevent Congress from using the Army to carry out a law; and once such a law is passed, the Army becomes *ipso facto* a "legislative agency." In the case at hand, the Army was by far the most important instrument of federal authority in the South, and it was the only available enforcer of national reconstruction policy, regardless of whether that policy was under executive leadership or congressional. Hence, the statement that the Army became a legislative rather than executive agency has no real meaning. Indeed, it is debatable whether Johnson really lost all control of the Army in the South by virtue of the 1867 legislation. The ultimate measure of control would seem to be the power to remove Southern commanders, and Johnson certainly exercised that power after July, 1867. The 1867 legislation on the high command of the Army was meant to reduce Johnson's powers as Commander-in-Chief, but the full extent of its effectiveness was never demonstrated, and the First Reconstruction Act would have made the Army a "legislative agency" even had the other measure not been passed.

Because Thomas and Hyman are primarily concerned with War Secretary Edwin M. Stanton, their work is very properly Washington-centered; but when one's primary concern is the Army during Reconstruction, one's focus must be carefully divided between Washington and the South. If insufficient attention is accorded to Washington, where the highest level political and military decisions were made, or to the South, where these decisions were executed, the picture that emerges will be one of the Army operating in a vacuum. Among the indispensable records for studying the Army during Reconstruction are the files of correspondence and orders kept at command posts throughout the South and now lodged in the National Archives. The bulk of these records has not been heretofore exploited by students of Reconstruction. Even though these records are vast, there are still gaps in them, and certain types of documents are sometimes missing for particular headquarters, especially at the post or garrison level. Both manuscript and printed copies of orders exist; outgoing correspondence was copied into chronologically organized large bound letterbooks; incoming correspondence was briefed in registers and the original copies put into boxes after receiving document file numbers. Other useful types of records, such as files of legal opinions and records of military courts, are also available.

Although the Army was generally careful to keep all important papers, it did not always keep them in a fashion to please modern investigators. Sometimes it is possible to find complete records of an event, with pertinent correspondence, all in the same place; but just as often one must piece the details together from scattered material. The system of passing papers up and down the chain of command, with each headquarters adding an endorsement, facilitates the tracing of particular cases; but since the headquarters that retained final possession of a document did not always add a concluding endorsement, one is sometimes hard put to ascertain the final disposition of a case. Further, military records do not always indicate how a particular incident turned out if the case passed from Army hands into the jurisdiction of the civil authorities. The Army's own records contain evidence on which to base criticism of military actions since letters of complaint from citizens received the same treatment as other correspondence.

The records kept at Washington headquarters must also be consulted, though previous historians have done more with these than with the ones kept in the South. The nature of the material is similar though even more voluminous. Most important are the records of the Adjutant General's Office, through which the bulk of official military correspondence passed. The Office of the Secretary of War and the Headquarters of the Army also maintained records, but they are of secondary importance to those of the Adjutant General. One characteristic of all military record collections is duplication. For any given piece of correspondence, the researcher can expect to find its text in the letterbook of the headquarters which sent it, the original signed copy in the records of another headquarters (not necessarily the one to which it was addressed), and copies of it in two or three other locations.

Official records cannot provide the whole story; collections of personal papers form an important supplement. Not all important individuals kept their private papers, however; and in some cases, because a general's family was with him in the South and he wrote few letters, the existing collections are thin on Reconstruction. Further, the aloofness which many officers displayed toward politics curtailed their correspondence with congressional and party leaders.

No investigator could possibly make a complete search through the hundreds of thousands of official documents and the many collections of personal papers that bear on military reconstruction, but I believe I have made a more thorough investigation of some parts of the official records than any of my predecessors, and have made extensive use of the sources as a whole. Indeed, if all the possible sources of information are counted, there is probably enough material to warrant short monographs on the Army's role in each Southern state. The following account, therefore, must of necessity omit repetitive illustrations and details. If the reader comes away from this account with a clearer understanding of the Army's role in the South, with some different insight into other aspects of Reconstruction, and perhaps with some ideas that prompt him to further inquiry of his own, then I shall be satisfied.

Acknowledgments

Without wishing to divest myself of responsibility for any short-comings in this volume, I would like to express my sincere gratitude of some of the many persons who have been of assistance during its many stages of preparation. The University of California, Los Angeles, through its program of research grants for graduate students, facilitated an essential trip to Washington, D.C. Of the many archivists and librarians who made available their knowledge and skills I especially want to thank Mr. Victor Gondos of the National Archives' Old Army Branch and his assistants, Mrs. Sara D. Jackson, Mr. Milton K. Chamberlain, and Mr. David C. Haas, as well as Dr. C. Percy Powell and other members of the staff at the Library of Congress Manuscripts Division.

Among the many instructors who have taken an interest in my work, my mentor, Professor Brainerd Dyer, deserves the greatest and most profound thanks. He did not seek to impose his own interpretations upon me; he made me wary of the problems and pitfalls of historical research and analysis of evidence; and he greatly improved the clarity and precision of my method of expression. I also wish to thank the other members of my doctoral committee for their interest and encouragement, and particularly Professors Eugene N. Anderson and Keith B. Berwick, who willingly subjected themselves to the reading of this work in its original, unrevised form as a dissertation and made many helpful suggestions and criticisms. Individual thanks are also due to Professor David G. Farrelly of the Political Science Department, a member of my committee for the first two years of its existence, for his investment of time and interest in my graduate work. Two of my former U.C.L.A.

instructors who are now at other institutions deserve special mention. Professor Bradford Perkins, now at the University of Michigan, always took a gratifying interest in my endeavors. Professor Harold M. Hyman, now at the University of Illinois, supervised some very early research on this topic for an undergraduate project in the spring and fall of 1960 and suggested the fruitfulness of pursuing the general topic for a dissertation. I also wish to thank Professor John Hope Franklin of the University of Chicago who, though not one of my instructors, has taken a kind interest in my career.

College undergraduates are undeservedly the "forgotten men" of acknowledgment pages in scholarly books. I desire to thank my U.C.L.A. students of 1961–64 for providing a pleasant, valuable, and challenging counterbalance to the trials and tribulations of graduate study, the manifestations of which in the moods and temperament of their "T.A." they staunchly endured. Similarly, my more recent students at San Fernando Valley State College deserve thanks for putting up with a measure of irritability during endless revising and rewriting for publication. Some colleagues and students alike have provided an ample amount of the moral support which authors seem to require.

Mr. Charles East and Miss June Wiley of Louisiana State University Press have been most helpful and generous with their time and patience while getting the manuscript ready for publication. Highly esteemed are the services of my two intrepid and persevering proofreaders—Mr. Donald A. McMaster with an early draft and Mr. Stephen C. Bedau with the final drafts and galleys. How anyone, while reading aloud my craggy prose and cryptogrammic footnotes, could stay as goodnatured as they did is a matter of marvel. Finally, there are hardly words to express appreciation for the understanding and encouragement my mother has provided over the years.

San Fernando Valley State College   J.E.S.
Christmas, 1966

Contents

List of Illustrations

List of Footnote Symbols

AAAG	Acting Assistant Adjutant General
AAG	Assistant Adjutant General
ADC	Aide-de-Camp
AG	Adjutant General
AGO	Office of the Adjutant General of the Army, Washington
BCA	Bureau of Civil Affairs
CG	Commanding General
CO	Commanding Officer
C/S	Chief of Staff
Dept	Department
Dist	District
Div	Division
Exec. Docs.	Executive Documents (of the House or Senate)
GCMO	General Court-martial Orders
GO	General Orders
HQA	Headquarters, United States Army, Washington (i.e., the headquarters of the General-in-Chief, not of the Secretary of War)
LC	Library of Congress (Manuscripts Division)
1MD, 2MD, 3MD, 4MD, 5MD	The five military districts established in the First Reconstruction Act of March 2, 1867
Misc. Docs.	Miscellaneous Documents (of the House or Senate)
NA	National Archives
PM	Provost Marshal
RG	Record Group (in the National Archives)
SO	Special Orders
USA	United States Army

A word of explanation may be in order concerning citation of material in the National Archives. These records are of three basic types: original copies of letters, telegrams, and other documents, filed in correspondence boxes; retained copies of correspondence, in letterbooks; and printed broadsides of orders. Each type requires a special form of citation. For original copies of correspondence and other items filed in boxes, the "document file number" and headquarters designation are always given, e.g., "file 208B1867, 4MD." Box numbers are not needed as long as these "file" numbers are provided. For correspondence in letterbooks, the headquarters designation is given first, followed by the book number (or letter), e.g., "Dept. Ark.,

2," or "HQA, C." Page numbers are not necessary since letters are entered chronologically. For orders issued by field commands, the number, headquarters, and date of the order are followed by the number of the relevant volume in the AGO collection, e.g., "GO 20, Dept. Ga., Jan. 25, 1866, Orders, 278." Volume numbers are not given for orders issued at Washington since those volumes are arranged and designated by year rather than number. The last part of each reference to National Archives material is the record group number, e.g., "RG94, NA." Where one footnote contains several individual references, all of which are in the same record group, the group designation is placed at the end of the note. Where a footnote contains more than one reference of any kind, the contents of the note are arranged in the same order as the employment of the material in the text.

THE UNITED STATES ARMY
AND RECONSTRUCTION

PART I

★ ★ ★ ★ ★ ★ ★

FROM APPOMATTOX
TO THE RECONSTRUCTION ACTS

After hostilities ended, the Army administered Southern affairs without specific guidance from Washington, pending the formulation of a national policy. President Johnson soon announced a program of reconstruction, which the Army administered for six months. But Congress disagreed with the President, and the Army watched with apprehension as Congress inaugurated its struggle with Johnson over control of policy. The result was a period of fifteen months during which the Army, amidst great confusion, administered a policy no longer purely presidential but not yet clearly congressional.

1

The First Confused Weeks

THE solemn scenes at Appomattox Court House which brought to a close four years of war launched the United States Army on another campaign—less costly in lives, with very different yet equally arduous requirements, and three times as long. In this new campaign the Army administered the national government's reconstruction policy throughout the defeated South. The Army was the only agency available, and it was ill-prepared for the task. American military history offered no precedents for the occupation of eleven states as conquered territory in time of peace.

The Army had gained some experience in military occupation and government from its efforts in Mexico under General Winfield Scott some twenty years earlier, but that situation and Southern reconstruction were fundamentally different. Mexico was a foreign country that had never been a part of the United States and was never seriously meant to become a part of it. To be sure, the exigencies of military government in Mexico led Scott to create the military commission to prosecute certain types of cases, and the military commission was of vital importance during the first five years of Southern reconstruction. But by 1865 the military commission had become a standard institution, and officers did not consciously look to 1847 for its origin.

It was also significant that of the thirty-five most important men who during the period 1865–77 held commands in the South appropriate to the rank of a general officer, seventeen either had not been in the Mexican War or had had service which did not bring them into direct contact with the problems of occupation. The lack of such personal experience was even greater among the field-grade and company offi-

5

cers who frequently commanded small posts and detachments in the South. Moreover, there is nothing to indicate that during the twelve postwar years the Adjutant General of the Army, in transmitting War Department or Executive instructions to commanders in the South, ever indicated precedents from the 1847 experience. Nor is there evidence that any of the highest field commanders noted such precedents, either in asking for guidance from Washington or in sending instructions to their subordinates.

A closer and slightly better precedent than Mexico, though still a highly imperfect one, was the experience gained in "reconstructing" parts of Louisiana, Arkansas, Tennessee, and Virginia from 1862 until the end of the war. But again, this wartime "reconstruction" was fundamentally different from that of the twelve postwar years. The existence of active military operations against hostile forces was the controlling factor during 1862–65, and the paramount goal of speedily concluding these operations eclipsed all "reconstruction" activities. Once hostilities had ended, "reconstruction" itself became the nation's main concern. Wartime "reconstruction" had affected only parts of four states; after Appomattox the entire South was involved, including considerable territory which had not been penetrated by Union troops until late in the war—Texas, western Louisiana, central Alabama, southern Georgia, most of Florida, and the interior of the Carolinas.

The government had made some attempt to provide a general guide for the policy to be followed during wartime "reconstruction" in Executive instructions to military governors and in the renowned "General Orders No. 100" of May, 1863. The latter, more descriptively titled "Instructions for the Government of the Armies of the United States in the Field," codified for military use those portions of international law governing the conduct of war and the relations of the conquering forces with the people in the occupied territory. But General Orders No. 100 and President Lincoln's instructions to the military governors were an imperfect basis for postwar occupation policy, and the Army recognized that fact. There is no evidence that after Appomattox Washington authorities or commanders in the South ever referred to these wartime guides. Nor did field commanders, in answering requests from subordinates for instructions, cite their own personal experiences in occupation duty prior to 1865.

If the actual practical experience which might have aided Army officers in their conduct of Reconstruction was slim, the constitutional and legal basis for their duties was equally unsatisfactory. The Constitution, though it anticipated the possibility of domestic insurrection, did not anticipate the possibility of a division of the Union by secession and was naturally silent on the political problems stemming from such an attempt. Consequently all provisions concerning the governing of territories or the admission of new states were inapplicable. Unless the war powers of the Executive be considered to extend beyond the immediate termination of hostilities, little of consequence can be found in the Constitution, other than those of the first ten amendments which provide procedural legal guarantees.

Statute law also afforded little guidance, since secession had never taken place before. No federal legislation passed before the war applied directly to the Army's Reconstruction activities. Among wartime measures, only two were significant. The Habeas Corpus Act of March 3, 1863, protected officers from prosecution or civil suit for actions performed under orders of the President or his subordinates during the war and allowed the transfer of such cases from state to federal courts.[1] The other was an act passed in February, 1865, governing the use of federal troops at state elections.[2] But since Congress always denied, during the early Reconstruction period, that the Southern states were in fact states, this law did not apply until after Southern representatives again sat in Congress.

The Articles of War drafted in 1806 governed purely military offenses such as desertion or violation of orders; but martial law, which armies customarily employ for governing the inhabitants of occupied territory, was not dealt with in any federal statute. Thus martial law, which existed continuously in any given area of the South from the time Union troops first occupied the locale until the particular state was readmitted to representation—sometime between the summers of 1866 and 1870—was for practical purposes anything the commander said it was, unless higher authority overruled him.

Aside from lack of satisfactory precedent and practical experience and the amorphous state of the written law covering the situation, other general factors made the Army's task difficult. The Army itself was undergoing rapid and far-reaching change. Volunteer regiments whose members had enlisted "for the duration" were anxious to go home, and so peacetime duties would have to be performed by regular units. In any reorganization of the regular regiments, some way would have to be found of balancing postwar military need with the traditional American desire to reduce military expenditures as much as possible. Of the officers who wished to remain in the service—and who succeeded in

[1]12 U.S. Statutes at Large 755.
[2]13 U.S. Statutes at Large 437.

getting appointments to regular regiments—many would have much preferred Indian fighting on the Plains to occupation duty in the South. The soldiers' Southern task required calmness, patience, tact, and an ability to use wide discretion wisely. The ruthlessness, impetuosity, and aggressiveness in combat which had made generals like Philip H. Sheridan popular war heroes also made them poor choices for Southern command. A thorough knowledge of law would have saved officers considerable grief, but of the high-ranking commanders only Alfred H. Terry had studied law extensively. And when the political cannonading between President Andrew Johnson and Congress became fierce, generals on Southern duty found themselves caught in the cross fire. In 1867, several months before being sent to Atlanta himself, General George G. Meade wrote to a brother officer: "Undoubtedly one might be better off than at Omaha; at the same time, it is very easy to be worse off, and that in the service too, vide our friends in the Southern Dept. where you have not only to be a soldier, but must play the politician, a part which I am sure both to you and me would be not only difficult but disagreeable." [3] Of course, since the nature of Reconstruction policy was the subject of bitter political quarreling, and since the Army was the principal executor of the policy, the political opinions and leanings of the senior commanders were a matter of considerable importance. Ill-prepared and with some misgivings, the United States Army thus embarked on a campaign which it knew would be unpleasant and hoped would be short. In the first respect it reckoned well; in the other it was to be sadly disappointed.

In the weeks immediately after Lee's surrender one of the principal tasks of the Army was the administration of government in Southern cities and towns—a large problem after the complete collapse of Confederate authority. A typical solution was that effected in New Orleans, where the government was in the hands of loyal citizens who acted under military authority and were subject to military supervision. [4] Commanders desired to have as many local administrative posts as possible filled by civilians in order to foster better relations with the inhabitants and to spare Army officers for purely military duties. In some cities specific regulations on various subjects were deemed necessary. The commander at Little Rock, Arkansas, set up strict garbage regulations,

---

[3]Meade to Col. P. Regis deTrobriand, Aug. 28, 1867, in M. C. Post, *Memoirs of Count Regis deTrobriand* (New York, 1906), 347.
[4]Gen. E. R. S. Canby to Gen. Carl Schurz, Sept. 8, 1865, Dept. Gulf, 79, RG98, NA.

prohibited dogs and other animals from running at large, arrested people who used vulgar language in public, prohibited children from running about unclothed, and established speed limits for riding horses and driving carriages through the town.[5] To prevent disloyal Georgians from using the mails, the commander at Savannah was ordered to require everyone receiving mail at that city's post office to present a certificate showing he had taken the oath of allegiance. In Richmond General Henry W. Halleck went even beyond the Georgia commander by requiring Southerners who wanted to be married to take the oath of allegiance. In forwarding his order to War Secretary Edwin M. Stanton, Halleck added with typical pomposity but rare humor, "You will perceive from paragraph V that measures have been taken to prevent so far as possible the propagation of legitimate rebels." [6]

Because of unsatisfactory sanitary conditions in the larger cities, commanders had to enforce health regulations of various kinds. In Augusta, Georgia, the Army ordered streets, alleys, cellars, and outbuildings thoroughly policed and cleaned, lime thrown in the streets and gutters, and all outbuildings, sheds, fences, and tree trunks whitewashed. Unless manpower could be had by arresting vagrants, the occupants of the premises had to provide the muscles while the Army provided the foremen and the lime. In Mobile, Alabama, all "public women" had to register with the local provost marshal.[7]

The Army found it necessary to conduct or supervise the relief of the needy and destitute because local governmental agencies were entirely unable to handle it. Both whites and Negroes who could find no other means of subsistence received daily rations. The number issued reached an average of 29,000 per day in Virginia during August, 1865, and the numbers were comparable in other states. This work had an undesirable effect, however, because many persons, particularly Negroes, did not bother to look for other means of support as long as free government food was available. One commanding general even saw a political advantage in the cessation of the Army's dole. "I think," wrote General Alfred H. Terry, "that if it were announced that the issue of

---

[5]Thomas S. Staples, *Reconstruction in Arkansas, 1862–1874* (New York, 1923), 75–76.

[6]AAG to Gen. C. Grover, April 19, 1865, Dept. South, 15, RG98, NA; Halleck to Stanton, April 28, 1865, in *The War of the Rebellion: A Compilation of the Official Records of the Union and Confederate Armies* (Washington, 1880–1901), Ser. I, Vol. XLVI, Pt. 3, pp. 990–91, hereinafter cited as *Official Records*.

[7]AAG to Col. S. M. Benedict, CO Augusta, Aug. 7, 1865, Dept. Ga., 1, RG98, NA; GO 53, Dept. Gulf, May 8, 1865, Orders, 890, RG94, NA; Walter L. Fleming, *Civil War and Reconstruction in Alabama* (New York, 1905), 417.

rations to destitute whites would cease at a given day and if the views which I have given [of the desirability of thorough Unionists being elected to office] were presented to the minds of the people they would be likely to exercise a salutary influence upon the selection of members of Congress and of the legislature." [8]

Military men supervised repair work on Southern railroads. General Edward R. S. Canby had the line from Shreveport, Louisiana, to Marshall, Texas, which was held as captured property, rehabilitated and operated under the control of his quartermaster officers. The sad state of some Mississippi River levees also received attention, though Secretary of War Stanton refused Canby's request that $200,000 of the funds available from the sale of sequestered property be appropriated for the repair work. [9]

[The soldiers saw the need of quickly restoring educational facilities. In eastern Virginia, schools operated by Army chaplains rapidly gained the appreciation of local residents.] General Joseph R. Hawley, an early abolitionist, Connecticut politician, and journalist, took the lead in establishing schools in Wilmington, North Carolina. Some commanders were sensitive to distinctions between white and Negro children. When the commanding general at Savannah established free schools for white children, his superior, General Quincy A. Gillmore—of all Southern commanders one of the most sincerely interested in the welfare of the Negro—objected. It was unfair to Negro children, he claimed, adding that most of the whites were disloyal anyhow. This attitude brought from Savannah the reply that Negro children were better provided for by charitable organizations than were the whites. The schools stayed. [10]

[Although these welfare and charitable activities were vital to the prostrate South, of much greater importance and delicacy in the long run were questions connected with the tenure of civil officials at all levels. Three courses were open. The first was to suspend completely all civil officials for an indefinite period and let Army officers perform all governmental tasks—in short, a military stewardship. The second was to permit the men who had held office under the Confederacy to continue to perform their functions, under military supervision, until elections for

[8] Terry to AAG Div. Atlantic, Sept. 15, 1865, Dept. Va., 14, RG98, NA.

[9] C/S to Gen. J. P. Hawkins, CG West. Dist. La., Aug. 10, 1865, Dept. Gulf, 79, RG98, NA; Gen. E. D. Townsend, AAG USA, to Canby, Oct. 11, 1865, AGO, 41, RG94, NA.

[10] Lt. Col. O. L. Mann, PM East. Dist. Va., to Hawley, April 23, 1865, in Hawley Papers, LC; Gillmore to CG Savannah, May 10, 1865, in *Official Records,* Ser. I, Vol. XLVII, Pt. 3, pp. 466–67; Gen. C. Grover to AAG Dept. South, May 13, 1865, *ibid.,* 492–93.

new officials could be held. The third was to refuse to recognize any erstwhile Confederate officials, with the national government establishing "provisional" or caretaker regimes until permanent officers could be elected.

The first course, though advocated by many in the North, both in and out of political life, would have been impractical, to say nothing of its basic repugnance to many soldiers. It would have required the maintenance of a large force at considerable and unpopular cost and would have imposed upon officers duties for which they were ill-equipped. Many soldiers would have seconded the views of General Meade:

We of the Army have done our work, the military power of the rebellion is shattered. It remains for statesmen, if we have any, to bring the people of the South back to their allegiance and into the Union. How and when this will be accomplished no one can tell. In the meantime I presume our armies will have to occupy the Southern States. I am myself for conciliation as the policy most likely to effect a speedy reunion. If we are going to punish treason, as perhaps strict justice would demand, we shall have to shed almost as much blood as has already been poured out in this terrible war. These are points however for others to adjust.[11]

The idea of allowing Confederate officials to continue at their posts temporarily, though it seemed to nullify the military result of the war, received consideration in some quarters. The command of General George H. Thomas embraced Tennessee and parts of northern Georgia, Alabama, and Mississippi. Addressing a general order to the inhabitants of that area on the day before Lincoln's assassination, Thomas recommended that all judges, sheriffs, commissioners, and justices of the peace continue to perform their duties according to the laws of the state as they existed prior to secession, "as far as it may be found practicable." Thomas promised them military aid and protection. Where vacancies existed, he said, "it is enjoined upon the loyal people of the neighborhood to hold regular elections and select officers competent to reorganize the civil courts, and uphold the authority of the civil laws." The order offered no criteria for "loyal people," though the mountainous regions of northern Georgia and Alabama had been among the strongest enclaves of Union sentiment in the South throughout the war.

Thomas' ideas met with mixed reactions. One Alabaman, complaining to President Johnson, expressed general faith in Thomas' loyalty but called the order "misguided" and asked that it be revoked—which it

[11]Meade to his wife, April 22, 1865, in Meade Papers, Historical Society of Pennsylvania.

was not. In Macon, Georgia, the *Daily Telegraph* hailed it as a truly liberal policy, and later castigated its readers for their seeming apathy in carrying out Thomas' suggestions.[12]

Recognition of Confederate governors and legislators raised more serious problems than recognition of lesser state officials. In several states governors who sought military permission to convene the Rebel legislatures were received coolly. Nothing came of a proposal to General Edward M. McCook by the Confederate governor of Florida that the state be brought back into the Union with all its existing officers still at their posts.[13] In Alabama many citizens signed a petition addressed to General Frederick Steele asking him to allow the governor to convene the legislature so that it could authorize a convention to be called. Steele sent the petition to Canby, the next higher commander, who in turn forwarded it to Secretary of War Stanton. In doing so Canby noted that he had received many such requests and had always replied that he lacked authority to entertain questions on the political status of the Southern states. He added that he thought the calling of a convention might be a good idea but warned that the legislature should be prohibited from doing anything else. The petition ultimately found its way to Johnson, who merely filed it.[14]

On May 10, 1865, Governor Joseph E. Brown, without asking the Army's permission, called a special session of the Georgia legislature to meet at Milledgeville on the twenty-second. Upon discovering that General James H. Wilson would not allow the legislature to meet without permission from Washington, Brown wired the President pleading that financial chaos and destitution made immediate legislative action imperative. Before Johnson could reply, General Wilson's superior, General Gillmore, sent a brigade of infantry to Milledgeville to "quietly" prevent the meeting and to detain any legislators who showed up. In explaining his action to Stanton, who approved it, Gillmore said, "I have feared that the assembling of the legislature might embarrass the future action of the Government by tending to perpetuate the political control over Georgia of men who have neither deep love for the nation nor sympathy in the national policy." [15]

---

[12]GO 21, Dept. Cumberland, April 13, 1865, Orders, 855, RG94, NA; Jeremiah Clemens to Johnson, April 21, 1865, in Johnson Papers, LC (Reel 13); Macon *Daily Telegraph,* May 24 and June 3, 1865.

[13]I. G. Harris to Johnson, May 21, 1865, in Johnson Papers, LC (Reel 14).

[14]Petition filed under May 1, 1865, in Johnson Papers, LC (Reel 14).

[15]Brown to Johnson, May 10, 1865, in Johnson Papers, LC (Reel 14); Gillmore to Stanton, May 10, 1865, in *Official Records,* Ser. I, Vol. XLVII, Pt. 3, p. 464, and reply, May 15, 1865, p. 505.

Nobody was entirely certain what the "national policy" was in May, 1865, but when finally announced it closely approximated the third of the possible courses—provisional regimes until permanent ones could be elected and installed. Before the fighting ended, and with increasing regularity during April and May, there had been much speculation concerning the course which the national government would pursue. Aside from the Wade-Davis Bill of 1864, to which Lincoln had given a pocket veto, the Congress had drawn up no formal plan of reconstruction. That body had adjourned in April, and President Johnson determined to proceed on his own authority rather than call a special session of Congress or wait until the new one convened in December.

Johnson received suggestions from politicians and ordinary citizens, from the informed and the uninformed, from the spiteful and the conciliatory. Many persons, believing that each Southern state should have a military governor, inundated Johnson's mail clerks with petitions and recommendations. From Natchez, Mississippi, came a request for General John W. Davidson, then in local command at that city. Loyal citizens of Ringgold, Georgia, stating that they could not think of a trustworthy native Georgian, asked for the colonel of the 18th Ohio, who had formerly commanded the post at Chattanooga. According to another writer who felt Georgia would do well under General William B. Hazen, one of that officer's best qualifications for the job was his pretty young wife, who kept him "free from that Rebel Petticoate [*sic*] influence so frequently and so successfully exercised over our officers in Tennessee."[16]

After some North Carolinians suggested General Innis N. Palmer, a fellow citizen objected, claiming that Palmer had fraternized with secessionists since coming to the state, that he had used his influence in New Berne in favor of the election of George B. McClellan in 1864, and that he had declared that Jefferson Davis should go unpunished. Then Palmer himself wrote to the President pleading to be spared the appointment.[17] When General Terry found out that Chief Justice Salmon P. Chase was touring the South at the President's request, he asked his chief of staff, who knew Chase, to listen for any intimation that he might be considered for military governor of North Carolina and if the idea arose, "to '*stamp upon it*' at once."[18]

[16]J. F. Hollingsworth to Johnson, May 25, 1865; W. C. Roberts, *et al.* to Johnson, May 26, 1865; and G. W. Ashburn to Johnson, April 30, 1865, all in Johnson Papers, LC (Reel 14).
[17]Petition dated April 29, 1865; J. W. Etheridge to Johnson, May 4, 1865; and Palmer to Johnson, May 30, 1865, all in Johnson Papers, LC (Reel 14).
[18]Terry to Hawley, May 6, 1865, in Hawley Papers, LC. Original emphasis.

Like Palmer and Terry, most generals preferred not to think of themselves as military governors, though there were some exceptions. General Robert H. Milroy, who had had difficulty as a field commander in the Shenandoah Valley in 1861 and was finding his current experience of a year on garrison duty at Tullahoma, Tennessee, "irksome," wanted to go to Alabama. His first choice was really to go to the Mexican border and help overawe Maximilian and the French, but if that could not be granted, the Alabama governorship would satisfy his desire for some active duty before leaving the service. He concluded (in vain), "Please try me." [19]

Making his suggestions on the installment plan, Chief Justice Chase described Southern conditions in a series of letters from various points along the Atlantic seaboard. In a letter from Hilton Head, South Carolina, written about midway through his tour, he presented a more systematic plan for restoring civil government than most of Johnson's volunteer advisers had offered. Prefacing his exposition with the firm belief that military supervision was necessary for a time, Chase explained that the mechanism of this supervision should resemble the regular state government as nearly as possible. Each state ought to be made into a separate military department with a commanding general or military governor. The commander should order a registration of loyal citizens of both races, either by provost marshals or by boards of loyal citizens in each county. Delegates would then be elected for a convention to write a new constitution or amend the old one. If the constitution were ratified by the people, a governor and other state officers should be elected. When these officers assumed their functions, the political duties of the military commander would cease, and his only remaining task would be the suppression of disorder in aid of the state authorities.

In choosing the commanders, Chase continued, care should be taken to select men completely loyal who were ready to maintain and promote the welfare of Negroes as well as whites—a revelation of one of Chase's favorite concerns. He thought that General John M. Schofield could be trusted with North Carolina. He regarded Gillmore very highly, probably because of Gillmore's concern for the Negro, and recommended him for Georgia. Rufus Saxton and John P. Hatch, he suggested, would be excellent command choices for South Carolina and Florida, respectively. [20]

Schofield himself had also been formulating a plan of reconstruction and had been in communication with Chase during the latter's tour.

[19]Milroy to Johnson, May 22, 1865, in Johnson Papers, LC (Reel 14).
[20]Chase to Johnson, May 17, 1865, in Johnson Papers, LC (Reel 14).

After receiving a letter from the Chief Justice, Schofield wrote to the General-in-Chief, Ulysses S. Grant, offering his own views. Chase was determined that Negroes should vote, and to facilitate this goal in North Carolina, he had favored basing suffrage on the state's constitution as it had stood in 1835. But Schofield demurred. Like numerous other officers, he believed the Negro population as a whole was not ready for suffrage, and he gave legal reasons for using the state constitution which was in effect immediately before the ordinance of secession.

The remaining details of Schofield's plan were similar to Chase's. He wanted all troops in the state put under the command of a military governor who would declare still in force such parts of the prewar state constitution and laws as did not conflict with federal law or Lincoln's wartime proclamations. The governor would appoint provisional sheriffs and other local officials. A registration of voters would precede an election for delegates to a state convention. Both candidates and voters would be required to take an amnesty oath and be otherwise qualified by state law—a reflection of Schofield's view that the federal government could not constitutionally prescribe state election qualifications. The convention thus selected would order an election for governor and legislators and for the ratification of its own acts. He expected this procedure to result in abolition of slavery, repudiation of secession, and restoration of normal federal-state relations. If it should fail, however, Schofield would feel that the people had violated their oaths and would consequently impose complete military government until they "should come to their senses." [21] In reply Grant agreed with Schofield's views but added that all the Army could do was to keep the peace until a uniform policy was adopted. A later note from Grant's secretary indicated that Stanton too had seen the letter and agreed with its contents. Johnson may not have known of Schofield's letter, but the Hilton Head message from Chase reached the President on May 22. [22]

⌈Andrew Johnson spent his first six weeks in office trying to determine a policy for the defeated South. He had been a stern military governor of Tennessee during the war, and he maintained this attitude for a short time after succeeding Lincoln in the executive chair. He soon realized, however, that he could not impose total military rule on the South without abrogating Lincoln's spirit of clemency and generosity. Nor could he withdraw all military supervision without risking the return to power

[21]Chase to Schofield, May 7, 1865, in *Official Records,* Ser. I, Vol. XLVII, Pt. 3, p. 427; Schofield to Grant, May 10, 1865, *ibid.,* 461.
[22]Grant to Schofield, May 18, 1865, *ibid.,* 529; C. B. Comstock to Schofield, May 25, 1865, *ibid.,* 571.

of men who had originally favored secession in 1860. The result was a plan which in spirit resembled Lincoln's and in detail strikingly resembled the proposals of Chase and Schofield. Johnson unveiled his plan in two proclamations of May 29, 1865. In the first he offered amnesty and pardon to most persons who had aided the rebellion, provided they took an oath of future loyalty to the government.

In the other proclamation Johnson appointed William Holden provisional governor of North Carolina and directed him to proceed with registration of "loyal" citizens, election of a convention, ratification of a new state constitution or amendments to the existing one, and election of state officials and federal legislators, much as in Schofield's plan. The principal difference between the two was that Schofield envisaged the provisional governor and the military commander as being the same individual; Johnson's plan conceived the two offices to be distinct, with the governor a civilian. As for the military commander, Johnson's proclamation directed him to aid the governor in carrying out his duties and "to abstain from in any way hindering, impeding, or discouraging the loyal people from the organization of a State government as herein authorized." [23] In the following weeks proclamations similar to that for North Carolina appeared for six other Southern states; in Arkansas, Louisiana, Virginia, and Tennessee the loyal governments set up under Lincoln's guidance were recognized by his successor.

On June 27, while Johnson was still issuing his proclamations, the War Department reorganized the various military divisions and departments into which the country was divided for purposes of command and administration and shuffled the commanding generals—a procedure which occurred with irksome frequency during the next several years.[24] A month later some forty-six general officers of volunteers who were becoming supernumerary due to the rapid muster-out of the volunteer forces were ordered to the Southern departments for whatever duty the commanding generals might assign them. When War Department affairs were under discussion in the Cabinet one day shortly thereafter, Postmaster General William Dennison inquired about these new orders.

[23]James D. Richardson (comp.), *A Compilation of the Messages and Papers of the Presidents, 1789–1897* (Washington, 1896–1901), VI, 310–14, hereinafter cited as *Messages and Papers.*

[24]Appendix A exhibits, as briefly as possible, the salient command changes during Reconstruction. An indispensable though hard-to-use guide is Raphael P. Thian (comp.), *Notes Illustrating the Military Geography of the United States* (Washington, 1881).

According to the Cabinet's indomitable diarist, Navy Secretary Gideon Welles, Stanton retorted peevishly that the question should be directed to Grant, since he himself had not given the General-in-Chief any advice on the subject. Stanton's disclaimer was probably not truthful because the preliminary drafts of the June order bear emendations in his handwriting.[25]

The largest unit of territorial command was the "military division," of which the June reorganization produced five: the Atlantic, the Gulf, the Tennessee, the Mississippi, and the Pacific. The first, embracing all the seaboard states from Maine to South Carolina, went to General George G. Meade, a West Point graduate of 1835 and the victor of Gettysburg. Rather spare, balding, and sharp-featured, "Old Snapping Turtle," as his men called him, was supposed by some of his contemporaries to have been a Democrat before the war, yet he always took pains to keep himself aloof from party politics. He favored a moderate treatment of the South and was determined to perform whatever duties he received without questioning the policies which induced them.[26]

Each of the three Southern states in Meade's command formed a separate "department." The Department of Virginia went to General Alfred H. Terry, who had attended Trinity College and Yale Law School rather than West Point. He maintained a close interest in Connecticut politics, but was without personal ambitions. His administration of Virginia affairs found favor in Republican circles. "I do not overestimate," wrote a friend of Terry's chief of staff, "when I say that among the Department Commanders, Genl. Terry holds the highest rank in public opinion for administrative capacity." [27]

The Department of South Carolina, at first intended for Terry, went instead to General Quincy Adams Gillmore, already in that state. Gillmore, a West Point graduate of 1849, was on friendly terms with Chief Justice Chase, having even enlisted his aid in 1864 to procure advance-

[25]GO 118, AGO, June 27, 1865, and GO 130, July 28, 1865, RG94, NA; Howard K. Beale (ed.), *The Diary of Gideon Welles* (New York, 1960), II, 355–56; undated draft of order on HQA stationery, filed under June 3, 1865, in Johnson Papers, LC (Reel 15); two similar drafts in Edwin M. Stanton Papers, LC, misdated by LC staff members as Dec., 1865.

[26]A handy compilation of information on the military careers of individual commanders is Mark M. Boatner, *The Civil War Dictionary* (New York, 1959). See also Francis B. Heitman, *Historical Register and Dictionary of the United States Army* (Washington, 1903). Additional data on senior officers is in *Dictionary of American Biography;* for lesser figures one must sometimes consult *The National Cyclopaedia of American Biography.*

[27]J. H. Almy to J. R. Hawley, Aug. 23, 1865, in Hawley Papers, LC.

ment in the Army. Although Chase thought well of him, another observer—and of Chase's political persuasion, too—thought Gillmore a "good officer" but "not fit for the post" he then held.[28]

It was easily settled that the Department of North Carolina should go to General John M. Schofield, also a West Point man. His political views, though seldom prominently expressed, were of the "moderate Republican" variety, and his feelings towards the defeated South were similar: "The imperative need of the Southern States at the close of the war was temporary military government, and permission, under such full military protection, to reorganize their civil governments." He believed that the Negroes should be protected, but he did not favor immediate enfranchisement.[29]

Below the level of the department, the territorial divisions and their disposition were ordinarily left to the pleasure of the generals commanding the departments. At first each divided his department into two or more "districts" or "subdistricts" and placed in command of these the volunteer-force generals they had received in July. Gradually, as these officers were mustered out and the number of troops in the South was reduced, the district and subdistrict organization in many states fell by the wayside, and officers commanding local posts reported directly to the department commander.

The chief position in the Division of the Gulf, embracing the states of Florida, Mississippi, Louisiana, and Texas, went to General Philip H. Sheridan, already at New Orleans. A classmate of Schofield at the Academy, though far below him scholastically, Sheridan was a particularly belligerent cadet and required an extra year to finish the prescribed course of study. A wartime incident illustrates his temperament. Once while traveling by train he detected an army news vendor harassing some soldiers. Without asking for an explanation he came up behind the offender, took him by the back of the neck, and battered his head against the side of the coach—though he had to stand on tiptoe to do it.[30] Sheridan had built up a well-deserved reputation during the war and was a favorite of both the public and Grant. He did not think the South's problems could be solved by legislation but preferred instead to "wait and trust to a little time and the working of natural causes." [31] He pre-

---

[28]Gillmore to Chase, March 10, 1864, in Chase Papers, Historical Society of Pennsylvania; Francis Hawley to J. R. Hawley, Sept. 24, 1865, in Hawley Papers, LC.

[29]John M. Schofield, *Forty-Six Years in the Army* (New York, 1897), 373.

[30]W. F. G. Shanks, *Personal Recollections of Distinguished Generals* (New York, 1866), 161.

[31]Sheridan to Johnson, Nov. 29, 1865, in Johnson Papers, LC (Reel 19).

ferred a stern though not malevolent policy towards the defeated South, whereas Johnson's policy was a comparatively milder one. Still, Sheridan's convictions need not have disqualified him for a Southern command had he been a man of more judicious and less irritable temperament.

General John G. Foster received command of the Department of Florida. An engineer officer, and a West Point graduate of 1846 along with such distinguished wartime commanders as George B. McClellan and "Stonewall" Jackson, Foster had held numerous commands along the Atlantic seaboard. Of undeterminable political views, he felt troops would be needed in the South for a considerable time.[32]

In a preliminary draft of the June order, the Department of Mississippi was slated for General John A. Logan; but Grant, in his own hand, crossed out Logan and wrote in "Slocum"—General Henry W. Slocum, who actually received the post. The reasons impelling Grant to make this change are a matter of speculation, but one distinct possibility exists. Logan had been a Democratic congressman before the war, and during the conflict his concern with politics exasperated Sherman to such a degree that he relieved him from command. On June 7, 1865, about the time the reorganization was in planning, Grant and Logan, by special invitation, attended a meeting arranged by New York City Democrats to show support for Johnson's reconstruction policy. During Logan's speech—Grant had contented himself with bowing in response to the crowd's cheers—the assembly acknowledged boisterously the purpose of the meeting. Logan replied: "So far as his administration has developed itself, I certainly have no fault to find with it. ['Good, Good'] What there may be to object to in the future I don't know; but if there is anything objectionable, then, as a matter of course, as the questions arise the country will have a right to decide for itself whether the President is in the right or in the wrong." [33]

Considered as a statement of American political practice Logan's remarks are unexceptionable. But Grant could still have been concerned that an officer with Logan's known penchant for politicking might not be well-suited to a Southern command. Moreover Grant had confided to a cousin in April that Johnson could understand "the wants and true interests of the country" better than anyone else.[34] Grant certainly knew

[32]Foster to AAG Div. Gulf, Dec. 11, 1865, in Sheridan Papers, LC.
[33]Undated draft, filed under June 3, 1865, in Johnson Papers, LC (Reel 15); George F. Dawson, *The Life and Services of General John A. Logan as Soldier and Statesman* (Chicago, 1887), 105–106. Original brackets.
[34]Grant to Silas A. Hudson, April 21, 1865, "Original Letters of General Grant," *Colorado Magazine,* XIV (March, 1937), 66–67.

Logan personally better than he knew Slocum; Logan's service had always been in the western theater, while Slocum had been in the Army of the Potomac until late 1863. Slocum, who had roomed with Sheridan at West Point, had led the Army of Georgia in Sherman's command at the close of the war. He did not last long in the South, however, for he resigned in September, 1865. He later became active in Democratic politics in New York.

General Edward R. S. Canby received command of the Department of Louisiana. A forty-eight-year-old Kentuckian, Canby graduated from West Point in 1839. His early action against the Confederates in New Mexico was instrumental in keeping that area (and California) for the Union. The close of the war found him in Louisiana. Sheridan soon came to doubt his administrative capacity, but Canby held various Southern commands during the early years of Reconstruction. He felt the Army's role was one of supervision rather than interference; and while he tried to keep aloof from questions of political policy, he believed the best course to be a firm but conciliatory one.[35]

The War Department entrusted the Department of Texas to General Horatio G. Wright, an engineer officer who was among the honor graduates in the Academy class of 1841. During the war he held both engineering posts and combat commands. He was chief engineer on the April, 1861, expedition to destroy the Norfolk Navy Yard, and later he commanded the VI Corps in the Army of the Potomac. He rarely expressed his political views.

The Division of the Tennessee, including the states of Kentucky, Tennessee, Georgia, and Alabama, went to General George H. Thomas, a forty-nine-year-old scholarly and distinguished Virginian. An Academy graduate of 1840, he later taught artillery and cavalry tactics there. He had earned the most complimentary of his many nicknames, "The Rock of Chickamauga," by preventing the defeat of General William S. Rosecrans' western army in September, 1863, from becoming a disaster. He was harsh on guerrillas and other marauders who infested the Tennessee area, where he served so long both during and after the war, but he favored a moderate policy towards the South as a whole. He hoped the Southern states would not be kept out of the Union for long.[36] Though many political factions sought to claim him, as they did every soldier with as illustrious a war record as Thomas', he was most taciturn and

---

[35]Max L. Heyman, *Prudent Soldier: A Biography of Major General E. R. S. Canby, 1817–1873* (Glendale, 1959), 271–73, 343–47.

[36]*House Reports,* 39th Cong., 1st Sess., No. 30, Pt. 1, p. 110 (the report of the Joint Committee on Reconstruction).

circumspect on partisan questions. As one newspaper columnist wrote: "Thomas—'Old Steady'—is to my mind the finest soldier and citizen the Regular Army has given us. He is eminently a national man, is just, able, unbending, and endowed with great administrative abilities. In many respects he more resembles the historic George Washington than any public man now on the stage." [37]

General George Stoneman headed the Department of the Tennessee— so labeled because of the War Office's addiction to naming commands after rivers wherever possible. A New Yorker, Stoneman had been commissioned in the dragoons following his 1846 graduation from West Point and had seen extensive prewar service in the Southwest. During the war he conducted several successful large-scale cavalry raids, although one during Sherman's operations in front of Atlanta resulted in the capture of himself and seven hundred men. He was a Democrat in politics, but no charges of partisanship in his conduct of Tennessee affairs were levied against him.

Choosing a commander for the Department of Georgia posed some problems. The first man considered was youthful General James Harrison Wilson, already in command at Macon and respected in that area for his "energetic yet moderate" rule.[38] A member of the West Point class of 1860, Wilson was but twenty-eight years old at the end of the war. Renowned for his skill at mixing claret punches and other "tropical tipples," he was well-liked in the service and was a favorite of Grant. After he took over the Cavalry Bureau in 1864 his administrative rigor and financial watchfulness was found so revolutionary by the government's horse contractors that they were instrumental in his being returned to active duty with the cavalry under Sherman. That was fine with Wilson, who habitually sulked when he had no active duty to perform.

But Georgia, with Stanton's acquiescence if not at his urging, went to General James B. Steedman, besides Terry the only non-West Pointer to be given high station in the South at this time. Steedman was perhaps the most politically oriented officer initially to receive a Southern command. He had been a member of the Ohio legislature before the war and "was always a democrat of the hard-money, anti-tariff, anti-bankrupt law and anti-abolition and negro equality school, and was always the leader of what was known as the uncompromising wing of his

[37]*Army and Navy Journal,* IV (March 30, 1867), 514, as reprinted from the Worcester (Mass.) *Spy.* This article is a general analysis of the supposed political views of many leading generals.
[38]Macon *Daily Telegraph,* June 14, 1865.

party." [39] He resigned from the Army in 1866, took part regularly in the many political conventions and rallies of that year, and as a friend of Johnson remained loyal to the President throughout the difficulties with the Congress of 1867–68. Steedman weighed over two hundred pounds and in appearance was "like a hale, hearty farmer, with stout, burly form, largely made, and of great physical power and endurance." [40]

General Charles R. Woods received the Department of Alabama. His first wartime service had been as commander of the ill-fated *Star of the West* expedition to relieve Fort Sumter in April, 1861. Thereafter he campaigned exclusively in the western theater, helping to open the Mississippi and later marching to the sea with Sherman. His administration of affairs in Alabama, though it proved to be vigorous, did not bring about charges of political partisanship.

The Division of the Mississippi—principally the Great Plains but also including Arkansas—went to General William Tecumseh Sherman, senior in rank to every officer in the Army save Grant and Halleck. He was a West Point graduate of 1840 along with Thomas, Winfield Scott Hancock, and the distinguished Confederate Richard S. Ewell, all of whom he outdid scholastically. He had seen service in California during the Mexican War; following his resignation in 1853 he had dabbled in banking on the West Coast and had been the president of a military academy in Louisiana (now Louisiana State University). After action at First Bull Run, Sherman's wartime service was in the West, culminating in his famous (or infamous) march from Atlanta to the sea and north into the Carolinas. Described by one observer as "the concentrated quintessence of Yankeedom," he was tall, lean, and sinewy, with "dingy red" hair and whiskers that continually looked as though their owner were a victim of incompetent barbering.[41]

Sherman emerged from the war with a reputation and popularity second only to Grant's, and political factions constantly sought his allegiance. But all were disappointed, for whereas many generals were apolitical, Sherman was anti-political, and usually outspokenly so. "Washington is as corrupt as Hell," he wrote to his wife in May, 1865, "made so by the looseness and extravagance of war. I will avoid it as

---

[39]*Ibid.,* July 11, 1865; Shanks, *Recollections,* 276–88. Since the general pronounced his name as if spelled "Steadman," it is frequently thus encountered in contemporary documents, though the correct spelling is "Steedman."

[40]Shanks, *Recollections,* 288.

[41]Boatner, *Civil War Dictionary,* 751, quoting Col. Theodore Lyman, a staff officer at Meade's headquarters; Shanks, *Recollections,* 57.

a pest house. . . ." [42] Rough language to one's wife, perhaps—but Mrs. Sherman was used to it. After capturing Savannah he wrote his brother, Senator John Sherman, "If you ever hear anybody use my name in connection with a political office, tell them you know me well enough to assure them that I would be offended by such association. I would rather be an engineer of a railroad, than President of the United States, or any political officer." [43]

Sherman's views brought disapproval from at least one newspaper commentator: "Sherman is organically wrong. He is a race-hater, and oligarchic by instinct. Though his brain may accept the issues of the war, his temperament will fight against their logical conclusions. He was a thorough Unionist, but intensely pro-slavery. He is of the same stripe still. I speak from some personal knowledge of his former opinions." [44] Perhaps Sherman was guilty as charged; he certainly did not favor Negro suffrage, which he felt was a trick "whereby politicians may manufacture just so much more pliable electioneering material." But another individual, who could speak from "personal knowledge of Sherman's former convictions" on the basis of their close association in Louisiana before the war, reminisced in 1875: "You [were] a Clay Whig (if you were of any party at all.)" [45]

Under Sherman the Department of Arkansas was commanded by General Joseph J. Reynolds, a friend of Grant, who had graduated from West Point with him in 1843 and served under him in the western theater during the war. At the end of the conflict Reynolds was already in Arkansas and was a logical choice for the command. He favored a cautious yet firm policy towards the South and believed that the former political leaders of Arkansas should not be allowed to participate in state politics until after the 1868 gubernatorial election. This goal he would have accomplished by a presidential grant of "amnesty as to all rights except the elective franchise." [46]

Except for one or two consolidations, this basic command structure remained in effect until the next major reshuffling in the summer of 1866, and these fifteen officers comprised the first group to be charged

[42]Mark A. DeWolfe Howe (ed.), *Home Letters of General Sherman* (New York, 1909), 352.

[43]Rachel Sherman Thorndike (ed.), *The Sherman Letters* (New York, 1894), 245.

[44]*Army and Navy Journal,* IV (March 30, 1867), 514, as reprinted from the Worcester (Mass.) *Spy.*

[45]Sherman to his wife, May 10, 1865, in Howe (ed.), *Home Letters,* 353; D. F. Boyd to Sherman, July 17, 1875, in W. T. Sherman Papers, LC.

[46]Reynolds to Attorney General Speed, July 5, 1865, Dept. Ark., 2, RG98, NA.

with the administration of federal reconstruction policy. Some of them—
Woods, Gillmore, Slocum, Steedman—would soon fade from the picture.
Others, along with comrades who in 1865 were on more traditional
military duty, were to gain protracted experience with Southern problems before the end of Reconstruction.

2

Working With (and Against) the Provisional Governors

JOHNSON's spring and summer proclamations of 1865 helped both the Army and the South by outlining a step-by-step process for Southerners to follow in re-establishing civil government. But Johnson's instructions to the Army about its role were general rather than specific, and the individual commanders were left to fill in the details, as local conditions might require. Most commanding generals issued detailed instructions to their troops setting forth their conception of the proper relation of the military power to state and local governments and to individual citizens. No slate of instructions could have foreseen all aspects of the problems that were to arise in the months to follow, but the order issued by General Steedman to his Georgia command was among the most comprehensive.

The numerous provisions of Steedman's order fall into five categories. First, the general declared that upon request the Army would furnish the provisional governor or his agents any military assistance necessary for the performance of their duties. Further, the Army was not to interfere in any way with official actions of the governor: "The military authority should sustain, not assume, the functions of the civil authority except when the unsettled state of society requires such assumption, as a last resource, to preserve peace and quiet." Second, the order dealt with military arrest of civilians. The Army was to protect all citizens in their lawful rights, but "no citizen will be arrested upon the complaint of another citizen unless the accusation, supported by the oath of the complaint [sic] would justify the issuing of a warrant in time of peace."

Third, military aid was available to civil officers of the federal gov-

25

ernment in performance of their duties and especially to agents of the Treasury Department who were engaged in collecting Confederate cotton. The fourth category embraced the problems of the Negro. Aid was to be given to the Freedmen's Bureau on request, and arrests could be made for an agent upon a full statement of the case. Persons arrested were to be held in military custody until they could be turned over to the civil authorities or until "duly authorized courts" could dispose of the cases. Plantation owners were not to force aged and helpless freedmen to leave their property, and able-bodied Negroes were warned not to be idle and vagrant. Finally, Steedman demanded that the troops maintain strict discipline and refrain from committing depredations upon private property. Officers were not "to obtrude upon families" but were to have social relations only with those who sought their company. Though the troops were naturally to prevent insult or indignity to the national authority, they were cautioned not to be offensive or provocative in their dealings with citizens.[1]

The first topic embraced in Steedman's order—relations between the military authorities and the provisional governments—was of paramount importance. The orderly progress of Presidential Reconstruction depended largely upon cordiality and cooperation by both sides. If the two jurisdictions worked at cross-purposes, much mischief could easily result since the civil governors had the responsibility for organizing the new government and the Army had the ability, through force or intimidation, to prevent any particular step in the process from being carried out. Naturally, civil and military authority overlapped in a number of areas: organization of local militia, administration of justice, appointment of subordinate local officials, and the rights of Negroes. But though both groups of authorities made an honest attempt to foster harmony in their relations, occasional notes of discord sounded.

One serious collision pertained to the organization of local militia in Mississippi. On August 19, 1865, Provisional Governor William L. Sharkey called upon the young men of the state, predominantly Confederate veterans, to form two companies of militia per county. He did not consult General Slocum, who would have been reluctant to approve the proclamation in any case. The general considered the existence of any such organizations not directly under federal military control to be a potential source of danger, and he was especially apprehensive of conflicts between the militia and the United States colored troops which were located in numerous garrisons throughout the state.

Slocum received reports from General Peter J. Osterhaus, in the

[1]GO 4, Dept. Ga., July 14, 1865, Orders, 278, RG94, NA.

northern part of the state, protesting the governor's action. Osterhaus claimed that the outrages which gave rise to the proclamation were all committed against Negroes, Northern whites, or government messengers; that they were probably gotten up purposely to afford an excuse for organizing militia; and that the persons responsible for them were likely to be the first ones to join the companies. Slocum therefore on August 24 prohibited the formation of militia companies. He was not unmindful of the ravages of outlaws and bandits, however, for his order also directed that any local commander receiving a report of lawlessness should send a detachment of troops to disarm everyone within ten miles of the place where the acts occurred. Anyone who refused to cooperate with the troops was to be arrested and held for trial; in addition the troops were to be quartered on his premises, and he was to be compelled to pay for their support.[2]

The matter had meanwhile received immediate attention in Washington. Two days after Sharkey's proclamation appeared, President Johnson had wired the governor advising against the formation of militia and suggesting that he call on Slocum for whatever military force was necessary to preserve order. This brought the reply that Slocum's force was too small to afford protection, included no cavalry, and contained too many colored troops who did "more harm than good when scattered throughout the country." [3]

The adequacy of Slocum's force was a matter of conjecture. Osterhaus had assured Sharkey that it was "amply sufficient" if the civil authorities cooperated with the military; but to Slocum he had complained that the governor thought "a few squads of young men, armed with fowling-pieces and the omnipresent revolvers, can suppress all irregularities, which the utmost vigilance and constant exertion of a large number of United States troops failed to suppress." In September, 1865, there were 13,873 troops in the state; and although this force was gradually being reduced, by December there were still twelve regiments of infantry (all but one of them colored) and two companies of light artillery occupying eleven central posts and numerous branches thereof.[4]

General Carl Schurz, on a tour of the South, was at Vicksburg while

[2]Osterhaus to AAG Dept. Miss., Aug. 21 and 22, 1865, in *Sen. Exec. Docs.*, 39th Cong., 1st Sess., No. 2, pp. 102–103; GO 22, Dept. Miss., Aug. 24, Orders, 900, RG94, NA.

[3]Johnson to Sharkey, Aug. 21, 1865, and reply, Aug. 25, in *Sen. Exec. Docs.*, 39th Cong., 1st Sess., No. 26, pp. 229–30.

[4]Osterhaus to Sharkey, Aug. 21, 1865, and to AAG Dept. Miss., Aug. 22, in *Sen. Exec. Docs.*, 39th Cong., 1st Sess., No. 2, pp. 103–104; Monthly Return, Dept. Miss., Sept., 1865, RG94, NA; Wood to AAG Div. Tenn., Dec. 6, 1865, Dept. Miss., 2, RG98, NA.

the controversy raged, and he urged the War Department to uphold Slocum's action in the interests of preserving order. "It would at once put a stop to all vagaries on the part of Provisional Governors." [5] Sharkey in the meantime had protested to Johnson, claiming that the President had in an oral interview "distinctly stated" that the militia could be organized. The ultimate result was a directive from the War Office that Slocum rescind his order, which he did. [6]

In evaluating the President's attitude and actions, it is possible to argue that he was so intent on supporting the governments he had created that he did not mind embarrassing the Army in the process by over-ruling its actions. [7] A sounder analysis, however, is that he wanted to give the civil authorities every opportunity to show that they could handle their own affairs while at the same time recognizing the necessity of military supervision. For although he felt that militia would bolster the authority of the civil government and allow the number of troops in the state to be reduced—which for financial reasons the North desired anyhow—he also made it clear that the Army would "detect and suppress on the first appearance any move insurrectionary in its character" on the part of the militia. [8] Moreover Johnson supported the Army in conflicts with the civil governments over trials of civilians by military commissions. The necessity for these trials was clearly an embarrassment to Johnson's reconstruction policy, but he realized they were unavoidable when civil governments failed or refused to administer justice.

The formation of militia and similar organizations caused trouble in other states. In Florida General Foster approved Governor William Marvin's organizing of militia, but with the understanding that the 7th Infantry would be dispersed in small garrisons throughout the state to preserve order and that the militia would only be called out in a great emergency. The Army in South Carolina objected to the formation of militia on much the same grounds as had Slocum in Mississippi. [9] Since one of the principal reasons for forming such organizations

[5]Schurz to Stanton, Aug. 29, 1865, in Stanton Papers, LC.

[6]Sharkey to Johnson, Aug. 30, 1865, in *Sen. Exec. Docs.*, 39th Cong., 1st Sess., No. 26, p. 231; GO 23, Dept. Miss., Sept. 4, Orders, 900, RG94, NA.

[7]Eric L. McKitrick, *Andrew Johnson and Reconstruction* (Chicago, 1960), 192–95.

[8]Johnson to Schurz, Aug. 30, 1865, in *Sen. Exec. Docs.*, 39th Cong., 1st Sess., No. 26, p. 232.

[9]Foster to Gen. E. D. Townsend, AAG USA, Nov. 23, 1865, Dept. Fla., 6; Gillmore to AAG Div. Atlantic, Nov. 7, Dept. South, 15; Gen. D. E. Sickles to Gov. James Orr, Dec. 17, Dept. South, 46, RG98, NA.

was the fear of a Negro insurrection around Christmas—why during the holiday season was never made clear—some local courts and judges ordered the establishment of "county patrols" to watch the Negroes. In Arkansas the commanding general outlawed such groups after the governor agreed they were illegal. But in Tennessee, a similar force organized to "drive out desperadoes" received arms from federal stockpiles at the commanding general's direction.[10]

Generals and governors also warred over the appointment of local officials. In July, 1865, South Carolina's provisional governor, Benjamin F. Perry, issued a proclamation allowing all men who were in office when the war ended to resume their duties upon taking the amnesty oath. He did so because he felt it would be impossible to find enough new men to fill all the positions vacated and because, with the state government not yet fully reorganized, local elections would be a difficult and dangerous proceeding. But General Gillmore thought Perry had transcended his authority and consequently annulled the governor's action.[11] In Louisiana the mayoralty of New Orleans was a subject of dispute. Hugh Kennedy had received the office from General Stephen A. Hurlbut. In May Hurlbut's successor, Nathaniel P. Banks, removed Kennedy for conniving with Governor J. Madison Wells to supplant Union office-holders with rebels wherever possible and in his stead appointed an officer of the 73rd Colored Infantry. Wells and Kennedy complained to Johnson, but apparently without effect; in the June reorganization the Louisiana command went to Canby, who reinstated Kennedy without noticeable pressure from Washington.[12] General Reynolds, on the other hand, cooperated with the Arkansas Governor on appointments and arranged for the discharge of military men who became citizens of Arkansas and as such were elected or appointed to civil office.[13]

One of the most delicate political duties of the troops was their role on election day. It was clearly prudent to have military force available

[10]AAG to Gen. C. H. Morgan, CO White River Dist., Oct. 27, 1865, Dept. Ark., 2; AAG to Lt. C. F. Rockwell, Nov. 28, 1865, Div. Tenn., 33, RG98, NA.
[11]Gillmore to Gen. L. Thomas, AG USA, Aug. 1, 1865, Dept. South, 15, RG98, NA; Gillmore to Chase, Aug. 22, in Chase Papers, Historical Society of Pennsylvania; Meade to Stanton, Aug. 28, in Stanton Papers, LC.
[12]Wells to Johnson, May 5, 1865, and Banks to Samuel Hooper and to Preston King, May 6, in Johnson Papers, LC (Reel 14); Canby to Schurz, Sept. 8, 1865, Dept. Gulf, 79, RG 98, NA.
[13]File 597A1865, AGO, and Gen. E. D. Townsend, AAG USA, to Reynolds, June 12, 1865, AGO, 40, RG94, NA.

in case of disorder, but it was desirable to avoid giving the impression of intimidating the voters. The Arkansas and Virginia commanders issued orders that illustrate the usual precautions: officers and men were strictly enjoined from approaching the actual polling places on election day unless a disturbance took place and they were called on for help by the civil authorities.[14] There is no clear evidence to show that the proximity of troops caused a different political result than the composition of the voting populace would normally have produced. In the Tennessee elections of July, 1865, for example, troops were dispatched to the areas of western and central Tennessee where conservative strength was greatest because the governor, William G. "Parson" Brownlow, feared disturbances. As a result election day was peaceful, and most of the conservative candidates won—which perturbed the good "Parson" since he had allied himself with the radicals. In at least one instance, however (Richmond, Virginia), the Army with President Johnson's sanction set aside the results of an election because too many unpardoned rebels had been elected.[15]

The administration of justice in the postwar South brought the Army more grief and headaches than almost any other aspect of its occupation experience. Four factors combined to make the problem a knotty one. The structure of the military judicial system itself was cumbersome and involved. Frequent conflicts of jurisdiction with the reopening civil courts occurred. The legal problems arising from the war were not always the easiest puzzles to unravel. Many officers had only a modicum of legal training, if that, and often this training had been confined to the law of the Articles of War. The wonder is not that some irregularities and unfortunate situations arose, but that there were not more of them.

The Army's courts were essentially of three types: the court-martial, the military commission, and the provost court.[16] The court-martial dealt with offenses committed by persons in the military service. Established by statute law and following specified rules of procedure, it tried cases arising under the Articles of War and the rules and regulations

[14]GO 93, Dept. Ark., Sept. 29, 1865, Orders, 829; GO 122, Dept. Va., Oct. 9, 1865, Orders, 983, RG94, NA.

[15]James W. Patton, *Unionism and Reconstruction in Tennessee, 1860–69* (Chapel Hill, 1934), 109–10; *Official Records,* Ser. I, Vol. XLIX, Pt. 2, p. 1093; *Harper's Weekly,* IX (Sept. 2, 1865), 547.

[16]For a general treatment of martial law and military legal systems see James G. Randall, *Constitutional Problems Under Lincoln* (Rev. ed.; Urbana, 1951), 140–85; Charles Fairman, *The Law of Martial Rule* (Chicago, 1930), esp. 197–205; and Robert S. Rankin, *When Civil Law Fails* (Durham, 1939).

of the Army. It had no jurisdiction over civilians and could not try infractions of civil law.

The military commission proceeded under rules similar to those for courts-martial, but it was not authorized by statute law. It derived its authority from the existence of martial law and from the powers of the military commander under the laws of war. It was used during the conflict to try civilians in occupied areas for military offenses or offenses against the laws of war, such as bushwhacking or guerrilla activities. It was a necessary instrument in such cases because the courts-martial could not adjudicate them and because the civil courts were not functioning.

After the cessation of hostilities the employment of the military commission continued, but with an alteration in principal function. Civilians were still tried for wartime military offenses, but the commissions were increasingly used to punish civilians for infractions of state and local laws in areas where the regular civil courts either had not yet been reestablished or refused to administer justice impartially. The Army felt that the commissions were necessary to ensure punishment of crime and that, since martial law continued after Appomattox, the legal basis for military commissions continued.

The provost court—the name derives from the Army's policemen being called provost marshals—was a peculiar institution which some commanders preferred not to use at all. It had the same source of authority as the military commission, though its jurisdiction was limited to cases of lesser degree. Its prime utility was to unburden the commissions of numerous petty criminal cases, and in this it served a desirable purpose. Whereas the rules of procedure for the military commission were fairly well standarized, those for the provost court were drawn up by the commander establishing them and often varied from one command to the next. Moreover, in some areas of the South provost courts heard minor cases involving Negroes and consequently clashed with the special courts operated by the Freedmen's Bureau.

Provost courts had been established in some commands during the war but had never been wholly satisfactory and had even incurred the displeasure of the Judge Advocate General. Before hostilities ended, General N. J. T. Dana had used them at Vicksburg and Natchez to handle various minor offenses by civilians—disobedience of military orders, charging soldiers exorbitant rates to ride on Mississippi River steamboats, and similar infractions. Unclear definition of jurisdiction led to considerable irregularity; in May, 1865, the Judge Advocate General decided the courts were illegal and Dana disbanded them. A similar fate befell the provost court at New Berne, North Carolina, its fault having been the adjudication of civil disputes between individual citizens.[17]

The most comprehensive system of provost courts set up after the war was that of General Gillmore in South Carolina. Bearing no clear resemblance to either a military or a civil court hierarchy, it contained both "superior" and "circuit" courts which were to have concurrent jurisdiction. Appeals could be taken to the subdistrict or district commanders under whatever rules those officers cared to establish. Whether one might appeal from a superior to a circuit court, seemingly a reasonable enough procedure, was unstated. The superior courts were to have one officer as provost judge who could select one or two citizens, preferably with magisterial experience, to sit with him. The circuit courts were comprised of one member of a superior court and one or two civilians.

This involved system could try all disputes between citizens and between citizens and soldiers and all violations of orders or federal laws which did not come under the jurisdiction of other military courts. It could also try violations of Freedmen's Bureau orders, but crimes by civilians requiring greater punishment than a $100 fine or six months in jail still went to military commissions. The courts could issue process to compel the attendance of witnesses and also decrees for possession of property and payment of debts. These courts were intended to be only temporary and were gradually phased out in areas of the state where the regular civil courts resumed operations. The temporary nature of this provost court system was in fact a blessing, since the possibilities for arbitrariness and irregularity were legion.[18]

Among the various legal Gordian knots the Army sought to unravel, disputes between Southern civilians over property rights were particularly troublesome. In some of these cases the title had been in dispute even before the war, and during hostilities the property might have changed hands several times. Many such cases were made still more complicated by the property's having been captured or abandoned during the war and thus coming under control of the federal government. In some instances the United States had sold the property to third parties; in others it had held the property for use by the Army or other government agencies. Postwar attempts of the original owners to recover the

[17]GO 31, Dept. Miss., March 15, 1865, and GO 43, May 6, Orders, 900, RG94, NA; Gen. J. A. Rawlins, C/S HQA, and Col. T. S. Bowers, AAG HQA, to Schofield, May 20, 1865, in *Official Records*, Ser. I, Vol. XLVII, Pt. 3, pp. 541–42.
[18]GO 102, Dept. South, June 27, 1865, Orders, 958, RG94, NA.

property led to much confusion since the Confiscation Act of 1862 was silent on the matter of restoration. Disentangling the resulting legal snarls was not infrequently beyond the meager legal knowledge of some officers.

A particularly involved case concerned the plantation of Mrs. Patience Eustis, near Beaufort, South Carolina. She had died in May, 1860, and had left her estate to several legatees, one of whom was her stepson, F. A. Eustis. Two attorneys, whom she had appointed her executors, administered the estate until Union forces seized it in the fall of 1861 on the ground that the executors were disloyal. The Army placed Eustis in control of the land, and he worked it during the rest of the war for the benefit of the former slaves. In November, 1865, General Gillmore took the part of the dispossessed executors and restored them to control. Eustis protested and the case went to General Oliver O. Howard, head of the Freedmen's Bureau. He admitted he did not understand all the legal points, but he thought the crops and their revenues belonged properly to Eustis and the Negroes and recommended the revocation of Gillmore's order. The Judge Advocate General concurred, and Eustis regained possession. The ultimate solution of the title question was left to the federal courts.[19]

In July, 1865, General Gillmore announced a policy for such property disputes. Property was not to be restored if it had been sold to a third party after having been seized or if the owner were excepted from the provisions of Johnson's amnesty proclamation and still unpardoned. Where the Army was still temporarily using the property, the claim was to be handled by Gillmore's elaborate system of provost courts, and decisions adverse to the claimants could be appealed to his own headquarters.

Gillmore provided some basic rules for adjudication. Citing wartime instructions, he defined property as "abandoned" when its owner was absent for purposes of aiding the rebellion. "Captured" property was that taken from hostile possession by federal troops. The meaning of the term "confiscable" property caused more problems. Gillmore began simply enough: it was property subject to confiscation under the Act of July 17, 1862. Then he elaborated: "Conclusive proof of disloyalty is not needed to authorize the seizing and holding of property as confiscable, but on the other hand property cannot be seized or held on the ground that the owner may possibly be a rebel. A prima facie case of disloyalty must be made out, and if the owner has taken an oath of

[19]Files 2567M1865 and 109P1867, AGO; Townsend to Sickles, Jan. 5, 1866, AGO, 42, RG94, NA.

allegiance there must be good reason to suspect that he has taken it fraudulently, or is not within its provisons to authorize the withholding of his property." This last statement was cryptic, to say the least, and judgments of confused provost courts only added to the general dissatisfaction with the whole provost court system.[20]

A safer and clearer policy concerning property rights than Gillmore's was that of General Canby in Louisiana. Referring to a specific claim, he held that the title to abandoned property automatically passed from the owner by the act of abandonment and that the claimant could only be reinstated by "executive remission" or through the United States Court of Claims. Canby thought the authority had not been delegated to subordinate officers of the War or Treasury departments and that his only function was to see that the property did not pass from the control of the government until proper authority had released it.[21]

In Tennessee, even though General Thomas returned property to the owner as soon as the Army had finished using it for military purposes, he still found himself engulfed by petitions not only for restoration but also for the payment of rent for the government's use of the property. The most troublesome individuals were disloyal owners who abandoned their property to serve in the Confederate forces or otherwise aid in the rebellion. When these persons could not get their way with Thomas they sometimes appealed to President Johnson himself.[22]

Vexatious situations sometimes arose from actions of the Confederate government or from wartime transactions based on Confederate currency. Shortly after the war ended General Halleck set up a special court of arbitration in Richmond to decide cases of property rights and debts where the contract involved Confederate money. This court was not to decide on property *titles,* but simply on rights of possession—provided the court's personnel could distinguish between the two—and its rulings were no bar to future legal action in civil courts. Perhaps fortunately, this court had a short life, for the civil tribunals soon reopened. But Virginia courts were notoriously slow in rendering verdicts—eighteen months in some instances—and General Terry disliked the injustice of these delays. He therefore extended over the whole state the jurisdiction of the city of Richmond's Court of Conciliation, so that it could decide cases of property belonging to Union men which had been seized under the Rebel Confiscation Act and sold. Proceedings in

[20]Gillmore to Gen. J. P. Hatch, CO Charleston, July 3, 1865, and to Capt. Lewis Reed, Provost Judge, July 29, Dept. South, 15, RG98, NA.
[21]Canby to Gov. of La., Aug. 5, 1865, Dept. Gulf, 79, RG98, NA.
[22]Thomas to Johnson, Aug. 26, 1865, Div. Tenn., 33, RG98, NA.

this court were summary and inexpensive compared to those in the regular state courts.[23]

The President finally took a hand in the matter of property rights, and in September, 1865, he had the War Department put a stop to most of the irregularities: "Military officers have no authority to interfere in any way in questions of sale or contracts of any kind between individuals or to decide any question of property between them without special instructions from this Department authorizing their action, and the usurpation of such power will be treated as a grave military offense." Johnson's edict seems to have been prompted by the case of an officer in Georgia trying to decide a dispute over 10,000 bales of cotton.[24]

The caution which General Steedman displayed in his guide concerning military arrest of civilians was typical of other commanders. Thomas had previously issued similar instructions in Tennessee, and Steedman's order was in fact closely modeled on that of Thomas.[25] This caution reflected not only the Army's general desire to leave as much as possible to the civil governments, but also the practical difficulty of finding sufficient competent officers to sit on a large number of military commissions. The generals' cautiousness did not mean, however, that they would sit quietly and see crime go unpunished. After all of the organized rebel armies had surrendered, anyone still remaining in arms against the government was subject to military trial as a guerrilla. Grant issued orders to this effect to the entire Army, and local commanders enforced them.[26] Military commissions also continued sentencing people to death for acts of guerrilla warfare committed before hostilities ended.[27]

The Army was especially concerned, too, about theft of government property. In September, 1865, an order from General Woods threatened Alabamans who stole government livestock with military trial and punishment as great as that provided by state law. A case the following month resulted in a sentence of four years at hard labor. In a

[23]GO 5, Div. the James, May 3, 1865, in *Official Records*, Ser. I, Vol. XLVI, Pt. 3, pp. 1074–75; GO 114, Dept. Va., Sept. 21, 1865, Orders, 983, RG94, NA; Terry to AAG Div. Atlantic, Oct. 2, 1865, Dept. Va., 14, RG98, NA.

[24]SO 503, AGO, Sept. 19, 1865, RG94, NA; GO 15, Dept. Ga., Sept. 20, Orders, 278, RG94, NA; *Army and Navy Journal*, III (Oct. 7, 1865), 99.

[25]GO 27, Dept. Cumberland, May 2, 1865, Orders, 955, RG94, NA.

[26]GO 90, AGO, May 11, 1865, RG94, NA; C/S to Gen. J. A. Mower, CG East. Dist. Tex., July 22, 1865, Dept. Gulf, 79, RG98, NA.

[27]GO 12, Dept. Tenn., Sept. 30, 1865, and GO 22, Dec. 22, Orders, 969, RG94, NA. Both trials took place in July.

similar case in Mississippi Johnson himself ordered a military trial.[28] Capital crimes such as murder and assault also claimed the Army's attention. In Arkansas a man accused of assault with intent to commit murder received the death penalty, but the commanding general in reviewing the case mitigated the sentence to ten years at hard labor. A Georgian was hanged for the murder of a Negro woman, both General Steedman and the President having approved the sentence. From Alabama, where the federal district court was not yet fully operational, came a request for permission, which Johnson gave, to try by military commission a man engaged in kidnaping Negroes and selling them into slavery in Cuba.[29]

Serious crimes by Negroes were not tolerated either. A Mississippi Negro received one year at hard labor on the Dry Tortugas for the attempted rape of a white woman. In Georgia a Negro was hanged for the murder of a white man, neither the commanding general nor the President seeing any reason to mitigate the sentence. And in the same state a Negro cook who failed to achieve her aim in serving her employer a special delicacy—butter flavored with strychnine—went to Fort Pulaski for one year, though the original sentence had been for three.[30]

In its administration of justice the Army had to work closely with civil officials. The soldiers sought to protect themselves and to minimize difficulty by issuing general instructions periodically and by asking higher headquarters for advice in doubtful cases. When acting to preserve order where the local authorities either could not or would not, troops in Mississippi were to go forth under the command of a "discreet" officer bearing written instructions "designating minutely, in every particular," what was to be done. The officer was to furnish a "minute written report" to higher headquarters.[31] Fairly typical were the directions sent to a young post commander in Tennessee: take a small detachment and go with the county sheriff to arrest a gang of outlaws; if the sheriff is reluctant to make the arrests, report him to headquarters. "You will consider your detachment simply as the Sheriff's posse, to be obedient to his requests and orders and those of his authorized

[28]GO 30, Dept. Ala., Sept. 4, 1865, and GO 1, Jan. 5, 1866, Orders, 815; Files 774G1865, 2227M1865, and 2250M1865, AGO; Townsend to Slocum, Aug. 21, 1865, AGO, 45, RG94, NA.

[29]GO 96, Dept. Ark., Oct. 3, 1865, Orders, 829; GO 32, Dept. Ga., Dec. 22, 1865, Orders, 278; Woods to Stanton, Dec. 9, 1865, file 1348A1865, AGO; Townsend to Woods, Jan. 4, 1866, AGO, 42, RG94, NA.

[30]GCMO 10, Dept. Miss., Sept. 28, 1865, Orders, 900; GO 14, Dept. Ga., March 12, 1866, and GO 27, Dec. 4, 1865, Orders, 278, RG94, NA.

[31]GO 36, Dept. Miss., Nov. 24, 1865, Orders, 900, RG94, NA.

deputies." Other generals sometimes gave the detachment commanders more discretion.[32]

On the whole the Army desired harmonious relations with the local authorities, but at times an overzealous officer or an indolent or incompetent civil official precipitated a conflict. The number of these civil-military clashes increased as more of the civil courts reopened. General Thomas H. Ruger, a subordinate commander in North Carolina, arrested three civilians for assaulting a Negro and held them for military trial. Provisional Governor Holden claimed the civil authorities ought properly to try the case and were willing to do so. But Ruger refused to remand the prisoners. He felt the state had not yet been fully restored and that preservation of order and punishment of crime were matters for the Army to handle.[33]

A more serious conflict arose in Mississippi. On July 4, 1865, a white man, Joseph L. Jackson, shot and killed a Negro. General Slocum had him arrested and brought to Vicksburg for trial before a military commission. Jackson appealed to Daniel Merwin, a local judge appointed by the governor, for a writ of habeas corpus. The judge issued it, but Slocum refused to comply, holding that Mississippi was still under martial law and that the state laws gave greater protection to whites than to Negroes. He also arrested Judge Merwin for issuing the writ. On the twentieth Merwin appealed to Governor Sharkey; the general's action, he said, was a "violent and strong-handed injustice" to him personally and also "a blow by the mailed hand of military power against the civil authority in the exercise of its most valued and hitherto most respected function."

Sharkey in turn appealed to the President through Secretary of State William H. Seward. He claimed that the state laws provided the same punishment for murdering a Negro as for murdering a white man and that even if martial law had existed in Mississippi previously—which fact he had never heard of—the President's proclamation establishing a provisional government had removed it. On the twenty-fourth the wires carried Seward's reply: "The President sees no reason to interfere with General Slocum's proceedings. The government of the State will be provisional only until the civil authorities shall be restored, with the approval of Congress. Meanwhile military authority cannot be withdrawn." [34]

More appeals from Sharkey dragged the case on into August. Seward

---

[32]AAG to Lt. John Carter, Sept. 4 and 5, 1865, Div. Tenn., 33, RG98, NA.
[33]*Army and Navy Journal,* III (Sept. 2, 1865), 24.
[34]Correspondence in *Sen. Exec. Docs.,* 39th Cong., 1st Sess., No. 26, pp. 55–60.

finally asked Attorney General James Speed for a legal opinion on the relative power of the civil and military jurisdictions. Speed narrowly construed the powers of the provisional governors, stating, "There are now no legal and constitutional administrative functionaries of government in Mississippi except the Army." Navy Secretary Welles noted some disagreement between Johnson and Speed when this opinion was undergoing discussion in Cabinet, but the President finally told Seward to wire Sharkey that it was still inexpedient to restore the privilege of the writ of habeas corpus. That ended that.[35]

Relations between governors and generals were not always stormy, though. In South Carolina General Gillmore and Governor Perry compromised on the court problem with the assistance of Gillmore's superior, General Meade. Jointly announced in a September proclamation and general order, the new policy was that the provost courts were to have exclusive jurisdiction of all cases involving Negroes, and that state courts under state law should hear other cases. Civil magistrates could make whatever arrests were necessary to apprehend criminals, but any Negroes arrested were to be remanded to military custody.[36]

The Army also had to work in close cooperation with federal civil officers, of whom the most important were agents of the Treasury Department and the personnel of the gradually reopening federal courts. After hostilities ended, treasury agents scoured the South collecting cotton which had been the property of the Confederate government and hence was subject to seizure by the United States. They then shipped this cotton to designated agents in Northern cities for disposal. In this work they had to rely on the Army for protection.

In June, 1865, General Grant wired commanders in the South that in their efforts to seize holdings of the Confederate government they should be careful not to endanger private property, and that they should aid the treasury agents in protecting and bringing to market cotton already in federal possession. Grant's message touched the most delicate questions of all in the cotton chaos, those of titles and ownership. *Did a particular lot of cotton actually belong to the Confederate government, or was it really private property?* Some local commanders tried to decide such matters, though higher headquarters frowned on the practice.[37] General Canby became so disgusted with the administration

[35]Correspondence *ibid.*, 60; 11 Opinions of Attorneys General 322–26; Beale (ed.), *Diary of Gideon Welles,* II, 366–67.
[36]*Army and Navy Journal,* III (Sept. 16, 1865), 49, 61.
[37]Grant to Sheridan, June 26, 1865, in Daniel O. Drennan Papers, LC; GO 7, Dept. Miss., July 31, 1865, Orders, 900, RG94, NA; AAAG to CO Macon, Miss., July 8, 1865, and to CO Enterprise, Miss., Sept. 1, 1865, 4MD, 85, RG98, NA.

of the cotton question in Louisiana that he telegraphed Stanton recommending that the government give up the whole idea and simply relinquish the property to the original holders. In return for this concession he advocated a tax of $5.00 per bale on all cotton brought to market. But the collectors stalked through the land well into 1866.[38]

Opportunities for fraud and corruption abounded. Railroad conductors deliberately tampered with manifests, and carloads of cotton got mysteriously sidetracked. Steamboat captains made unscheduled stops at private docks. Treasury agents themselves perpetrated many of these frauds, and in consequence the Army had to guard not only the agents against irate Southerners but also the government against its dishonest employees. Numerous complaints about irregularities reached Treasury Secretary Hugh McCulloch, who enlisted the Army's aid to stop the abuse. He informed General Reynolds in Arkansas that any agents who took cotton which they could not prove was Confederate property overstepped their authority, and he asked Reynolds to do what he could to stop such theft. McCulloch also directed customs officers to assume the duties of receiving property in certain cases.[39]

General Woods was especially vigilant in ferreting out shady deals by Alabama cotton agents. In October, 1865, he ordered a military commission to try Thomas J. Carver for fraud. During August and September Carver, the agent for Choctaw County, had conspired with a private citizen to buy 227 bales of government cotton for himself at a price far below the market value. He was found guilty, fined $90,000, and sentenced to hard labor for one year and until the fine was paid. Woods, convinced that Carver was "the tool of more designing parties," remitted the imprisonment in consideration of Carver's advanced age and the fact that he gave evidence implicating numerous others. Woods was sure that more than 50,000 bales of government cotton had been stolen in Alabama and shipped out of the state or moved about from place to place so that all trace of it had disappeared. The Carver case furnished his first clues.[40]

Perhaps the most spectacular episode in the whole cotton drama was the case of T. C. A. Dexter, which the Carver prosecution had brought to light. On November 13 Woods convened a military commission to

---

[38]Canby to Sec. War, Aug. 12, 1865, Dept. Gulf, 79, RG98, NA. *Sen. Exec. Docs.,* 43rd Cong., 2nd Sess., No. 23, contains statistics on all cotton collected.
[39]Reynolds to CO Ouachita Dist., Dec. 16, 1865, Dept. Ark., 2; C/S to Gen. J. A. Mower, CG East. Dist. Tex., July 22, 1865, Dept. Gulf, 79, RG98, NA.
[40]GO 55, Dept. Ala., Oct. 30, 1865, Orders, 815, RG94, NA; Woods to Gen. L. Thomas, AG USA, Nov. 9, and to McCulloch, Nov. 10, Dept. Ala., 1, RG98, NA.

try Dexter on two charges: defrauding the government, in that he had appropriated for his own use 3,426 bales of government cotton, and malfeasance in office, in that he had sold a subordinate position to a friend for $25,000. On the twenty-second, after the commission began the case, Dexter appealed to a newly-arrived federal carpetbagger judge, Richard Busteed, for a writ of habeas corpus. Busteed issued the writ, but Woods refused to comply, stating that Dexter was held by order of President Johnson and General Thomas and that the privilege of the writ had not been restored in Alabama. The next day Busteed ordered Woods arrested for disobeying the writ and ordered the commission to stop its proceedings. Since the general declined to be arrested and the judge had no physical force to compel it, the latter was stymied. An appeal to Johnson brought presidential approval of Woods's course, and the commission continued without interruption. On February 17, 1866, came the announcement of the judgment—and what a judgment: $250,000 fine, imprisonment for one year and until the fine was paid, and permanent disqualification from holding any office of honor, trust, or profit under the United States.[41] This was apparently the only instance during Reconstruction in which the sentence of a military commission included a political disability.

But the Dexter case did not rest there. Before announcement of the findings, the War Office had directed Woods to supend the execution of whatever sentence the commission imposed until the Judge Advocate General could review the case. The review was a slow process, and in the meanwhile Busteed made another unsuccessful attempt to make the blue tunic bow to the black robe. Late in March Dexter filed a damage suit for $500,000 against Woods and the members of the commission, and the War Department promptly hired civilian counsel to defend them. The case was postponed, however, and on April 14 Woods turned Dexter over to the federal court in compliance with instructions from Washington.[42]

General Woods had displayed a commendable zeal in trapping miscreants, though at the same time a censurable lack of faith in the regular federal courts. He claimed that the military commission had begun

[41]GO 8, Dept. Ala., Feb. 17, 1866, Orders, 815, RG94, NA; copy of writ, Woods's return, and Court Clerk's briefs, Dec. 22–23, 1865, and Woods to Stanton, Dec. 13, Dept. Ala., 1, RG98, NA; *Army and Navy Journal,* III (Dec. 2, 9, and 23, 1865), 225, 242, 278.

[42]Townsend to Woods, Feb. 10, 1866, and to Henry Stansbury [Stanbery?], March 30, 1866, AGO, 42, RG94, NA; Woods to Gen. L. Thomas, AG USA, Feb. 19, 1866, and to McCulloch, April 15, and an undated response to a writ entered under April 9, 1866, Dept. Ala., 1, RG98, NA.

before Busteed arrived in Alabama to establish his court, which may have been true. Yet in December, 1865, Woods requested permission to try federal offenses by military commission, claiming that the district court was not yet established and ready to handle cases, even though the judge was clearly in the state and firing writs at the general by mid-November. On the other hand, Busteed's motives are hard to fathom, especially in view of his Janus-like course with respect to reconstruction in 1867–68. Public sentiment in Alabama was on his side in the dispute, though this probably reflected a general desire to have the civil authorities deal with such affairs rather than any personal approval of Busteed, who seems to have been as notorious a scamp as Dexter himself.[43]

In addition to maintaining a close watch on miscreant treasury agents the Army was even directed on occasion to investigate federal courts themselves. In June, 1865, the War Department ordered a military inquiry into the Florida court. Irregularities had been complained of in certain prize and confiscation cases, and the investigating officer was expected to review the character and loyalty of the judge and marshal, the procedural rules of the court, the completeness of the evidence presented, *and the propriety of the judgments.* Nothing ever came of the incident, however, and it was indeed fortunate that such singular labors were not given to the Army as a regular matter of course.[44]

Even though conflicts with federal courts did arise on occasion, the generals nonetheless saw the need for speedy reestablishment of the courts and urged Washington to take the necessary steps. As the Texas commander put it: "Cases are constantly arising which are properly referrable to the District U.S. Court, and which call for prompt adjustment; and as they often involve nice points of law, I have not the means for properly deciding them, even if I conceived myself authorized to entertain them." [45]

Emancipation created a critical social and economic problem for the South and a different though equally serious one for the Army. In the spring of 1865 Congress formed the Bureau of Refugees, Freedmen, and Abandoned Lands, primarily to protect the interests of former slaves. It was a bureau of the War Department and its head was a regular Army officer, General Oliver Otis Howard. The existence of this bureau did not relieve the occupation forces from concern with the Negro;

[43]Fleming, *Alabama,* 413–14.
[44]Gillmore to Gen. I. Vogdes, CG Dist. Fla., June 22, 1865, Dept. South, 15, RG98, NA.
[45]Gen. H. G: Wright to AAG Div. Gulf, Nov. 20, 1865, in Sheridan Papers, LC.

indeed, it made the Army's task rather more difficult for three reasons. First, the organization and operation of the bureau at its lowest local level were slow in being perfected. Second, conflicts of jurisdiction among the bureau, the occupation forces, and the civil governments often occurred; and the local agents of the bureau were sometimes civilians, sometimes Army officers. Third, the natural dislike of many white Southerners for the bureau also manifested itself against the occupation forces since they were, in fact, the only power with which the bureau could enforce its policies.[46]

Freedom and the end of hostilities had a mischievous pyschological effect on some Negroes, who wandered about from place to place, congregated around military posts, and generally thought ill of having to work for a living, if indeed they understood the practical necessity of doing so. In the weeks immediately after Appomattox, whites feared the Negroes would form gangs to loot and pillage, which did occur in some places. From the upper reaches of the Cape Fear River one North Carolinian asked for military protection after an armed gang of Negroes, claiming vaguely to be acting "under orders"—whose orders they did not say—raided his house. "They said their object and business was to examine papers, secure arms, get *forage,* drive Negroes off from the farms, and rectify the country, generally." [47]

Though turbulence on the part of the Negroes was not widespread, the Army still felt that prudent restrictions on their actions would speed the return of order to society. In eastern Virginia General George H. Gordon proclaimed that the Negro "must earn his own bread by the sweat of his own brow" and warned, "For the idle and lazy vagabond the penitentiary is provided, where compulsory labor lessens expense." General Francis Herron ordered the Negroes of northern Louisiana to stay on their former plantations and get the crops in, threatening to arrest and punish those found wandering about. He also forbade steamboats on the Red River to haul freedmen who could not show military passes. Other local commanders also took steps to prevent vagrancy and idleness.[48]

The Freedmen's Bureau made comparable regulations, and when

[46]The most recent and thorough treatment of the bureau is George Bentley, *A History of the Freedmen's Bureau* (Philadelphia, 1955). It should be supplemented by John A. Carpenter, *Sword and Olive Branch* (Pittsburg, 1964), a biography of General Howard.

[47]J. F. Oliver to Hawley, May 15, 1865, in Hawley Papers, LC. Original emphasis.

[48]*Army and Navy Journal,* II (May 20, 1865), 615; *Official Records,* Ser. I, Vol. XLVII, Pt. 2, pp. 854–55, and Vol. XLIX, Pt. 2, pp. 916, 1043–44.

some of the legislatures elected under the auspices of the Johnson governments met they too passed laws of similar nature—the Black Codes. Though on some subjects the latter were harsher than the military decrees, there is a remarkable similarity in the measures of the Army, the bureau, and the states which highlights the magnitude of the problem and makes passage of the Black Codes more understandable.[49]

These restrictive measures did not quiet public fears, however, and rumors of a Negro insurrection planned around Christmas time were heard with increasing frequency as the year wore on. In western Tennessee concern became so great that two white regiments, the 11th Missouri and 12th Iowa, had to be brought in from other parts of the state to offset possible danger caused by the presence of colored troops. In other states the newly-formed militia companies sought to disarm Negroes, an action which Army commanders disapproved. When asked about this matter with regard to Mississippi, President Johnson decided that only the Army had authority to disarm anybody, and that if the Army had to do so at all, it should disarm all troublemakers of whatever color.[50] In Louisiana, General Canby at Grant's direction forbade colored soldiers who were being discharged from the Army to purchase their arms.[51] This deviation from the standard practice can only be explained as a precaution to avert apprehended bloodshed.

Generals, bureau officials, and state legislators alike realized that the restoration of a stable economy required a reliable labor supply. The disinclination of some Negroes to work, induced by the tenacious belief that free lands would be given them at the end of 1865, and the bewilderment of some with their new freedom, which some planters used to the Negroes' disadvantage, proved major stumbling blocks to the solution of the problem. Army and bureau urged the Negroes to make written contracts with their employers, and one of the bureau's prime functions was to approve and supervise the execution of these pacts.

---

[49] A convenient if selective compilation of the bureau's circulars is *House Exec. Docs.,* 39th Cong., 1st Sess., No. 70. Similar works for the Black Codes are *Sen. Exec. Docs.,* 39th Cong., 2nd Sess., No. 6, pp. 170–230, and Walter L. Fleming, *Documentary History of Reconstruction* (Cleveland, 1906), I, 244–310. I first noticed the similarity among Army orders, bureau circulars, and the Black Codes several years ago in an unpublished seminar paper. More recently the same point has been made by Theodore B. Wilson in his study, *The Black Codes of the South* (University, Ala., 1965).

[50] AAG to Gen. J. E. Smith, CG Dist. West. Tenn., Dec. 26, 1865, Div. Tenn., 33, RG98, NA; Gen. T. J. Wood to Gov. B. G. Humphreys, Nov. 28, 1865, and Dec. 20, 1865, Dept. Miss., 2, RG98, NA.

[51] Gen. J. A. Rawlins, C/S HQA, to Sheridan, Oct. 26, 1865, in Drennan Papers, LC.

But the contract system did not always work well due to frequent violations, by design on the part of unscrupulous employers and by ignorance or laziness on the part of the Negroes. In some areas Negroes would only work on the crops themselves, neglecting ditches, fences, and outbuildings.

From time to time officers suggested other approaches, though none seemed to work with complete success. In Virginia General Terry considered a "peasant proprietor" system, wherein competent freedmen would be settled on abandoned land under bureau control with the understanding that through industry and frugality they could ultimately become owners. Terry also believed that working for a share of the crop was better than working for wages since the Negro had little concept of the value of money and would be more productive if he were paid in kind.[52] Bureau circulars and state Black Codes also sought to improve the situation. Although progress with many aspects of the Negro's elevation from slavery to freedom seemed slow, officers like General Canby realized that Southern society could not be transformed suddenly:

It is scarcely reasonable to expect, that we shall get out of the wilderness in forty days, or that society disintegrated and demoralized by a war of four years, and the emancipation of a race, can at once be restored to order and regularity. The facts stated by Mr. Sandodge, furnish in my opinion no just ground for his gloomy views of the present, or his desponding anticipations of the future, and it is neither policy nor wisdom, to condemn the policy the Government has adopted, or may hereafter adopt in relation to the colored population, until it has been fairly tested. On the contrary it is the duty of all well disposed persons to give to that policy such support as will ensure its being fairly tested.[53]

Protecting the Negro's civil rights caused the Army serious difficulties. The generals were quick to proclaim whites and Negroes equal before the law and also quick to enforce that equality. But they understood the desirability of having the civil authorities take the lead in this field and interfered only where prejudice marked the latter's course. In Mississippi General Slocum objected to his subordinates' taking Negroes from civilian custody where an intention to be fair had been displayed. "The object of the Government," he said, "is not to screen this class from just punishment; not to encourage in them the idea that

[52]Gen. C. Devens to Gen. L. Thomas, AG USA, Sept. 12, 1865, Dept. South, 15; Sickles to AAG Div. Atlantic, Dec. 14, 1865, Dept. South, 46; Terry to AAG Div. Atlantic, Sept. 15, 1865, Dept. Va., 14, RG98, NA.
[53]Canby to Gov. of La., July 24, 1865, Dept. Gulf, 79, RG98, NA.

they can be guilty of crime and escape its penalties; but simply to secure to them the rights of free men, holding them, at the same time, subject to the same laws by which other classes are governed." [54]

In Virginia General Terry prohibited restraints on Negroes that did not also apply to whites but added that vagrancy would not be tolerated. Terry's chief of staff, General Joseph R. Hawley, received word of Northern public reaction. From a college fraternity brother: "I tell you his capital order hit the North exactly; it has made a hero of him again." From an Army colleague: "By the way, Senator Wilson was in high extasy [*sic*] over Gen. Terry's order in relation to the blacks in Virginia, and told me that he had been to Gen. Grant, and tried to have him order all other generals commanding Depts. to issue orders like it." From a Connecticut state legislator, noting the order's universal approval: "These F.F.V.'s find it difficult to learn that slavery is dead. They will learn after a while." [55]

But while the Army was sensitive to the necessity of legal equality for the Negro, social equality evoked different opinions. "I am in favor of elevating the Negro to the extent of his capacity and intelligence," General George A. Custer wrote from Hempstead, Texas, "and of doing everything in our power to advance the race morally and mentally as well as physically, also socially. But I am opposed to making this advance by correspondingly debasing any portion of the white race." [56] Even General Gillmore, a sincere friend of the Negro who had expressed his eagerness to "aid in the satisfactory solution of the great social question which this war has thrust upon us," complained about the bureau keeping possession of all Charleston schoolhouses, remarking, "There would seem to be neither reason nor justice in the Freedmen's Bureau retaining possession of all the houses, or in forcing the white and colored children to be mixed together in the same rooms to the annoyance and mortification of both races." [57]

The generals also endeavored to prevent the Negroes from being given unsound and inflammatory advice. Complaining about such goings-on in Charleston, Gillmore declared, "There has been too much public talking, and too little quiet and unobtrusive work." Launching a blast

---

[54]GO 10, Dept. Miss., Aug. 3, 1865, Orders, 900, RG94, NA.

[55]GO 77, Dept. Va., June 23, 1865, Orders, 983, RG94, NA; Charles Dudley Warner to Hawley, July 12, 1865, Gen. J. C. Abbott to Hawley, July 7, and V. B. Chamberlain to Hawley, July 8, in Hawley Papers, LC.

[56]Custer to Mr. and Mrs. Daniel S. Bacon (his parents-in-law), Oct. 5, 1865, in Marguerite Merington (ed.), *The Custer Story* (New York, 1950), 175.

[57]Gillmore to Howard, June 26, 1865, and to AAG Div. Atlantic, Oct. 28, 1865, Dept. South, 15, RG98, NA.

against unscrupulous former masters in addition to well-meaning Northern "friends of the Negro," Slocum observed: "The colored man can be improved and elevated; not by making him the tool of politicians; but by impressing upon him the importance of education and of forming habits of industry and economy." [58] Army officers themselves sometimes gave advice to the freedmen, and by so doing called forth objections from the bureau. In Mississippi, after receiving such complaints from the state's assistant commissioner, General Thomas J. Wood prohibited his officers from making speeches or issuing written addresses to the populace. This concern over freedmen receiving bad advice probably stemmed from the generals' common belief that Negroes were not yet qualified for the franchise. Custer opined, "As to trusting the negro of the Southern States with the most sacred and responsible privilege—the right of suffrage—I should as soon think of elevating an Indian Chief to the Popedom of Rome." [59]

Protests were lodged against officers suspected of anti-Negro prejudice, though upon investigation they often were proved false. Chief Justice Chase complained about one general who "promised [,] if he did not use [,] military force in compelling persons heretofore slaves of a railroad corporation to return to its service." Chase's reference, not at all clear, is probably to General James H. Wilson, then in Georgia; if so Chase was in error, as Wilson's correspondence shows him to be strongly anti-slavery. Vague, unspecific allegations that General John P. Hatch at Charleston was callous toward Negroes fell flat upon investigation and brought the observation from Hatch's superior that there were as many complaints about his being severe with Rebels as being unsympathetic towards Negroes. [60] At Savannah, however, a captain in a Connecticut regiment who showed great unfairness to Negroes while functioning as a provost judge was mustered out of the service. [61]

[58]Gillmore to Howard, July 2, 1865, Dept. South, 15, RG98, NA; GO 10, Dept. Miss., Aug. 3, 1865, Orders, 900, RG94, NA.

[59]Wood to AAG Div. Tenn. Dec. 6, 1865, Dept. Miss., 2, RG98, NA; GO 46, Dept. Miss., Dec. 12, Orders, 900, RG94, NA; Custer to Mr. and Mrs. Daniel S. Bacon, Oct. 5, 1865, in Merington (ed.), *Custer Story*, 175.

[60]Chase to Johnson, May 23, 1865, in Johnson Papers, LC (Reel 14); Wilson to AAG Div. Tenn., June 15, 1865, in Johnson Papers, LC (Reel 15).

[61]*House Reports*, 39th Cong., 1st Sess., No. 30, Pt. 2, pp 232–33. The statement in John Hope Franklin, *Reconstruction After the Civil War* (Chicago, 1961), 119, concerning troops oppressing Negroes is potentially misleading. Although no citation is given, the source appears to be Francis B. Simkins and Robert H. Woody, *South Carolina During Reconstruction* (Chapel Hill, 1932), 66–67. Franklin closely paraphrases a statement by Simkins and Woody based on some instances in South Carolina in 1867 and incorporates it in a paragraph

One of the basic problems complicating the Army's relations with the bureau was the latter's amorphous position in the hierarchy of military administration. It was a branch of the War Department; its head or commissioner was a general officer of the regular Army and senior in lineal rank to most of the occupation commanders; each state was under the jurisdiction of an assistant commissioner, and all of the first appointees to these posts, except in Louisiana, were also Army officers; the local agents were a variety of civilians, soldiers, and even a few Negroes (who did not last long). In May, 1865, Secretary Stanton directed the occupation commanders to detail temporarily to the bureau whatever officers and men it might request and to furnish such aid as it might require to carry out its duties.[62]

This directive had two defects. First, it meant that officers would frequently be absent from their commands and their more purely military duties, with consequent deterioration in morale, discipline, and effectiveness among the troops; and it raised the question of whether an officer on detached duty with the bureau was still responsible to his regular military superior. Second, it left unclear whether the Army had any discretion at all in furnishing aid to the bureau and in prescribing the duties of troops on such expeditions.

The first problem became even more severe as the number of troops in the South gradually diminished during 1865, and within the Army itself there were mixed feelings as to how the difficulty could be alleviated. In Virginia General Terry found it desirable in some localities to combine the offices of provost marshal and bureau agent. In Arkansas General Reynolds wanted civilian "labor agents" appointed to relieve officers of their present duties concerning contracts and employer-employee relations. He thought the best men would be persons who had never owned slaves and if possible had not lived in the Confederacy during the rebellion.[63]

Exactly the opposite sentiments prevailed on the Atlantic seaboard where the Carolina commanders, desiring to eliminate all civilians from the bureau, denounced them as "more mischievous and troublesome than beneficial—mere doctrinnaires and agitators." But they could not prevail on the assistant commissioners to let the post and subdistrict com-

---

dealing with military activity in all states from 1867–77. If Franklin intends the statement as a broad generalization, it does not hold true.

[62]GO 102, AGO, May 31, 1865, RG94, NA.

[63]Terry to AAG Div. Atlantic, Sept. 15, 1865, Dept. Va., 14, RG98, NA; GO 5, Dept. Va., Jan. 24, 1866, Orders, 984, RG94, NA; Reynolds to Howard, July 13, 1865, Dept. Ark., 2, RG98, NA.

manders act as bureau agents ex-officio.[64] Perhaps the least objectionable resolution of a basically insoluble problem would have been to merge the office of assistant commissioner with that of department commander, and to let the local commanders serve as ex-officio agents with a trustworthy resident to aid them. During later years the first part of this plan was used in a few states, but it did not make Army-bureau relations fully satisfactory.

Discretion in aiding the bureau was a knotty problem for all concerned. Some commanding generals tried to phrase their instructions broadly to allow their own subordinates considerable leeway. Thus troops in Texas received orders to render all "proper and necessary aid" to bureau agents; Mississippi forces were cautioned not to interfere in cases unauthorized by law or orders. This latitude was desirable provided both the detachment commander and the bureau agent were discreet and cautious individuals, but such was not always the case. Any attempts of bureau officials to exercise military command over troops sent to aid them evoked resistance from the commanding generals. In Georgia one officer was told not to consider himself "Chief of Police for the Agents of the Freedmen's Bureau" but to exercise supreme command over his area until civil law was reestablished and to aid the bureau "in every reasonable way, consistent with the laws of the United States and the orders from these Headquarters." [65]

The existence of a special court system within the bureau led to frequent collisions with the occupation forces. There were minor variations from state to state, but typically these courts were comprised of three members, a Bureau official and two local citizens. Their jurisdiction encompassed all cases relating to compensation of Negroes up to $300, all other cases between whites and Negroes, and all criminal actions against Negroes where conviction would lead, at the most, to a fine of $100 or a jail term of thirty days. More important cases were heard before local civil courts where these existed and showed evidence of impartiality, or before military commissions.

Friction was most likely to arise in commands where an elaborate system of provost courts existed, as in South Carolina. The Army wanted to try cases involving Negroes in the provost courts whereas the bureau preferred its own. Gillmore and Assistant Commissioner Saxton finally

---

[64]Gillmore to Gen. Rufus Saxton, Aug. 10, 1865, and to AAG Div. Atlantic, Oct. 28, 1865, Dept. South, 15; Sickles to Howard, Jan. 21, 1866, and to Grant, Jan. 22, 1866, Dept. South, 46, RG98, NA.

[65]C/S to Mower, July 22, 1865, Dept. Gulf, 79, RG98, NA; GO 10, Dept. Miss., Aug. 3, 1865, Orders, 900, RG94, NA; AAG to Gen. E. L. Molineaux, CG Dist. Nor. Ga., July 8, 1865, Dept. South, 15, RG98, NA.

reached a compromise: the provost courts would handle all Negro cases except where the bureau agent was located at a considerable distance from the nearest military force. In Georgia the policy was to try all cases involving Negroes by military commision in the absence of a bureau agent.[66] The bureau's court system may have had some beneficial effects in protecting the Negro from prejudice in the civil courts, but as a complicating factor in the Army's administration of justice, it was at best ill-advised.

All commanders were very sensitive to the last subject dealt with in General Steedman's prototype set of instructions—proper conduct of troops in their dealings with civilians. They had a difficult enough task as it was, and making the population hostile by ruthless and unprincipled action would only make it more so. The garrisons of Alabama were warned, "All complaints on the part of citizens for outrages committed by officers or enlisted men will receive an honest investigation, and if sustained after due consideration in the case, the offenders will be held to a strict accountability, and visited with prompt, severe punishment." In neighboring Mississippi General Wood announced, "Commanding officers will be held to the strictest official and pecuniary responsibility for any unorthorized [*sic*] interference with the people of this State, and for all marauding, pillaging, or any other depredations committed by their commands, whether in camp, barracks, or en route." In Texas, any of Custer's cavalrymen who committed depredations on the persons or property of civilians had their heads shaved and took twenty-five lashes on the back. He claimed it was an effective punishment.[67]

As one officer pointed out, soldiers were likely to get into trouble because the fragmentation and dispersal of small commands bred a deterioration in discipline and because the men were "removed from the restraints of home." The midsummer mugginess of Tennessee got the better of some Knoxville soldiers, who resorted to raiding private watermelon patches and milking cows belonging to citizens—and even to officers. In New Orleans some soldiers thought the uniform gave them license to ride the streetcars without paying. Georgians looked askance at the "shameless indecency" of troops at Macon going swimming on

---

[66]Gillmore to AAG Div. Atlantic, Oct. 28, 1865, Dept. South, 15; AAG to Gen. J. M. Brannan, CO Savannah, Aug. 22, 1865, Dept. Ga., 1, RG98, NA.
[67]GO 36, Dept. Ala., Sept. 15, 1865, Orders, 815; GO 36, Dept. Miss., Nov. 24, 1865, Orders, 900, RG94, NA; Merington (ed.), *Custer Story*, 172–73.

Sunday afternoons in a public park undaunted by the quartermaster's neglect to issue them swimming trunks along with their uniforms.[68]

Drunkenness and brawling were common. "I want you to deal more vigorously with liquor sellers," was the directive of the Richmond commander to his provost judge. He was determined to punish both civilians and soldiers and added, "Let it be prima facie evidence to you, that when a crowd of drunken soldiers are collected in a rum shop, liquor has been sold. . . . I will not permit soldiers together in grog shops throughout the city creating noises and disturbances; and Citizens who permit it to be done under their roof must be held responsible." In Vicksburg a colonel was acquitted after having staggered down the street roaring: "Come out and show yourselves, you G—d d——d rebel s——s of b——s. War has been declared against you for insulting me. G—d d——n your Ethiopian hearts, you dare not come out and face me now. I have come amongst you both in my uniform and in citizen's dress, and you dare not meet me. I have cowhided one G—d d——d rebel s—n of a b——h, but I'll shoot the next one who insults me, by G—d!" [69] From Madison, Georgia, came complaints about cavalry officers letting Negroes take animals from nearby farms and swarm into the camps. The correspondent added, "And the Negro girls for miles and miles are gathered to the camps and debauched. In some instances this has occurred where ladies have taken the same pains to protect their virtue that they have exercised towards their own daughters." [70]

Relations between soldiers and civilians were made more delicate by the presence of colored troops in the South. Except for three regular Army regiments organized in the fall of 1866, these were volunteer regiments recruited during the last years of the war in both Northern states and occupied areas of the South. The problems raised by the presence of colored troops became more serious as 1865 went on. A large number of white regiments were mustered out, and the proportion of colored troops in the South consequently increased. The white volunteers were all anxious to go home soon after hostilities ended, even though the terms of enlistment of some regiments did not expire until well into 1866. The colored units, however, were more willing to stay in the service, since many Negroes did not have homes to which to return or much

[68]*House Reports,* 39th Cong., 1st Sess., No. 30, Pt. 3, pp. 139–40; C/S to Col. H. G. Gibson, CO Knoxville, July 17, 1865, Dept. Tenn., 22, RG98, NA; Macon *Daily Telegraph,* July 3, 1865.

[69]Gen. John W. Turner to Col. J. McEntee, Dec. 19, 1865, 1MD, 72, RG98, NA; GCMO 5, Dept. Miss., Sept. 14, 1865, Orders, 900, RG94, NA.

[70]N. G. Foster to Gen. W. T. Sherman, May 10, 1865, in Johnson Papers, LC (Reel 14).

prospect of employment if they did leave the Army. Other reasons mitigated against keeping colored troops in the service. Most colored regiments had been organized late in the war and were less well trained and disciplined than the white volunteer units, which had been in service longer. Several cases of mutiny occurred in colored regiments but apparently none in white regiments serving in the South.[71]

A greater degree of antagonism naturally prevailed between colored troops and white civilians than when both parties were white, and this antagonism was the fault of both troops and populace. In referring to a petition from citizens of the Louisiana parishes of LaFourche and Terre Bonne, the commanding officer pointed out improprieties by both sides. The Army was willing to correct abuses by its own men, he said; but he added, correctly, that citizens were unwilling to accept from colored soldiers what they would have found less objection to in a white soldier.[72] On the other hand a North Carolinian—rather petty for the "leading man of the county"—worked himself into a "perfect fever" because a Negro soldier offered the "insult" of bowing and wishing him a good morning as he sat on his "piazza." In Florida it was possible to solve the problem partially by placing the colored troops in the coastal garrisons and larger seacoast towns, leaving the interior to be held by white volunteer forces or the small number of regulars available.[73]

The commanding generals were keenly aware of the difficulties which colored troops caused, and they did not like to have so many of them in the South. Every time muster-out orders were received which would seriously alter the proportion of white regiments to colored, the generals protested, citing the frequent calls made for replacement of colored garrisons.[74] Just after the surrender, Ord and Halleck had found it necessary to remove the whole XXV Corps from occupation duty in Virginia because its officers were incompetent, discipline was bad, the men had committed many crimes against civilians including numerous cases

---

[71]I base this statement on a survey of court-martial proceedings, and hence the affray caused by the 165th New York in Charleston is excluded, there having been no formal charge of mutiny in that case. For instances of mutiny in colored regiments see GCMO 12, Dept. Miss., Nov. 11, 1865, Orders, 900; GO 22, Dept. Tenn., Dec. 22, 1865, Orders, 969; GO 12, Dept. South, Sept. 19, 1866, Orders, 959, RG94, NA.

[72]Canby to Wells, Aug. 10 and 26, 1865, Dept. Gulf, 79, RG98, NA.

[73]*House Reports,* 39th Cong., 1st Sess., No. 30, Pt. 2, p. 178; Gen. J. G. Foster to Sheridan, Oct. 29, 1865, Dept. Fla., 6, RG98, NA.

[74]Sheridan to Stanton, Aug. 19, 1865, in Drennan Papers, LC; AAG to Gen. J. E. Smith, CG Dist. West. Tenn., Sept. 19, 1865, Dept. Tenn., 22, RG98, NA.

of "atrocious rape," and because its presence had a bad influence on the Negro population. It was replaced with a corps of white troops from the Army of the Potomac. In South Carolina, where out of 14,000 troops only 2,500 were white, General Gillmore complained:

I have found so many bad men among the non-commissioned officers and privates of some of my colored regiments—men, who by their false representations and seditious advice, have exercised a most baleful influence upon the plantation laborers,—that I have been forced to devolve upon the white troops—to a much greater degree than their numbers would justify— the onerous and delicate duties of instructing the inhabitants of the country in their rights and responsibilities as well as the ratifying and enforcing of labor contracts. In many instances nearly all the laborers on large plantations under extensive cultivation have violated their contracts and suspended their work in consequence of the pernicious influence of a few bad colored soldiers, who were formerly slaves in the neighborhood.

But while Gillmore did not want colored troops in the service, he felt reluctant to muster out those from Southern states because the discharged men would have caused trouble in the community.[75]

In September General Grant finally urged Secretary Stanton to have all colored regiments raised in Northern states mustered out. This, however, did not markedly reduce the number of colored troops remaining, because many regiments had been raised in the South. During the last half of 1865 and the first months of 1866 the proportion of colored to white troops in some parts of the South was 3 to 1 or higher. The order to muster out numerous white volunteer regiments in August, 1865, left General Stoneman in Tennessee with the 16th Infantry, a couple of batteries of artillery, and thirteen colored regiments of all arms. Five of these colored regiments were ordered to Alabama—where at the moment white troops predominated—so that General Woods could muster out five white regiments. In December, 1865, only one of twelve infantry regiments in Mississippi was white, and in the following month Sheridan reported 6,550 white and 19,768 colored volunteers in Texas and Louisiana. During 1866 the colored volunteer regiments were gradually mustered out, but some remained as late as November of that year.[76]

[75]Halleck to Grant, April 29 and 30, 1865, and reply, April 30, in *Official Records,* Ser. I, Vol. XLVI, Pt. 3, pp. 1005, 1016; Gillmore to Gen. L. Thomas, AG USA, Aug. 20, 1865, Dept. South, 15, RG98, NA.
[76]Grant to Stanton, Sept. 6, 1865, in Stanton Papers, LC; Thomas to Grant, Aug. 23, 1865, Div. Tenn., 33; Wood to AAG Div. Tenn., Dec. 6, 1865, Dept. Miss., 2, RG98, NA; Sheridan to Grant, Jan. 7, 1866, in Drennan Papers, LC. Thus it would seem that the statistical data on the number of colored troops

The mere fact of colored troops being from the South did not justify keeping them there on occupation duty; indeed, the consistent application of any such principle as "duty-in-one's-home-territory" would have made it impossible to garrison frontier posts adequately. As the records of the subsequently organized 9th and 10th Cavalry demonstrated, colored units could have been sent to the frontier as easily as not. On the question of colored troops the Army and the white Southerners were in substantial agreement. Although they did not always share the same reasons, the agreement is understandable for, as a policy, keeping colored troops in the South was very clearly ill-advised.

Troops frequently performed acts of charity and kindness for citizens, like the soldier in Atlanta who, denouncing in thick Gaelic-English the laziness of the Negroes, helped an elderly woman each week with her washing and woodcutting. Or like General Edward O. C. Ord, who had his engineer officer supply a group of Virginia ladies with calcium lights so they could stage a tableau for the benefit of the poor. Or like General Thomas, who objected to the Quartermaster General's order directing the seizure of all government animals found in the hands of citizens. Thomas admitted that some of them had acquired the animals illegally, but he thought that in the interests of promoting agriculture the government should forget that fact.[77]

Popular sentiment toward the Army varied from place to place. In some areas which had always been heavily Unionist in sentiment or which had seen federal troops since early in the war, relations were better than in others. If a general evaluation applicable to the largest area of the South could be found, it might perhaps be that used by General James H. Wilson to describe the situation around Macon, Georgia: neither true loyalty and love for the Union nor hatred and desire for opposition, but some middle ground of willing acquiescence due to the thoroughness of the military defeat.[78] From this general attitude towards the Union it follows that the prevalent attitude towards the troops, as symbols of the Union, would be a showing of disdain and boorishness to make it obvious to the conquerors that what could not be prevented was at the most being endured. As one observer remarked, Southerners tended to divide Northerners into two groups, those who had

---

given in Franklin, *Reconstruction,* 35–36, while accurate, is potentially misleading.

[77]Myrta L. Avary, *Dixie After the War* (New York, 1906), 118–19; Macon (Ga.) *Daily Telegraph,* May 20, 1865; Thomas to Stanton, Dec. 14, 1865, Div. Tenn., 33, RG98, NA.

[78]Wilson to AAG Div. Tenn., June 15, 1865, in Johnson Papers, LC (Reel 15).

not been in the Army and those who had. The former were called "d——d Yankee s——s of b——s," while the latter were called "d——d bluebellied Yankee s——s of b——s." [79]

Some Southerners were polite and friendly, of course, but evidence of malevolence towards Union troops was easy to find. There were continual petty insults and indignities; officers' wives found Southern hospitality lacking in the Lake Charles, Louisiana, restaurant where they were refused service because it might "affect the custom of the house." The women of the South seemed to be strongly anti-Yankee. General Grant visited parts of Secessia late in 1865, and in Charleston one of his companions noted: "As we rode through the city I saw several who called themselves ladies make faces at the Yankee officers with us. It is useless to say they are only women—they express openly what their husbands and brothers feel but do not show." [80]

On Christmas, 1865, some citizens of Marshall, Texas, actuated by something other than the proper seasonal spirit, treated some soldiers of the 46th Illinois to liquid refreshment and then prompted them to shoot a Negro. After the post commander arrested the soldiers the city authorities demanded custody, but the commanding officer refused. The civil officials would probably have punished the soldiers not so much for murdering the Negro as for being soldiers. General Carl Schurz, who toured the South during the autumn of 1865, reported to the President that much hostility still existed and that the exceptions were "not numerous enough to affect the rule." Larger bodies of troops were not molested, but he did hear of frequent shootings of single soldiers and individual government couriers. Even so, a personal friend of Johnson, General C. C. Andrews, had written to the President from Selma, Alabama, that contact between the troops and the populace was desirable. "It has done our cause great good by having the people of the South see and converse with our brave, frank, and generous common soldiers. It causes a reaction." [81]

The Army often expressed its opinion that the best-disposed people in the South were the former Confederate soldiers, and the worst were those who had somehow escaped active duty. From a private stationed near Atlanta came the observation, "There is no feeling of enmity between the *true* soldiers of the two armies. Each has tried the other in

---

[79] *House Reports*, 39th Cong., 1st Sess., No. 30, Pt. 4, p. 126.

[80] C. B. Comstock, ms Journal, Feb. 2, 1866 and Dec. 1, 1865, in Comstock Papers, LC.

[81] *House Reports*, 39th Cong., 1st Sess., No. 30, Pt. 4, p. 49; *Sen. Exec. Docs.*, 39th Cong., 1st Sess., No. 2, pp. 7–8, 57–58; Andrews to Johnson, May 11, 1865, private, in Johnson Papers, LC (Reel 14).

the stern ordeal of the battlefield, and have [*sic*] learned to respect his sturdy valor." In Arkansas the returned soldiers of both sides were generally well-behaved, though some ex-Confederate officers caused trouble. Even Northern journalists who toured the South reported good relations between the erstwhile foes.[82]

The commanding generals read Southern newspapers regularly for evidences of disloyal attitudes and stopped the publication of some journals, though they did not carry out a wholesale suppression of adverse opinion. General Reynolds found fault with two Arkansas papers for editorials advising voters to violate a state law passed in May, 1864, prescribing an oath to be taken by voters. The Little Rock *Gazette* escaped suppression, but Reynolds closed the *Pantograph* after its editor refused to identify the offending author. Two Georgia papers, one at Macon and one at Americus, incurred military displeasure; and General Ruger stopped the *Daily Union Banner* of Salisbury, North Carolina.[83]

A Louisiana journal was the center of a more serious dispute. In the little town of Franklin two teenage boys, one a Negro and one white, got into a brawl. The mayor and the local provost marshal then argued over the disposition of the case, with the mayor wanting to make a grave case of assault and battery out of it and try it before the district court. The officials' dispute led to intemperate articles in the Franklin *Planters' Banner,* for which the provost marshal jailed the editor. The case ultimately found its way to Governor Wells and General Canby; the general settled it by releasing the editor, relieving the provost marshal, and urging the governor to remove the mayor. Canby ventured the correct if crusty remark that the affair would never have happened if the mayor and provost marshal "had been imbued with an ordinary degree of common sense." [84]

In Virginia General Terry carried on a running battle with the Richmond press. In July, 1865, the *Whig* undertook to call Johnson's amnesty proclamation "heathenish" and a law of Congress "mean, brutal, and cowardly, revoltingly absurd and atrociously unjust." For this Terry had his provost marshal general close the office, though after ten days he allowed the paper to resume operations. The editor had previously

[82]Letter signed "Blue Jacket," Macon (Ga.) *Daily Telegraph,* June 2, 1865, original emphasis; Reynolds to E. W. Gantt, Oct. 12, 1865, Dept. Ark., 2, RG98, NA; Sidney Andrews, *The South Since the War* (Boston, 1866), 95, 386.

[83]Reynolds to Atty. Gen. Speed, Sept. 12, 1865, Dept. Ark., 2; AAG to Gen. J. T. Croxton, CO Columbus, Aug. 10, 1865, Dept. Ga., 1, RG98, NA; *The Nation,* I (Aug. 10, 1865), 162.

[84]Townsend to Canby, Oct. 18, 1865, AGO, 41, and file 1507B1865, AGO, RG94, NA.

been loyal, had expressed his regret, and Governor Pierpont had urged clemency. Reading through the *Commercial Bulletin* in September, Terry found an article which he considered an "indecent insult" to the memory of President Lincoln and "an almost equally offensive reflection" on President Johnson. He had the paper closed and the editor arrested, there having been previous difficulty with the same journal.[85]

Some citizens manifested their dislike for the Army by instituting suits against officers and men for acts done during the war under orders of superiors. These suits usually stemmed either from false arrest for suspected disloyalty or from damages done to property. Criminal cases, most often for murder or assault, were less common. A complicating factor in these cases was the alleged loyalty of the aggrieved parties. They usually claimed to have been fierce Unionists during the war in the hopes of being more successful, though whether many of them actually were devoted to the Union is another matter.

A citizen most often began his quest for monetary redress with an appeal to the commanding general in his particular state. Such was the course followed by E. S. Chappell, of Mobile, who claimed that while he had been absent from his property for a time piloting Union troopships on the Mobile River, the 24th Indiana and 76th and 96th Illinois camped near his house and tore down his garden fence for firewood. Livestock thus invaded his garden and ruined it, the whole loss amounting to $2,000. His claim made the rounds of lower commanders before finally being sent to Washington. At length he received a reply: the troops in question being no longer in the service, the War Department could not compel them to pay; the government itself could not compensate him since no funds had been appropriated for the purpose; therefore such claims would have to wait until Congress decided to act in the matter. Shortly thereafter the Judge Advocate General issued a general ruling that Congress would have to act before anything could be done in such cases. In order to be prepared in case Congress did act, the War Department sometimes appointed boards to estimate the loss, as in the case of alleged damages done to the Armstrong farm in Dinwiddie County, Virginia. The Armstrongs were not paid, however, and most of the paperwork done by such investigating boards was left to gather dust in the War Department files.[86]

---

[85]GO 87, Dept. Va., July 11, 1865, GO 92, July 21, and GO 119, Sept. 30, Orders, 983, RG94, NA.

[86]Townsend to Chappell, Nov. 10, 1865, AGO 41, and file 1483C1865, AGO; Circ. 51, AGO, Nov. 27, 1865; Townsend to Terry, Sept. 22, 1865, AGO, 40, and file 1026A1865, AGO, RG94, NA.

Chappell gave up his case but others were more determined and took their claims to court, like the Louisianans who sued the officers who had used their homes as headquarters during the war.[87] If the judge were biased, a decision adverse to the soldier was very likely, and most of the defendants had little money to appeal the verdict to a higher court. These cases were alarming enough when pressed in Southern courts, but when they were initiated in federal courts in the North, even greater anxiety resulted. In Vermont a suit by a citizen against a provost marshal for false arrest, which originated in the state courts in August, 1864, and was transferred to the federal courts under the 1863 Habeas Corpus Act, resulted in an award of $1,000 to the citizen.[88]

Southern commanders closely watched the actions of Southern courts in these cases. In Texas, a captain of the 18th New York Cavalry while acting as provost marshal had seized the property of some gamblers, who then proceeded against him in the civil courts. Sheridan instructed the officer's superior, General Wesley Merritt at San Antonio, not to interfere in the slightest with the proceedings of the court but, once the decision was arrived at, to give the captain full protection against it. Acting on their own authority, most Southern commanders issued orders prohibiting state courts from entertaining such cases, whether civil or criminal; this policy received official sanction from Washington in January, 1866.[89]

While the Army did, on the whole, attempt to administer Southern affairs fairly and reasonably, in some cases an ill-advised action brought the perpetrator deserved reproach. One such affair was the great Alabama prayer crisis. Before the war the Methodist Episcopal Church had offered a prescribed prayer for the President "and all in civil authority." During the war this became a prayer for Confederate officials; and in June, 1865, Bishop Richard Wilmer of Alabama recommended, in a letter to the clergy, that the prayer not be said at all. He claimed that since it was a prayer for those in "civil authority," and the only authority in Alabama was military, the prayer should be dropped since nobody could reasonably pray for the continuance of military rule.

But General Thomas, a deeply religious man, took offense at this attitude and ordered General Woods to suspend the bishop and prohibit those clergymen who followed his suggestion from holding services.

[87]Canby to Howard, Nov. 6, 1865, Dept. Gulf, 79, RG98, NA.
[88]*Walker vs. Crane*, Fed. Cas. No. 17067 (USCC, Dist. Vt., Oct. 1865).
[89]Forsyth to Merritt, Oct. 21, 1865, in Sheridan Papers, LC; GO 42, Dept. Ala., Sept. 26, 1865, Orders, 815; GO 113, Dept. Va., Sept. 21, 1865, and GO 124, Oct. 11, Orders, 983; GO 3, AGO, Jan. 12, 1866, RG94, NA.

The order Woods issued was practically a prayer itself. He interpreted the Methodist invocation as simply one

For the temporal and spiritual weal of the persons in whose behalf it is offered—it is a prayer to the High and Mighty Ruler of the Universe that he would with his favor behold and bless his servant, the President of the United States, and all others in authority—that He would replenish them with the grace of His holy spirit, that they might always incline to His will and walk in His ways, that He would endow them plenteously with heavenly gifts, grant them in health and prosperity long to live, and finally after this life to attain everlasting joy and felicity. It is a prayer at once applicable and appropriate, and which any heart not filled with hatred, malice, and all uncharitableness could conscientiously offer.

He considered its omission as a violation of the canons of the church and evidence of a "factious and disloyal spirit" on the part of Wilmer and the clergy. "Such men are unsafe public teachers, and not to be trusted in places of power and influence over public opinion." Wilmer and the clergy could not resume services until they agreed to offer the prayer and also take the President's amnesty oath. Each clergyman constituted a separate case and had to apply individually to headquarters.[90]

The suspension caused a public outcry, understandably loud in the South but also in the North. Wilmer complained to Johnson, who declined to interfere other than to have the bishop's letter directed to Thomas. Three days before Christmas Thomas decided to reverse himself, and got out of his difficulty as neatly as he could manage. First he castigated Wilmer's action as an attempt to hinder "the spread of popular approbation and grateful appreciation of the magnanimous policy of the President in his efforts to bring the people of the United States back to their former friendly and national relations with one another." The bishop had been "animated with the same spirit through which temptation beguiled the mother of men to the commission of the first sin—thereby entailing eternal toil and trouble on earth." He (Wilmer) "took advantage of the sanctity of his position, to mislead the minds of those who naturally regard him as a teacher in whom they could trust, and attempted to lead them back into the labyrinths of treason." But Thomas concluded that since Alabamans were honestly trying to be loyal in spite of Wilmer's pernicious influence, the previous order stood revoked, and Bishop Wilmer was "left to that remorse of conscience consequent to the exposure and failure of the diabolical schemes of designing and corrupt

[90]GO 38, Dept. Ala., Sept. 20, 1865, Orders, 815, RG98, NA.

minds." [91] Perhaps Wilmer and the clergy *were* disloyal, but military interference with religious worship was clearly beyond the bounds of propriety and necessity.

By December, 1865, the South had made definite progress towards full restoration to the Union. New state governments elected under the auspices of Johnson's provisional appointees were functioning in all states except Texas, where the convention had not yet met. Economic progress, though slow, was increasing, and society was gradually recovering from the war. The Army's work had on the whole assisted rather than retarded this recovery. Without the Army, Johnson's governors would have been powerless, and the efforts of the Freedmen's Bureau to help the Negro would have come to naught. The soldiers also contributed materially to Southern economic recovery through the local purchase of supplies and equipment. But Northerners in the winter of 1865–66 focused their attention on the political aspects of Reconstrution—readmission to representation, punishment of traitors, and related questions. The forthcoming political conflict over such subjects was to increase the difficulty of the Army's task in the South. Writing from the plains of Kansas during the autumnal election excitement of 1866, General Custer expressed a view that was perhaps too infrequently heard in Washington in January of that year: "For the Government to exact full penalties, simply because it is constitutionally authorized to do so, would, in my opinion, be unnecessary, impolitic, inhuman, and wholly at variance with the principles of a free, civilized and Christian nation, such as we profess to be." [92]

[91]GO 40, Div. Tenn., Dec. 22, 1865, republished in GO 2, Dept. Ala., Jan. 10, 1866, Orders, 815, RG94, NA.
[92]Custer to unknown, Oct. 23, 1866, in Merington (ed), *Custer Story*, 187–88.

3

A Struggle for Control of Policy

THE first session of the Thirty-ninth Congress opened in December, 1865. All eyes, North and South, focused on Washington, anxious to learn what action the solons would take with respect to the South. After determining to reject consummation of the President's plan of reconstruction by excluding Southern representatives, Congress established the Joint Committee on Reconstruction. This group divided itself into four subcommittees which then spent three months hearing testimony on conditions and attitudes in the South.

Witnesses, 139 in all, paraded through the capitol meeting rooms. Army officers were a potentially valuable source of information, but only twenty-six testified, not counting Freedmen's Bureau personnel. Moreover, only a minority of this small number were on duty in the South at the time or their testimony or immediately before. More up-to-date military opinion could have been obtained had the subcommittees held hearings in the states with which they were concerned. Or if the investigators had been enterprising, they could have mailed questionnaires to a number of officers in the South for their written replies. Only Sheridan's views were thus solicited, however. Few of the officers who testified held high commands. Only three—Terry, Thomas and Sheridan—commanded an area of one or more states. The 113 nonmilitary witnesses included Freedmen's Bureau agents, native Southerners who had remained loyal during the war, and former Confederates such as Robert E. Lee and Alexander H. Stephens.

Although few in number, the Army officers who testified did have important things to say. Fifteen out of twenty-six observed that employers generally were harsh and exploited the Negroes whenever they could.

All six who were asked if the South would willingly let the Negro vote replied in the negative. Most officers were not asked for their opinions on the desirability of congressional legislation touching the Negro, but the query, directed to Sheridan, brought this response: "I believe the best thing that Congress or State [*sic*] can do is to legislate as little as possible in reference to the colored man beyond giving him security in his person and property. His social status will be worked out by the logic of the necessity for his labor. It is the only labor that can be obtained in the southern States for some time to come." [1]

The examiners were especially anxious to know the extent of pro-Union sentiment in the South. Twelve officers found the attitude generally sullen and hostile; eleven emphasized that the amount of local variation made a general statement impossible. Those who thought that attitudes had changed over a period of time said that they had become worse rather than better. Some examiners asked questions about the effect of the President's liberal pardoning policy on Southern attitudes. Nine officers thought it had a deleterious effect; Sheridan found no change due to that policy; and Terry rather neatly sidestepped the issue with respect to Virginia by remarking cryptically that he could not trace results to specific causes. Proceeding on the premise that election results were a good indication of popular attitudes, some questioners asked whether Rebels or Unionists most often triumphed. The answers varied depending on the state or portion thereof in question. Four of the five officers who testified concerning Arkansas were certain that the senators and congressmen elected from that state and at the time seeking admittance to Congress were loyal men; but it was nevertheless to be over two years before an Arkansan would sit in Congress. Other committeemen thought Union sentiment could be measured by probable loyalty in case of a war with some European power, "say, France or England." Most of the respondants declared the South would side with the foreign enemy in hopes of thus securing its independence.

The few officers who were asked about the civil courts all declared them to be prejudiced against Union men. The committee also probed into the matter of personal relations between individual Southerners on the one hand and soldiers and Northern civilians on the other, but with inconclusive results. Remarking that he had no social relations with any-

---

[1]*House Reports,* 39th Cong., 1st Sess., No. 30, ·Pt. 4, p. 123. For a full treatment of the committee and its work see Benjamin B. Kendrick, *The Journal of the Joint Committee of Fifteen on Reconstruction* (New York, 1914), which contains an analysis of the entire body of testimony, though its treatment of the military viewpoint is much shallower than that given here.

one except known Unionists, General Terry said of the Virginians under his rule: "They do not seek me; and it is neither becoming to my position as the commanding officer of the department, nor consistent with my self-respect, to seek them first." [2]

One of the most important questions put to the witnesses was whether maintaining federal military control over the South was necessary or desirable. When asked if troops should remain there, twenty-one replied in the affirmative without offering substantive reservations or explanations; four more agreed but emphasized that the need was simply for small bodies of troops in specified areas; only one, speaking of Arkansas, said they were not necessary. Although a large proportion favored retention of troops, in only one instance was an increase in the current force recommended. That was in a report of an inspection tour through the White River District in northern Arkansas, included as part of the evidence concerning that state.[3] A closely related and equally important question concerned the admitting of Southern delegates to Congress. Only five officers of the twenty-six were asked for an opinion. Three favored admission of Southern representatives as a means of aiding the growth of loyal sentiment; two opposed it. General Thomas told the committee he thought Tennessee ought properly to be readmitted because "that State, of her own accord, has complied with every instruction of the President, and has done all that it was believed it would be necessary for her to do in order to gain admission into Congress." Tennessee had repudiated the Rebel debt, adopted the Thirteenth Amendment, disfranchised Rebels, allowed Negroes to testify in court, and elected loyal representatives and senators. Thomas believed admission of Tennessee would set a precedent for other states: "They can see at once the reasons why the Tennessee members are admitted, and that if they expect their members to be admitted they must do as she has done." [4]

As a general summary, most of the officers who testified probably would have agreed in substance with the evaluation offered concerning Texas and Louisiana by the flamboyant Custer: since Southerners had thus far failed "to manifest a penitent spirit for the great crime committed against the nation, or to give a proper and sufficient guarantee of future good conduct," federal control should be maintained for the time being.[5]

2*House Reports*, 39th Cong., 2nd Sess., No. 30, Pt. 2, p. 141.
3*Ibid.*, Pt. 3, pp. 168–70.
4*Ibid.*, Pt. 1, p. 110.
5*Ibid.*, Pt. 4, p. 78.

The testimony of the nonmilitary witnesses followed the same lines, but there was a tendency to paint a gloomier picture of conditions and attitudes. Freedmen's Bureau officers magnified the problems of the Negro. Northern civilians who went South on business complained of the rude and sullen treatment accorded them, and emphasized the need of federal protection. Plantation owners complained of the laziness of the Negro, and of course, former Rebel officers lauded the increasing loyalty of the region.

The 776 pages of closely printed testimony which accompanied the committee's final report received wide audience in the North and in the fall of 1866 served as a Republican campaign document. But certain characteristics of the testimony impeach its validity and usefulness. The amount of military testimony ought properly to have been greater since the Army was administering federal policy in the South. Some of the questions were entirely hypothetical, such as Senator Jacob Howard's favorite query: "Suppose they [the Southerners] got into power again, with their full representation in Congress, and with a President who, like Mr. Buchanan, should disavow the right of the government of the United States to coerce a state, and should decline to use the military force of the government to prevent secession; would they or would they not, in your opinion, again secede from the Union and attempt to set up an independent government?" [6] The answer was ordinarily affirmative, but Howard never asked for proof.

More important, the committee was not governed by legal rules of evidence and it accepted hearsay, *ex parte* testimony which would have been inadmissable in a court. At times solid factual evidence was presented, with details of specific cases; but too frequently the exchanges were elaborations of this condensed model:

Q: What is the general state of feeling towards the Union?

A: It is intensely hostile and bitter. The people have no love for the Union as a governmental system, for the individual Northern man, or for the Negro.

Q: Can you cite an example of individual cruelty or maliciousness towards Negroes or Union men?

A: Many reports of whipping Negroes have come to me from the interior, which is a generally lawless and turbulent portion of the State. The people have determined ideas of what they will do to the freedmen and Union men when the troops are withdrawn.

[6] *Ibid.*, Pt. 2, p. 142.

Q: Do you have personal knowledge of such threats having been made?
A: I have not heard them myself but they are frequently reported to me.
Q: By men in whose trustworthiness you have confidence?
A: Yes.
Q: Give us an instance.
A: Several days ago one of my staff officers reported a conversation he overheard on the cars to Atlanta, between two men who from their dress and manner of speech he judged to be Southerners. They expressed the intention of forming patrols to "regulate" the Negroes and drive the "Yankees" out, once the troops had left.

After receiving more vague and general replies the questioner would pass on to another subject.

The unreliability of some testimony evoked comment from officers in the South. The commanding general in Mississippi blasted those witnesses who "seem to think it necessary in order to acquire temporary celebrity to seize hold of isolated cases of abuse of the freed people to make out a theory of general oppression of this class of the community by the dormicant [*sic*] or white race." Calling this practice "injurious to a just public sentiment," he noted two specific cases. A captain on bureau duty in Amite and Pike counties failed to report any abuses for months on end and then, when he was relieved, made a report "as marvelous as unreliable" and painted for the committee a picture of general oppression. General Wood also scored a regimental commander who, notwithstanding the size of his force, failed to make a single arrest or even ask for a military commission to try the outrages he had been reporting. "Such officers," the general closed, "expose themselves to the dilemma of having neglected their duty or of having made false reports; I leave them to choose which horn they will take." [7]

While the committee was endeavoring to find out the attitude of the South, the Army and the Southerners were wondering about the attitude and future policy of the federal government. It was apparent that Southern delegates would not be seated for a while, since the resolution establishing the committee charged it with reporting whether any of the rebel states were entitled to representation. Presumably the Congress would not act until the committee reported, and gathering evidence was a long process. Thus, for the time being the Army would continue to administer Southern affairs in much the same way as it had previously

[7] Wood to AAG Div. Tenn., March 27, 1866, Dept. Miss., 2, RG98, NA.

done. No change had taken place in the legal status of the Southern states, and no new formal instructions came down from the War Office.

One of the most significant legislative questions facing the new Congress was the size, organization, and structure of the peacetime regular Army. It was a paradoxical situation. Although Republican politicians thought that the condition of the South warranted the continued presence of an occupation force, the country as a whole, weary after four years of costly war, demanded reduction of the Army as a means of reducing governmental expenses. The first military bill of the new session, presented by Senator Henry Wilson, provided for five regiments of artillery, twelve of cavalry, and fifty-five of infantry, or a total of 60,000 men. This figure was a marked increase over the size of the regular Army before the war; the act of March 3, 1855, set the strength at 12,698 and new legislation of the summer of 1861 raised it to 39,273. In contemplating such an increase Congress was concerned not only with the Army's Southern duties, but also with the policing of the Plains and the Mexican border. Wilson's bill received the support of some officers and also of the *Army and Navy Journal*.[8] By the time it reached the House the number of regiments had been reduced and other changes made. Both houses then bogged down in minor questions of organization and small-item appropriations.

By May, 1866, Grant became anxious about the new legislation and wrote to Stanton in an effort to speed up action on it. After nearly seven months of arduous if intermittent debate the bill reached its final form late in the session. Much of the time had been consumed by interminable haggling over minor points, such as the number of commissaries of subsistence allotted to each regiment, or the special provisions applicable to majors of artillery but not to majors of cavalry. The new law authorized a force only slightly smaller in total strength than the 60,000 Wilson had first recommended in January. It also provided for one General (Grant), one Lieutenant General (Sherman), five major generals (Halleck, Meade, Sheridan, Thomas, and Hancock, in order of seniority), and ten brigadiers (McDowell, Cooke, Pope, Hooker, Schofield, Howard, Terry, Ord, Canby, and Rosecrans).[9] Not all officers

[8] *Army and Navy Journal,* III (Jan. 20, 1866), 341.
[9] The progress of the legislation can be followed in *Army and Navy Journal,* III (Jan.–Aug. 1866), *passim,* and the *Cong. Globe,* 39th Cong., 1st Sess. The officers listed were not designated in the act but were appointed to fill the positions authorized.

were pleased with the product, however; Sheridan objected to the insufficient amount of cavalry and to the provisions for disabled soldiers. He also thought the total strength inadequate for the size and condition of the country. With respect to the South he informed Senator Wilson, "My own opinion is that there should be a good compact force at two or three different points in these States for some time; not to interfere in civil affairs, but for precautions suggested by the history of all Rebellions, and by common sense." [10]

Another topic which received legislative attention was the prosecution of Union soldiers by civil authorities for acts done under orders during the war. Congress had already afforded some protection in the 1863 Habeas Corpus Act. Section 4 of that law made any order issued by the President or on his authority a defense against all civil and criminal proceedings for any search, seizure, arrest, or imprisonment done under such order or under any law of Congress. Section 5 allowed removal of cases from state to federal courts upon petition of the defendant; Section 6 allowed appeals to the United States Supreme Court; Section 7 was a two-year statute of limitations running from the date of the alleged offense.[11] In January, 1866, General Orders No. 3 from the War Department directed commanders in the South to "protect" soldiers from such proceedings in state courts and from any penalties or damages that might be adjudged.[12] This order notwithstanding, cases still continued and now began reaching the highest level of state courts. Critical questions were involved; for example, was a Union soldier punishable in a state court for a robbery committed in September, 1863? Yes, held the Supreme Court of Missouri.[13]

Considering the 1863 act to be insufficient and citing as an example the fact that more than 1,500 cases had arisen in Kentucky alone, Congress decided on new legislation. A bill to amend the old law emerged from the House Judiciary Committee in March, 1866, and became a law with the President's signature on May 11. [14] It was indeed blanket protection. It declared that the 1863 act applied to anything done by written or verbal order of the President, Secretary of War, or any officer in local command. Such acts were covered whether done by the person to whom the order had been given or by anyone aiding him. The defendant could remove a case to the federal circuit court at almost any stage in the proceedings in the state court, even after a final judgment

[10]Sheridan to Wilson, private, June 29, 1866, in Henry Wilson Papers, LC.
[11]12 U.S. Statutes at Large 755.
[12]GO 3, AGO, Jan. 12, 1866, RG94, NA.
[13]*Missouri vs. Rogers,* 37 Missouri 367 (1866).
[14]*Cong. Globe,* 39th Cong., 1st Sess., 1368, 1387–90, 1423–26, 1530, 2052–66.

there. The new law stretched the rules of evidence considerably. If the order in question were a written one, either the original or a certified copy would be sufficient evidence. For telegrams, courts were told, "the production of the telegram purporting to emanate from such military officer shall be prima facie evidence of its authenticity; or if the original of such order or telegram is lost or cannot be produced, secondary evidence thereof shall be admissable, as in other cases." The law did not specify what evidence would be sufficient to prove that the action was based on a verbal order. Curiously, the law had begun by referring to acts done "during the said rebellion" but later stated that the defense provided did not apply to things done "after the passage of this act." [15] This provision was a rather neat way of skirting the important legal question of how long after April, 1865, the rebellion had continued; and of course, if the "rebellion" still had a legal existence in the spring of 1866, many occupation activities of the Army would be protected.

Grant with his General Orders No. 3 and Congress with its two statutes had the same goal of safeguarding soldiers, but the methods employed were different. Grant's instructions to "protect" were vague enough so that some individual commanders could prohibit damage suits completely, as some did, whereas Congress in both the 1863 and 1866 laws clearly provided that the suits could continue. Congress in effect declared that if it could be proven in court that the defendant had *not* acted under orders (admittedly difficult to prove), then the plaintiff was entitled to redress.

On one legal technicality or another cases continued to arise. In August, 1866, a trial court in Tennessee convicted a soldier of a murder committed in June, 1865, holding that since the orders under which he had acted were illegal, he was liable to prosecution. The state supreme court ruled the evidence insufficient, reversed the conviction, and ordered a new trial.[16] The rule of law used by the Tennessee trial court also figured in a Kentucky case shortly thereafter, although the facts were different. In July, 1864, a provost marshal had, under orders, taken a group of slaves from their master. Citing a federal decision of the 1850's, the state supreme court held the provost marshal liable to prosecution since his superior had no legal authority to issue the order, there being no immediate military necessity at the time.[17] The Supreme Court of Arkansas believed differently, however; private soldiers, it ruled,

---

[15]14 U.S. Statutes at Large 46.

[16]*Riggs vs. State of Tennessee,* 3 Coldwell (Tenn.) 85 (1866).

[17]*Jones vs. Commonwealth of Kentucky,* 1 Bush (Ky.) 34 (1866). The federal case was *Mitchell vs. Harmony,* 13 Howard 128 (1852). A later Kentucky case on the question of orders being illegal is *Eifort et al. vs. Bevins,* 1 Bush 460 (1867).

might justify the taking of property under the orders of their commanding officers but the latter, having some discretion, were liable if property were taken without sufficient warrant.[18]

Early in the session Congress took up the future status of the Freedmen's Bureau. Even though Sheridan had recommended legislating sparingly on Negro affairs, many people were telling the Joint Committee on Reconstruction that the bureau had to stay in the South for the good of the Negro. On January 11, 1866, Senator Lyman Trumbull reported a bill to enlarge the bureau's powers and functions. The organization was to continue indefinitely and was now to encompass the border states as well as Secessia. Its agents and employees, whether Army officers or civilians, were all to be under "military jurisdiction and protection." Trumbull and his Judiciary Committee may have felt they were improving relations between the bureau and the Army by this provision, though a more complete consolidation might have been more successful. During the spring of 1866 the Army continued to aid the bureau, and subordinate officers commanding small units in towns or rural areas still wrote to their commanding generals for instructions in specific cases. These requests most often brought a reply of the following pattern: aid the bureau whenever possible and furnish details upon request, provided the men can be spared from their military duties without detriment to the interests of the service.[19] In at least one state, however, the commanding general was reluctant to furnish numerous small details because of the resulting fragmentation of his forces, which included many new recruits.[20] Most individuals attempted to maintain harmony; a complaint that "improper interference and injudicious advice" by Army officers were interfering with bureau policy towards the Negroes brought a gruff order from department headquarters: "Public harrangues [sic] or written addresses by such officers to the inhabitants of this Department, are strictly forbidden. Such officers are reminded that their duties are purely executive, to be carried out literally under the orders and regulations promulgated from time to time by competent higher authority." [21]

The heart of the Freedmen's Bureau bill was in the seventh and eighth

[18]Taylor vs. Jenkins, 24 Arkansas 337(1866).
[19]AAG to Maj. T. D. Ogilby, May 4, 1866, Dept. Ala., 1, RG98, NA.
[20]Terry to AAG Div. Atlantic, March 1, 1866, Dept. Va., 14, RG98, NA.
[21]Wood to AAG Div. Tenn., Dec. 6, 1865, Dept. Miss., 2, RG98, NA; GO 46, Dept. Miss., Dec. 12, 1865, Orders, 900, RG94, NA.

sections. The President, through the commissioner of the bureau, was to "extend military protection and jurisdiction" over all cases in which, because of a state or local law, custom, or prejudice, any of the civil rights and immunities belonging to white people were denied to Negroes or in which Negroes were subjected to punishment different from that of whites for the same offense. Such discrimination was to be a misdemeanor punishable at most by a $1,000 fine or one year in jail or both. Bureau officers were to hear and decide all such cases, under whatever rules and regulations the War Department might provide; this jurisdiction was to continue until readmission of the particular state and full restoration of the civil courts to their functions were effected. The vastness of this grant simply increased the abuses of power by the existing bureau courts; unfortunately an attempt to amend the bill to allow appeals from bureau decisions to federal courts fell in defeat by the strict party vote of 37 to 8. [22] The bill also contained provisions designed to confirm the Negroes in their possession of lands on the Sea Islands of Georgia, South Carolina, and Florida, and to acquire other lands for their use. "The proposition now before Congress," objected General Daniel E. Sickles, "cannot secure lands to more than a few thousand, yet *all* will expect land and will do *nothing* meanwhile but plunder and draw rations. How will you discriminate in making grants, and what will our soldiers and the widows and orphans of the fallen say when they see the lands in the South given away to Negroes and none being reserved for them? It is a great error." [23]

In spite of potent constitutional arguments against the vast jurisdiction of bureau agents, which Trumbull and his colleagues could answer but weakly, the Senate passed the bill on January 25 and the House on February 6. [24] Many people hoped Johnson would approve the measure, but on February 18 he vetoed it on many of the same grounds its congressional critics had urged. The Senate upheld the veto and it was not until July that Congress was able to pass a new bureau bill— basically the January one with some modifications—and this over another presidential veto. Southern commanders were publicly circumspect about Johnson's course, whatever they may have thought privately. Sherman wrote his brother, who in the Senate had voted to override the veto: "Sumner and Stevens would have made another civil war in-

[22]*Cong. Globe.,* 39th Cong., 1st Sess., 399–400, 416.
[23]Sickles to Howard, Jan. 21, 1866, and to Grant, Jan. 22, Dept. South, 46, RG98, NA. Original emphasis.
[24]*Cong. Globe.,* 39th Cong., 1st Sess., 314–23, 415–21.

evitably [*sic*]—the President's antagonistic position saves us war save of words, and as I am a man of peace, I go for Johnson and the Veto." [25]

Making its way through Congress along with the Freedmen's Bureau bill was the Civil Rights bill, a measure of equal if not greater import. Reduced to its simplest terms, this bill prohibited racial discrimination by state or local law or custom in civil rights and immunities. These included making and enforcing contracts, being parties to civil suits, giving evidence in court, purchasing and holding real and personal property, being protected in one's life and property, and receiving the same punishment for a crime as anyone else would. Enforcement of the law was in the hands of the federal courts; any official serving a warrant or other process could call the Army to his aid and was protected from suit or prosecution in state courts for acts done while enforcing the law. [26]

This bill received heavier fire in congressional debate than did its companion measure, but the objections were quite similar: lack of constitutional authority to pass the bill and impropriety as well as illegality of military enforcement. In countering the constitutional argument, the proponents stretched the "war powers" and the Thirteenth Amendment to their limits. In countering the objections to military enforcement they revealed the principal reason for the bill: fear that local Southern officials could not be trusted to treat the Negro fairly. Inveighing against "rebels steeped in treason and rebellion to their lips," Indiana's Senator Henry S. Lane claimed that without military aid in enforcement the law would be "a mockery and a farce." [27] Speaking immediately after Lane, Senator Henry Wilson of Massachusetts pointed to the "black codes" which several Southern legislatures had passed, implying that the bill under consideration would void these discriminatory measures. As Wilson said, the enforcement of the "black codes" had already been suspended by military orders in some states. On January 12, as part of his directive in General Orders No. 3 to protect soldiers and loyal citizens against damage suits, Grant had also instructed the Army to protect Negroes from being punished more severely than a white man would be for the same offense. [28] Wilson considered that the "black codes" had made this order necessary and that it had doubtless been issued with

[25]Sherman to John Sherman, Feb. 23, 1866, in Thorndike (ed.), *Sherman Letters*, 263.
[26]*Cong. Globe.*, 39th Cong., 1st Sess., 211–12.
[27]*Ibid.*, 603.
[28]GO 3, AGO, Jan. 12, 1866, RG94, NA.

the approval of Johnson. There is no positive evidence of such approval or, for that matter, of any disapproval. However, the order appeared the day after Trumbull reported the Freedmen's Bureau and Civil Rights bills out of committee, and the relevant part of the order was clearly designed to achieve the same purpose as the two bills. The proximity in dates may reflect a sudden and unilateral decision by Grant to institute the policy of the two bills immediately by military action in case Congress were delayed in enacting the measures, or it may be unverifiable circumstantial evidence of cooperation between the general and the senator. Or then it might have been sheer coincidence.

In objecting to the "black codes," the North gave the impression that Southern legislatures had passed them overwhelmingly and with great delight. Such was not always the case, however, as Army officers could attest. From South Carolina General Sickles informed Grant that the legislature had passed a "black code" with much hesitation and that the governor was reluctant to approve it. Not much encouragement on Sickles' part was required to induce the governor to withhold the necessary proclamation.[29]

During the early months of 1866 local commanders safeguarded the rights of Negroes in pursuance of Grant's January order. The Army peremptorily told Georgia's Governor Charles Jenkins that part of the state code which discriminated against Negroes could not be enforced. In Florida military influence was more subtly applied. The legislature passed a law prohibiting Negroes from bearing arms, thus ignoring the provision of the new state constitution which prohibited discrimination based on color. Instead of simply suspending the law, General Foster suggested that the governor ask the state attorney general, John Galbraith, if the law were not unconstitutional. When Galbraith came to that correct conclusion, Governor Walker directed the civil authorities not to enforce the law. Application of the Mississippi vagrancy law to recently discharged colored soldiers in Vicksburg brought a request from the commanding general that they first be given time to find employment.[30]

In following the spirit of Grant's order, commanding generals at times took questionable actions. In January, 1866, the Virginia legislature passed a vagrancy law. The classification "vagrant" included "all persons who not having the wherewith to support their families, live idly

---

[29]Sickles to Grant, Jan. 22, 1866, Dept. South, 46, RG98, NA.
[30]Gen. J. M. Brannan to Jenkins, Jan. 17, 1866, Dept. Ga., 1; Foster to Gen. L. Thomas, AG USA, March 13, 1866, Dept. Fla., 6; Wood to Mayor of Vicksburg, Jan. 18, 1866, Dept. Miss., 2, RG98, NA.

and without employment, and refuse to work for the usual and common wages given to other laborers, in the like work, in the place where they then are." On its face this looked like a reasonable and innocent statute; but General Terry, who had been a court clerk before the war and regarded himself as a lawyer by profession, detected a potential inequity. In some localities, he claimed, employers' meetings had led to "unjust and wrongful combinations" to depress freedmen's wages below their real value, thus making inadequate wages the "usual and common" ones. Reflecting the widespread Northern distrust of the white Southerner's intentions toward the Negro, Terry somehow found it "easy to foresee that even where no such combinations now exist, the temptation to form them, offered by the Statute, will be too strong to be resisted. . . ." He consequently forbade state civil officers to apply the law to any Negro.[31] However good Terry's intentions might have been, his order was wide open to an objection on grounds of principle, had anyone come forth to make it. The state law had not discriminated on the basis of color, whereas Terry in affording a shield against its operation had done so. As a practical matter it may not have been important since most laborers in the state were Negroes, but it amounted to the same discrimination, in reverse, to which the proponents of the Civil Rights bill had objected in many state laws.

The Virginia lawmakers had copied the errant provision verbatim from the Code of Pennsylvania, but nobody in the North worried about that fact in denouncing the law and applauding the order. In answering one approving letter the general explained that his order was intended to protect the Negroes from unfairness and "to show these people [whites] that there is yet 'a God in Israel.' " Wilson commended the order in the Senate debate on the Civil Rights bill but a Delaware Democrat, Willard Saulsbury, asked on what grounds Wilson thought Terry had the authority to issue it. Wilson's reply was primarily an oration in favor of passing the bill, in which he dismissed the point of Saulsbury's question by briefly remarking that Virginia was under martial law.[32]

Presidential approval of the Civil Rights bill was not forthcoming. Johnson met the bill with an able veto message which used some of the congressional arguments against the measure and emphasized the lack of constitutional authority for its passage. In arguing for overriding the veto Trumbull noted the President's observation that there was little

[31]GO 4, Dept. Va., Jan. 24, 1866, Orders, 984, RG94, NA.
[32]Richmond *Daily Dispatch,* Jan. 27, 1866; Terry to Hawley, Feb. 1, 1866, in Hawley Papers, LC; *Cong. Globe,* 39th Cong., 1st Sess., 603.

necessity for the bill and that adequate remedies already existed. Trumbull met this point by citing Terry's order and other similar military actions which he claimed were done and approved by presidential authority.[33] Thus Trumbull was trying to use presidential policies to refute presidential polemics. The argument had some theoretical validity, for in climbing up the chain of command from the generals one ultimately reaches the President as Commander-in-Chief; but in actual practice there was not as much presidential supervision or prior approval of generals' actions as Trumbull wanted to make it seem. Congress did not need too much convincing, however, and shortly voted to override the veto.

On July 3 Grant issued General Orders No. 44 concerning arrests in the South. It included no direct reference to the Civil Rights bill, but anticipation of military enforcement of that measure seems the best explanation for the instructions set forth. Grant ordered soldiers at all command levels in the South to arrest persons charged with crimes against "officers, agents, citizens, and inhabitants of the United States" where the civil authorities either could not or would not do so. The order did not contemplate military trials, but directed the culprits to be held "until such time as a proper judicial tribunal may be ready and willing to try them." This was a rather sweeping order, and Grant did not want the Army to take too drastic action under it, an attitude illustrated by a cautionary wire to the Florida commander emphasizing that, as a rule, arrests under No. 44 should be made only where the civil officials refused.[34]

The crisis over the Civil Rights bill was a high point in the friction which had gradually been developing between Johnson and Congress during the spring. To the increasingly stormy events the Army was an interested if usually circumspect witness. In December, 1865, the *Army and Navy Journal* had predicted there would be no clash at all, and until the Freedmen's Bureau question came to a head in mid-February that view had appeared to be sound. Sherman, who hated politics but always took firm stands, took one on Johnson's action: "Of course I agree substantially with the President. If we do not design to make a

---

[33]*Cong. Globe,* 39th Cong., 1st Sess., 1759.

[34]GO 44, AGO, July 3, 1866, RG94, NA; Grant to Foster, Aug. 7, 1866, HQA, C, RG108, NA. It is difficult to concur with Benjamin P. Thomas and Harold M. Hyman, *Stanton: The Life and Times of Lincoln's Secretary of War* (New York, 1962), 490, who see this order as "strengthening" General Orders No. 3. The two really deal with different problems.

complete revolution in our form of Government, but rather to preserve it, you must, sooner or later, allow representation from the South, and the longer it is deferred the worse will be its effect." [35]

Some officers left the Army and took an increased interest in politics. One such was Steedman, who after returning from his Georgia command became vice-president of a Washington National Union Club formed to support Johnson. Others kept watch on developments from their headquarters, like Terry, who closely followed Republican party affairs of his native Connecticut.[36] Another officer, General Custer, had returned from Texas and was spending a leave in Washington preparing to go Indian-fighting on the Plains. While the House debated passage of the Civil Rights bill, "Dear Old Sweetness" received this self-inflating news from her husband: "I think if I stay here much longer and Andy Johnson remains firm, the Constitution will be able to stand alone. . . . At least, that seems the present policy." A week later, this: "My confidence in the strength of the Constitution is increasing daily while Andy is as firm and upright as a tombstone. He has not uttered any speeches lately, but I am nightly expecting an outburst of his peculiar eloquence. However, I'm not partial to speechmaking. I believe in acts, not words. But, unlike some public characters, he does not swallow his own words. He has grown. . . ." [37]

The President believed in actions as well as words, and his veto of the Civil Rights bill on March 27 had been a vigorous specimen of both. A week later, on April 2, there appeared another product of his pen. This was his proclamation declaring that the rebellion had been suppressed and peace restored in all parts of the United States save Texas. He omitted that state apparently because it had not yet completed the election and organization of its new legislature. At any rate the proclamation came as a surprise to most people. Among the Cabinet only Seward had had prior knowledge of it, and even he had not been consulted until late the preceding afternoon. Navy Secretary Welles first learned about it in his morning newspaper on the third. Probably the President intended the proclamation as a counterstroke to the congressional enactments, since their supporters had been urging continuance of the "war powers" as justification for them. Welles so interpreted it

[35]*Army and Navy Journal,* III (Dec. 9, 1865), 243; Sherman to John Sherman, Feb. 28, 1866, in Thorndike (ed.), *Sherman Letters,* 265.

[36]Printed platform and list of officers of the club, March, 1866, in Stanton Papers, LC; Terry to Hawley, Feb. 1, 1866, in Hawley Papers, LC.

[37]Custer to Elizabeth, March 12 and 18, 1866, in Merington (ed.), *Custer Story,* 177–79. Original ellipses.

and thought a "sudden determination" had possessed Johnson. If there were a "sudden determination" it could conceivably have been brought on by a letter from a pardoned Southerner running a plantation near Pine Bluff, Arkansas. Complaining about a few officers of the local command who were "burdened with self-importance" the planter observed, "They seem inclined to take advantage of the *fact* that the President has never issued a Proclamation, affirming that 'Peace' *existed* in the country, and until that was done they had a right to presume that *war* existed still, and of course *War remedies.*" [38]

Just after Johnson's proclamation the United States Supreme Court further disturbed the already turbulent legal atmosphere with its decision in the Milligan case. Lambdin P. Milligan, a civilian, had been tried and convicted during the war by a military commission in Indiana while the civil courts there were open. His plea for a writ of habeas corpus brought the case to the Supreme Court. All the justices agreed that the military commission had been without authority and that he was thus entitled to the writ. Since there was disagreement over some aspects of the case, the formal written opinions were deferred until the following December term.[39] But in the interim any application of the decision to the South on the ground that military commissions could not function where civil courts were open would cast grave doubt on the legality of an important part of the Army's practice there.

If the President and Congress were playing a political version of chess, perhaps the most strategic move of the whole game was the passage late in the session of the Fourteenth Amendment. A prodigious number of resolutions proposing amendments had been introduced sporadically during the early months of the session, and these ideas had been refined and synthesized into the Fourteenth Amendment as passed and adopted. It embodied the principles of the Civil Rights bill and was in part made necessary by the doubtful constitutionality of that measure. Much of the constitutional oratory on the Civil Rights and Freedmen's Bureau bills was reiterated in debate over the amendment, but questions of military power and domination did not arise since the amendment included

---

[38]Beale (ed.), *Diary of Gideon Welles*, II, 473–74; S. R. Cockrill to Johnson, March 26, 1866, in Johnson Papers, LC (Reel 21). Original emphasis. There is no certainty that this letter reached the President by April 2 as the earlier practice of date-stamping incoming letters had apparently been abandoned by this time. I do not suggest that Cockrill's letter provoked the *drafting* of the proclamation, since internal evidence in the original draft shows it had been prepared earlier, but merely that the letter might have precipitated its *issuance* at that particular time.

[39]*Ex parte Milligan,* 4 Wallace 2 (1866).

no direct provision for military enforcement. On May 10 the House passed its version of the amendment; on June 8 the Senate passed a different one, to which the House agreed five days later. In one of its last actions, shortly before adjournment, the House admitted representatives from Tennessee after that state had ratified the amendment.

Congress adjourned on July 28. Its accomplishments of the past eight months included important legislation, to be sure, but whether that bundle of laws qualified as a "plan" of reconstruction in the same way that Johnson's May, 1865, proclamations had was quite another question. In truth Congress had adjourned without producing a step-by-step procedure for the South to follow in regaining admittance. Congress certainly expected ratification of the Fourteenth Amendment as a condition of restoration, but nobody in the South was certain what other requirements might later be imposed. The situation was as uncertain for the Army as for the South. Before December, 1865, there had been a clearer procedure for the South to follow; but from March, 1866, to March, 1867, the South and its military overseers were left with the congressionally discredited institutional remnants of Johnson's rejected plan, plus the legislative products of the spring which, as federal laws, had to be enforced and observed. In this fogbank of conflicting policies the task of giving prudent direction to the South's course was one that taxed the abilities of the well-disposed among Southern leaders; maintaining order and overseeing affairs in general taxed the abilities of the commanding generals.

4

The Fruits of Confusion

G LORY to God in the Highest!! for your magnanimous Proclamation
of the ever memorable 2ᵈ Apl. 1866! Proclaiming Peace throughout the United States of America! and encouraging *Good will* to all
Mankind!" That laudation greeted Johnson as he read his mail one day
just after releasing his peace proclamation. Reading on, the President
must have been somewhat let down as the eloquence of the writer's
beginning descended to the supplication of his close, "Please find something for me to do." Just another of the multitudinous office-seekers
who had beleaguered the President for the past year! That message had
come from urban New Jersey; from rural Mississippi came more serious
substance and less flowery prose: "We have just heard of your proclamation declaring the war at an end and that the writ of Habeas Corpus
is again restored, & that for the future we are to be governed by the
Civil instead of the Military laws, thank God for it. We are tired of
Military [rule], we are tired of war, and wish to be again as we were
before the late terrible and calamitous rebellion." [1] This was the
interpretation which many Southerners gave to the proclamation. Rural
Arkansans read in their weekly newspaper an editorial claiming the
President had removed standing military occupation, martial law, and
suspension of the habeas corpus privilege.[2]

But *had* the proclamation actually done the things Southerners credit-
ed it with doing? All Johnson had *proclaimed* was that the insurrection
was at an end and was henceforth to be so regarded. The rest had all

[1]S. Corden to Johnson, April 3, 1866, and G. W. Williams to Johnson, April
12, in Johnson Papers, LC (Reel 22). Original emphasis.
[2]Batesville *North Arkansas Times,* April 14, 1866.

been in the proclamation's preliminary statements and constituted part of standard American governmental philosphy:

Whereas standing armies, military occupation, martial law, military tribunals, and the suspension of the privilege of the writ of *habeas corpus* are in time of peace dangerous to public liberty, incompatible with the individual rights of the citizen, contrary to the genius and spirit of our free institutions, and exhaustive of the national resources, and ought not, therefore, to be sanctioned or allowed except in cases of actual necessity for repelling invasion or suppressing insurrection or rebellion. . . .[3]

The Army was quick to see that more than one interpretation was possible and acted cautiously pending settlement of the matter. Department headquarters in Virginia temporarily suspended military arrests and trials of civilians. In Georgia the bureau chief asked Washington if the proclamation removed martial law, adding that the department commander was hesitant about making arrests now. In a day or two this inquiry brought forth a wire from General Townsend to the department commander: ". . . the Secretary of War, *with the approval of the President,* directs me to inform you that the President's Proclamation does not remove martial law or operate in any way upon the Freedmen's Bureau in the exercise of its legitimate jurisdiction. It is not expedient, however, to resort to military tribunals in any case where justice can be attained through the medium of civil authority." The same instructions went out to all other military commanders.[4]

In Atlanta Townsend's telegram was rephrased thus for a local commander: "You should bear in mind that the right of the exercise of the writ of Habeas Corpus is not restored, but that the Military relinquish to the civil authorities the exercise of all power, compatible with the safety of the public and justice to all." [5] For his Louisiana command General Canby elucidated in greater detail what the proclamation meant.

[3]*Messages and Papers,* VI, 431–32.

[4]AAG to Maj. P. W. Stanhope, and to Gen. N. A. Miles, April 5, 1866, Dept. Va., 14; Brannan to AAG Div. Tenn., April 7, Dept. Ga., 1, RG98, NA; File 122F1866, AGO, and Townsend to Brannan, telegram, April 9, AGO, 42, RG94, NA. Emphasis added because the treatment of this point in Thomas and Hyman, *Stanton,* 478, is misleading. From their account it appears that Stanton and Grant, by sending a "secret circular," were circumventing Johnson without his knowledge. This would have constituted grounds for Stanton's instant ejection from the Cabinet. Moreover, there is no subsequent evidence that Johnson issued other instructions later on, which he would probably have done had the ones of April 9 not corresponded to his own view. The language of Townsend's telegram seems to clearly indicate Johnson's foreknowledge.

[5]AAG to Maj. R. Crofton, CO Savannah, April 19, 1866, Dept. Ga., 1, RG98, NA.

It did not remove martial law or affect the bureau. It did not allow state courts to interfere with persons legitimately held in federal custody. It did not impair the Army's power to stop forceful opposition to federal laws. It did not affect the jurisdiction of military tribunals over acts committed before the proclamation, but it did suspend that jurisdiction over subsequent acts. It had no effect on the protection against civil suits provided in Grant's January order. Military power was to be used when necessary to enforce federal court processes but unnecessary interference with the civil authority was barred. Officers called upon to act in jurisdictional conflicts between federal and state courts should be guided by the Supreme Court's 1859 opinion in *Ableman vs. Booth*— the general did not brief the case for his subordinates but did furnish them the proper citation from the printed reports.[6] In spite of the official interpretation, some officers still felt hampered by the proclamation; Thomas complained that it "virtually denies to the Military all supervision of the civil [power], all exercises of the functions of the civil [power], or the right to enforce their orders, where they in any degree collide with the decision of a civil Magistrate. . . ." [7]

On August 20 the President issued another proclamation. Now Johnson declared the rebellion ended in Texas, as well as in other states, since civil authority could enforce the laws there and the people were "well and loyally disposed." Johnson reiterated most of what he had set forth in April including his strictures on military government. The original draft of the August document contained a lengthy proviso concerning what the Army had previously done:

It is to be understood, however, that such military orders as have been heretofore issued with reference to any or all of the several States or any of them under the act to establish a Bureau for the relief of freedmen and refugees, approved March third, one thousand eight hundred and sixty-five and the act passed at the late session of Congress continuing the same in force, and all military orders now existing for the purpose of sustaining the civil authority of the Federal Government and the laws of Congress with reference to a possible renewal of resistance to that authority, are not affected by this proclamation, and the same will remain in force until hereafter specially revoked, or countermanded.[8]

This section did not appear in the proclamation's final form. Johnson may have felt that the substance of the omitted section was covered by

[6]*Army and Navy Journal*, III (May 5, 1866), 586.
[7]AAG to G. E. Grishan, June 11, 1866, Div. Tenn., 34, RG98, NA.
[8]Ms draft, filed under Aug. 20, 1866, Proclamations, in Johnson Papers, LC (Reel 49). The draft being a clerical one, it is impossible to determine whether Johnson or some advisor was responsible for the change.

language already included: "Whereas adequate provision has been made by military orders to enforce the execution of the acts of Congress, aid the civil authorities, and secure obedience to the Constitution and laws of the United States within the State of Texas if a resort to military force for such purpose should at any time become necessary. . . ." [9] The original section, applying to all eleven states, was admittedly broader than this one, and the Army would probably have felt better had it been included.

As it was, the Army still worried about its legal position. After the proclamations appeared, Thomas used his troops sparingly in Tennessee, and then only when essential to help the civil authorities.[10] From the Gulf states also came signs of doubt. The Florida commander complained to Sheridan that some officials, thinking the proclamation amounted to total restoration of civil supremacy, were arresting soldiers and federal employees right and left for trifling infractions of municipal ordinances. Sheridan sent the letter on to Grant with an endorsement pointing out the "increasing insolence" of Florida and Texas officials since the proclamation's appearance. Louisiana he did not consider such a problem because there the proclamation had never been "officially promulgated." Since General Orders No. 3 and 44 had never been rescinded, Sheridan said, he had kept on in Louisiana as if no proclamation existed.[11]

Sheridan was not alone in thinking the President's actions had produced increasing hostility towards the government. Even in April the Baton Rouge commander had noticed such an attitude as a result of Johnson's first proclamation. According to him prominent men averred that if Congress tried to force distasteful measures on them, "another *tea party* will be gotten up." [12] On the question of the proclamations' effect on No. 3 and No. 44, Grant informed Sheridan in October that he considered the proclamations nullified the orders.[13] December instruc-

---

[9]*Messages and Papers,* VI, 438.

[10]Thomas to Stanton, Nov. 29, 1866, Div. Tenn., 34, RG98, NA.

[11]Foster to AAG Div. Gulf, Sept. 20, 1866, and endorsement of Oct. 6, in Sheridan Papers, LC. Sheridan's use of the phrase "officially promulgated" obscures his meaning, since commanding generals always received official copies of laws and proclamations in the form of general orders from the War Department. He probably meant that he had taken no steps to announce the proclamation in Louisiana.

[12]Col. A. J. Edgerton to AAG Dept. La., April 30, 1866, in Sheridan Papers, LC. Original emphasis.

[13]Maj. G. K. Leet, AAG HQA, to Sheridan, Oct. 17, 1866, in Sheridan Papers, LC. The treatment of this point in Thomas and Hyman, *Stanton,* 498–99, seems confused in that it credits Grant with sending out devious and contradictory instructions, to the end that Johnson's edicts would not hamper the Army. They mention an alleged letter from Grant to Sheridan of Oct 17, in which Grant told

tions to subordinates from Headquarters, District of Texas show that this opinion of Grant's was the policy subsequently followed in that state, although one post commander probably went too far in refusing military aid to the bureau under it.[14] The Army's chief lawyer, Judge Advocate General Joseph Holt, was also drawn into the question. A wartime statute had limited to the duration of the war the authority of commanders of "separate brigades" to review court-martial proceedings. After Johnson's August proclamation, one of Sheridan's subordinates in Texas had exercised this authority, but Holt ruled that the proclamation had ended the rebellion in law and that the officer's action was thus incorrect. Since courts-martial only try soldiers for military offenses, the specific legal question involved did not concern civil-military relations; it was Holt's ruling on the effect of the proclamation on the rebellion that was significant.[15]

The uncertainties which Johnson's proclamations had raised concerning the Army's legal position in the South became greater due to the unsettling effect of the Supreme Court's action in the Milligan case. In October, 1865, Crawford Keyes and several friends had attacked a group of United States soldiers in South Carolina, killing several, for which a military commission tried them in January, 1866. Since the commission decreed the death penalty, the President had to review the case; and in July, upon Stanton's recommendation, Johnson commuted all the sentences to life imprisonment. The Secretary was unwilling to carry out a death sentence in view of the Milligan decision. In November, 1866, after the prisoners were transferred to Fort Delaware, they induced a federal judge to release them on a writ of habeas corpus on

---

Sheridan the proclamations did not really revoke the general orders. They provide no footnote reference for this letter, and it could not be located in the Grant or Sheridan Papers. From *Leet's* dispatch of Oct. 17 (which Thomas and Hyman do not mention at all) it seems quite clear that Grant considered No. 3 and No. 44 nullified. Thomas and Hyman claim that in Grant's alleged letter of the seventeenth he told Sheridan to pretend he had never "officially received" Johnson's proclamation; actually it was Sheridan (in his endorsement on Foster's letter, referred to *supra,* note 11) who first suggested this, and Grant's concurrence in the idea is doubtful since Leet's letter of Oct. 17 transmitted, at Grant's order, official copies of the proclamations. Thomas and Hyman place the phrase "officially received" in quotes, as if it appeared in Grant's alleged letter of the seventeenth.

[14]AAAG Dist. Tex. to Maj. S. H. Lathrop, Dec. 19, 1866, and to Capt. J. H. Bradford, Dec. 26, 5MD, 111, RG98, NA.

[15]"Memo" filed under Sept. 26, 1866, in Sheridan Papers, LC. The treatment of this point in Thomas and Hyman, *Stanton,* 499, while technically correct as far as it goes, omits the most significant part of the problem.

the ground that the federal courts in South Carolina had been open during the trial.[16]

Another South Carolina military commission had tried eighty-year-old James Egan for the murder of a Negro boy and had sentenced him to life in the federal penitentiary at Albany, New York. In June, 1866, Justice Samuel Nelson of the United States Supreme Court, sitting as a circuit judge in New York, granted Egan a writ of habeas corpus. Nelson's opinion was an important statement of the proper bounds of martial law, which he defined as the will of the commander, capable of overriding all civil law. But, he said, martial law could only be used in times of necessity and must end when the necessity ends. In addition, the existence of the necessity must be shown by those employing martial law. In this case, Nelson held, the necessity ended with the suppression of the rebellion and the reorganization of the state government by Johnson.[17] This opinion was in tune with the Milligan edict of April; and since Nelson was a Supreme Court justice, the opinion seemed to suggest what might be forthcoming when the nation's highest court met in December. Yet this decision of Nelson's left two critical questions unanswered. First, at what date had the rebellion been suppressed? Among the conceivable points were the surrender of Lee, the surrender of Kirby Smith, and Johnson's April proclamation, with practically a year between the first and last. And second, when had Johnson reorganized the state government? One might choose his appointment of a provisional governor, the election of members of Congress, or Johnson's annual message of December, 1865, announcing the reorganization of the state. Small wonder that the Army could not look to the courts for clear guidance.

Concern for the Negro had been one force motivating the enactment of the Freedmen's Bureau and Civil Rights bills, and events of the first half of 1866 showed the reality behind this concern. Among these events were prolonged riots in Memphis. On May 1 some discharged colored soldiers became disorderly and a police attempt to arrest them proved futile. The entire police force then mobilized and with the aid, whether asked or unasked, of numerous citizens made a general onset against the Negroes in South Memphis. The affair promptly got out of hand and troops had to be summoned. The department commander, General George Stoneman, cautioned his men to use discretion, especially if the

---

[16]*Army and Navy Journal,* III (July 14 and 21, 1866), 742, 758; *House Reports,* 39th Cong., 2nd Sess., No. 23; *United States vs. Commandant of Fort Delaware,* Fed. Cas. No. 14842.

[17]*In re Egan,* Fed. Cas. No. 4303.

mayor called upon them for aid. The soldiers were to assist the civil authorities in maintaining order but were to use firearms "only in case of extreme necessity of which you must be the judge." He also thought it advisable to patrol part of Memphis and to have some of his white troops keep the 3rd Colored Heavy Artillery at Fort Pickering to prevent the men from entering the city.[18] The riots continued sporadically until the fourth when additional troops ordered from Nashville arrived and comparative quiet was restored. Stoneman, who did not trust either the sincerity or the ability of the civil functionaries, addressed a long and tart letter to the mayor: "In conclusion I have to assure you and through you the people of Memphis that if they cannot govern themselves as a law abiding and Christian community that [*sic*] they will be governed—and that hereafter it will be my duty and privilege to see that there is [*sic*] no more riotous proceedings or conduct either on the part of whites or blacks or city authorities." [19] The subsequent military investigation placed principal blame on the civil officials and set the monetary loss to the Negroes at a total of $72,000, including both thefts and property damage.

Some question arose concerning what, if anything, the Army could do with respect to collection of damages and prosecution of the culprits responsible. On July 7 Grant sent a sheaf of papers to Stanton with the suggestion that legal proceedings ought to be pressed against the city of Memphis for damages caused by the riot and that the leaders should be arrested by the Army and held until the civil authorities should be willing to try them. In so doing Grant was apparently looking to action under his General Orders No. 44, issued four days previously and covering exactly such situations. Stanton and the President referred the question to Attorney General James Speed who returned his opinion a week later. The riots, he ruled, were no offense against the laws or dignity of the United States and the Army's role at Memphis ended with the suppression of violence. There being no war, and both federal and state courts in Tennessee being open, the people would have to appeal to them; the Army was powerless to redress private grievances or carry on "prosecutions for public wrongs." [20] In mid-August the wires brought a cipher telegram from General Thomas: the fulminators of the riot were known; the grand jury, long in session, had ignored the matter;

[18]*Army and Navy Journal,* III (May 19, 1866), 615; Stoneman to Capt. A. W. Allyn, May 1, 1866, and AAG to same, May 2, Dept. Tenn., 22, RG98, NA.
[19]Stoneman to Mayor John Park, May 5, 1866, Dept. Tenn., 22, RG98, NA.
[20]Grant to Stanton, July 7, 1866, HQA, C, RG108, NA; 11 Opinions of Attorneys General, 531–32.

should not the culprits therefore be arrested under No. 44? Grant sent the paper on to Stanton with the endorsement that he wished the arrests could be made in order to have a salutary effect on the civil officials but that he did not feel authorized to order such action.[21] "A strict and prompt enforcement of this order is required."—this had been Grant's gruff conclusion to No. 44, and the Memphis agitators were a clear case in point. If he did not feel authorized to order an arrest under a policy he had himself set forth, he must have been either exceptionally weak-willed or else doubtful of the legality of No. 44 in the face of Johnson's April proclamation.[22]

Of even greater significance than the Memphis disorder were disturbances in New Orleans just after Congress adjourned; they were almost a testimonial to the need for the legislation recently passed. The difficulties began when a remnant of the pro-Union 1864 state convention undertook to hold a session in New Orleans. The governor considered the meeting legal; the lieutenant-governor, attorney general, and mayor were determined to prevent it. On July 25, 1866, the mayor informed General Absalom Baird, commanding the Department of Louisiana, of the expected meeting. The mayor made it clear that he considered the meeting ilegal; that it was "calculated to disturb the public peace and tranquility"; that he was conseqently obliged to disperse the meeting; and that he intended to do so by arresting its members, provided the convention lacked military sanction. Baird replied that the convention had never applied for permission to meet but that moreover, all loyal citizens had a right to assemble peacefully to discuss governmental questions. Considering the turbulent state of public opinion in postwar Louisiana, the general displayed singular political naïveté and wishful thinking: "If the assemblage in question has the legal right to remodel the state government, it should be protected in so doing; if it has not, then its labors must be looked upon as a piece of harmless pleasantry, to which no one ought to object." He questioned the propriety of a mere mayor assuming to decide on the legality of a state convention and thought the governor (and ultimately the federal government) should be the ones to deal with this question. As to the use of troops, Baird promised the civil authorities military and naval aid if public hostility

[21]Thomas to Grant, Aug. 15, 1866, and endorsement of Aug. 16, in Stanton Papers, LC. There are no further endorsements beyond Grant's.

[22]This case seems additional evidence of the incorrectness of the view in Thomas and Hyman, *Stanton*, 478, 498–99, that Grant was secretly circumventing Johnson's policy during 1866.

to the convention was such that the mayor's police force could not control the populace and protect the covention in its sessions.[23]

There the matter rested for a day or so, until speeches began to be made in preparation for the meeting. On the twenty-eighth the lieutenant-governor wired President Johnson describing affairs and asking if the Army would interfere with the contemplated arrest of the convention members under process from the local court. Johnson doubted the legality of the convention and also desired to maintain order; he consequently wired back to the lieutenant-governor: "The military will be expected to sustain, and not to obstruct or interfere with, the proceedings of the courts." [24] This telegram went out from the White House at 5:40 P.M.; four and a half hours later a telegraph key filled a room in the War Department with the staccato clicking of another message.

HON. EDWIN M. STANTON, SECRETARY OF WAR: A CONVENTION HAS BEEN CALLED, WITH THE SANCTION OF THE GOVERNOR WELLS [SIC] TO MEET HERE ON MONDAY. THE LIEUTENANT-GOVERNOR AND CITY AUTHORITIES THINK IT UNLAWFUL, AND PROPOSE TO BREAK IT UP BY ARRESTING THE DELEGATES. I HAVE GIVEN NO ORDERS ON THE SUBJECT, BUT HAVE WARNED THE PARTIES THAT I COULD NOT COUNTENANCE OR PERMIT SUCH ACTION WITHOUT INSTRUCTIONS TO THAT EFFECT FROM THE PRESIDENT. PLEASE INSTRUCT ME AT ONCE BY TELEGRAPH. A. BAIRD, BREVET MAJOR GENERAL.[25]

The War Minister failed to show the dispatch to the President and failed to send any reply on his own. These were perhaps the most crucial decisions made by anyone during the entire affair.

Sunday the twenty-ninth was quiet enough, but on Monday the convention met and a riot took place in which 37 Negroes were killed and 119 injured. In the relative quiet of Monday evening, after his troops had arrived and cleared the streets, Baird penned Stanton an account of the events. The military etiquette and stereotyped formality of his opening words hardly fit the subsequent details: "I have the honor to inform you that a very serious riot has occurred here today." The trouble

23John T. Monroe to Baird, July 25, 1866, and reply, July 26, in *House Exec. Docs.*, 39th Cong., 2nd Sess., No. 68, pp. 6–7. This is a compilation of relevant correspondence and telegrams, plus the findings of a subsequently established military board of investigation.

24Albert Voorhies to Johnson, reply, and Johnson to Gov. J. Madison Wells, all July 28, 1866, *ibid.*, 4.

25*Ibid.*, 4–5.

began when some Negroes, parading in Canal Street near the convention hall, got into a scuffle with a group of white citizens. As the dimensions and intensity of the affray increased, the police force, which had been massed and held ready by the mayor, made an all-out attack on the pro-convention elements of the crowd and inflicted numerous brutal and unnecessary injuries, predominantly on unresisting Negroes. The police, acting in concert with the anti-convention segments of the mob, brought the convention hall itself under siege and ultimately broke up the meeting. Since Jackson Barracks were three miles below the city, the troops did not arrive at the scene until after much bloodshed had occurred; but they did succeed in restoring order. Baird declared martial law in the city and appointed a military governor.[26]

As the week progressed, more details came to light, and attempts were made to shift the blame from one principal to another. In some respects these attempts were largely academic, for surely there was enough blame to go round. Sheridan, Baird's superior, returned from a visit to Texas just after the riot, and on August 1 he wrote Grant a dispatch calling the convention leaders "political agitators and revolutionary men" but throwing chief responsibility for the riot on the conduct of Mayor John T. Monroe's police. The White House released this dispatch to the press with the latter opinion omitted; and the publication of this version led to a journalistic cross fire between the pro- and anti-Johnson newspapers, an indignant complaint from Sheridan, and ultimate publication of the dispatches in full.[27]

Baird came in for his share of abuse, though some of it was undeserved. In the tumult of the thirtieth a Northern correspondent lashed at the general: "In the face of all these tremendous conditions, our own military commander sits down quietly to dinner, while the blood of such men as the former class [Unionists] is poured at his feet by the latter [Rebels] as if it were a libation to his incapacity and egotism." [28] Baird's troops had indeed appeared too late to prevent the riot, but this is not necessarily attributable to the commander's indifference. The gen-

[26]*Ibid.*, 6. Baird did not have all the details at the time he wrote this letter. It can be augmented by the findings of his board of investigation, summarized *ibid.*, 36–43. The inevitable congressional investigation resulted in *House Reports*, 39th Cong., 2nd Sess., No. 16.

[27]*House Exec. Docs.*, 39th Cong., 2nd Sess., No. 68, pp. 19–22; New York *Times*, Aug. 3, 1866; New York *Tribune*, Aug. 4–10. The question of the garbled dispatch is satisfactorily dealt with in McKitrick, *Andrew Johnson and Reconstruction*, 426–27 and n.

[28]New York *Tribune*, Aug. 6, 1866.

eral was under some misapprehension (perhaps deliberately perpetrated by the civil authorities) as to the time of the convention's meeting; he had expected it to start at 6 P.M. whereas it actually began at noon.

Stanton and Johnson also received censure. For the failure of Baird's telegram of the twenty-eighth to reach the President, the War Secretary alone is responsible. Stanton's motives, however, are less easy to determine. To ignore an officer's plain request for instructions from the Commander-in-Chief is at the least sheer incompetence. But the grounds for charging Stanton with deliberate deceit and conniving are much less firm. Stanton differed with the President on many points of policy towards the South, and perhaps he would not have minded seeing the President embarrassed by trouble in New Orleans. But the charge of deliberately fomenting bloodshed seems insupportable. Stanton's later defense was that Baird's telegram showed no fear of immediate violence and that Baird's "existing instructions" to preserve peace covered the case. This was a weak argument, however; any observant person, as aware of the state of affairs in Louisiana as Stanton was, could hardly have underestimated the urgency of Baird's request.[29]

The matter of Baird's "existing instructions" was an equally weak point in Stanton's defense. Of course Baird was expected to preserve the peace; he did not need the President to tell him that. The thorny question was, what course should Baird take with respect to the action of the courts? Troops all over the South had been called upon from time to time to help this sheriff or that marshal execute a civil process, and Army officers were not always certain what was the extent of their power in such cases. It seems clear that had Baird received definite instructions on the specific point of his relation to the civil authorities, the chances of any serious disturbance would have been slim. Had Baird received instructions to support the police in their execution of a court order to arrest the delegates, the convention would probably have melted away without the violence which actually transpired and which was the result of the police acting without any restraint. Had Baird's instructions been to prevent the arrest of the delegates, there would still have been little trouble since the New Orleans police would hardly have engaged in a pitched battle with regular United States troops. As was the case throughout Reconstruction, the moral and psychological effect of the blue uniform was great, but in this instance the War Secretary's inaction prevented the timely application of this suasion.

[29]Thomas and Hyman, *Stanton*, 496–97.

Some of Johnson's contemporaries believed that the President had helped to foment the trouble.[30] But this is farfetched. Three Johnson dispatches to the civil officials, two on the twenty-eighth and one on the thirtieth, show that he had three desires: that the convention, being of doubtful legality, should not meet; that the Army should uphold the court process; and that peace should be preserved. The crucial message was probably the one to the lieutenant-governor which left the Executive Mansion at suppertime on the twenty-eighth: "The military will be expected to sustain, and not to obstruct or interfere with, the proceedings of the courts." This had gone forth in response to an inquiry from the lieutenant-governor as to the Army's course.[31] Johnson was here informing a state official what he wanted the Army to do, without sending a simultaneous message to the Army officer concerned— seemingly an irregular procedure for the Commander-in-Chief to follow.[32] But there is an explanation. If Stanton thought Baird did not need to be told to keep the peace, Johnson thought Baird did not need to be told to uphold the civil courts. Johnson had always wanted the civil authorities to have as much freedom as possible, with the Army exercising a supporting role. Hence he was simply informing the civil functionaries of a policy he then believed was already clear enough to the military power. Had he received Baird's message which came to the telegraph office five hours later he would have realized the policy was *not* clear to Baird and would most likely have sent him the same wire he had sent to the lieutenant-governor.

The blame distributed in Washington falls in greatest measure at the Secretary's door; that distributed in New Orleans belongs principally to the mayor and his police. After the affair Sheridan wrote: "It was no riot; it was an absolute massacre by the police, which was not excelled in murderous cruelty by that of Fort Pillow. It was a murder which the mayor and police of this city perpetrated without the shadow of a necessity; furthermore, I believe it was premeditated, and every indication points to this." The military investigation bore out most of this opinion. Conflicting testimony was offered on almost every important point,

[30]New York *Tribune*, Aug. 1, 1866. Thomas and Hyman, *Stanton*, 497, accept this idea.

[31]*House Exec. Docs.*, 39th Cong., 2nd Sess., No. 68, pp. 4–5. It is difficult to concur in the opinion of Thomas and Hyman, *Stanton*, 497, that in this message Johnson was "acting in direct contradiction" to the position he had taken earlier in July with respect to the Tennessee legislature. The two situations were not parallel.

[32]Thomas and Hyman, *Stanton*, 497, censure Johnson for this.

but without much doubt Monroe was determined to break up the convention and wanted his police to have a free hand in doing it.[33]

Passions in New Orleans took a long time to cool. Nearly a month after the riot Captain William B. Armstrong, a quartermaster, sent Senator Lyman Trumbull a badly-spelled estimate of affairs: "You know that we union and military men live here rather insecurely in this rebelious riotous city, constantly exposed to the bullet or dager of the assasan [*sic*]." [34] Fortunately, conditions were not quite that bad every place in the South. Northerners, particularly ones of Republican proclivities, regarded the Memphis and New Orleans affairs as typical of Southern attitudes during 1866. It was not an accurate estimate, though, for violence on the scale of Memphis and New Orleans was the exception rather than the rule. But if such riots were not typical of 1866, they were more extreme than anything that had occurred in 1865. The malevolently disposed among Southerners probably thought they could get away with more in view of the conflict between Congress and the President. And whereas the President's intransigence likely alienated some moderate Republicans, it seems equally plausible that Congress' intransigence in refusing to accept Johnson's policy (even though the basis for the intransigence was natural and understandable) discredited the moderates among influential Southerners who had honestly counseled acquiescence in Johnson's plan on the assumption the President's actions would be ratified by Congress.

In protecting Negroes—and white Unionists as well—the Army was not often required to suppress large-scale riots so devised that the victims would be principally from those two "objectionable" classes. A more customary occurrence was military interposition in individual cases, sometimes specifically under the powers vested in the bureau or under the Civil Rights Act. Some difficulty arising from the conduct of the Natchez police force during a riot occurred in March, 1866, and the post commander felt it desirable to disarm the police. General Wood disapproved. Such action he thought was not in line with "what is believed to be the true policy for correcting the evils which exists [*sic*] in the society of the states lately in rebellion." Wood thought the "true policy" was not to modify state and municipal laws, but to deal with individual cases of abuse, and thus "educate a public sentiment which

[33]*House Exec. Docs.,* 39th Cong., 2nd Sess., No. 68, pp. 11, 36–43.
[34]Armstrong to Trumbull, Aug. 24, 1866, in Lyman Trumbull Papers, LC.

will finally (and it is hoped at no distant day) result in a system of laws, and such in [*sic*] enforcement of them, as will secure equal and impartial justice to all classes of the community." Nullifying existing laws or customs would just create chaos and extend the necessity for military rule. As to the Natchez police, when individual officers abused their power and harmed anyone, white or Negro, the post commander ought to report it to the city government and ask for redress. Only if the local officials refused to correct the abuse should the offenders be arrested. "If the mayor cannot control his police," Wood remarked sharply, "and see that they do not carry on the business of public highwaymen, the government of the City will of necessity revert to the Military, the necessity of which will be deplored by the General Commanding as much as it can be by good citizens." [35]

After the Civil Rights bill had become law, however, Wood took a stronger position with respect to "nullification" of local laws. In July, 1866, he told a justice of the peace in the little town of Kosciusko that three sections of the Mississippi black code which forced Negroes to make written contracts and have fixed homes were in conflict with the Civil Rights Act since they did not apply equally to whites. If Negroes *made* agreements and then did not live up to them, he said, they could be proceeded against for breach of contract, but not by the summary remedies set forth in the state law. [36]

On one occasion in South Carolina General Sickles prevented a white man from being lashed under a court order; on another he threatened to relocate the freedmen of Edgefield, Laurens, and Newberry districts and provide for them at local expense unless they were treated more fairly. Grant ordered Sheridan to see that all stockholders of the Buffalo Bayou, Brazos, and Colorado Railroad got to share in the reorganization of the company and did not suffer from usurpation of control of the road during the rebellion. When the mayor of Norfolk, Virginia, tried to interfere with a Freedmen's Bureau court case, the commanding general told him to desist. While General Charles Griffin commanded in Texas, he wrote many letters to Governor James W. Throckmorton requesting pardons for people unjustly convicted by civil courts. [37]

Protecting people's rights by interposition in specific cases naturally

[35]Wood to Col. H. A. McCaleb, March 19 and 26, 1866, Dept. Miss., 2, RG98, NA.

[36]Wood to E. M. Wells, July 10, 1866, Dept. Miss., 2, RG98, NA.

[37]Simkins and Woody, *South Carolina*, 57; Grant to Sheridan, Feb. 28, 1866, HQA, C, RG108, NA; AAG to Mayor of Norfolk, Feb. 8, 1866, Dept. Va., 14, RG98, NA; Griffin to Throckmorton, fall-winter 1866, *passim*, 5MD, 111, RG98, NA.

required close relations between the Army and civil officials, who varied in attitude from cooperative to recalcitrant. The simplest way of dealing with scoundrelly civil functionaries would have been their removal, but the Army was reluctant to make wholesale purges for misconduct. In March of 1866 Sheridan urged that New Orleans hold a municipal election to improve affairs there. "The present mayor is a military appointee," he wrote, "but defied General Canby, who appointed him, and conducted affairs as though he had been elected by the people; but if the courts found him at fault, he defied them by the facts [*sic*] that he was a military appointee and only subject to military jurisdiction; so he had a pretty good thing of it, not being particularly responsible to anyone." [38] In North Carolina General Ruger ordered the mayor of Wilmington to replace the marshal, but this action brought disapproval from Grant. "The eligibility of civil officers to office is a question for the courts and law officers of the Government to decide," he wrote, adding that state officials ought not, as a rule, to be interfered with unless found guilty of some offense. When, however, it turned out that the marshal was an unpardoned rebel general, Ruger's course was upheld.[39] The War Office wanted to keep close watch on projected removals and in July directed another commander to make a detailed report to Washington and await special instructions in each instance before removing anyone. Johnson too involved himself in the question of removals and ordered the Virginia commander to prevent the recently elected mayor of Portsmouth from exercising his functions until pardoned.[40]

During 1866, as at other times during Reconstruction, the fact that local conditions varied from place to place and over periods of time made it difficult for Washington to formulate general instructions for the field commanders. Consider Arkansas. An inspection tour through the northern part of the state early in the year resulted in a report of mixed popular sentiment. The only open resistance described took place at a little crossroads with the disarmingly peaceful name of Evening Shade, where a small command attempting to make some arrests was fired upon. The fire was returned and there were no casualties, but the desperadoes the Army was after escaped. The area around Jacksonport,

---

[38]Sheridan to Lt. Col. C. B. Comstock, ADC HQA, March 2, 1866, in Daniel O. Drennan Papers, LC.

[39]E. G. Parker, Mil. Sec. HQA, to Gen. T. Ruger, Apr. 5, 1866, HQA, C, RG108, NA; File 130R1866, AGO, and Townsend to Ruger, April 9, 1866, AGO 42, RG94, NA.

[40]Townsend to Gen. J. C. Robinson, July 13, 1866, AGO, 43, and to Terry, May 29, AGO, 42, RG94, NA.

however, thirty-five miles away, was peaceful enough to warrant a rec-ommended reduction in the local garrison. By the time annual report-writing time had arrived in the autumn, General Sherman could report the state as doing very well and not causing "a particle of trouble." [41]

Other parts of the South exhibited similar variances. In July the Florida commander found conditions in his state generally good but thought troops would be needed for one or two years, if not longer, to protect Negroes and Northern investors. Sheridan agreed in his annual report that Florida was doing well and that its people realized "that their best interest was to take off their coats and go to work to repair the disaster of the rebellion." This was quite a contrast to the most vexatious portion of Sheridan's command—Texas—where he found conditions "anomalous, singular, and unsatisfactory" and remarked that Indians killing white men on the frontier caused much greater con-sternation than white men killing Negroes in the interior.[42] As to the Carolinas, Sickles wrote, "In my Dept. I have not yet seen the American flag raised by a Carolinian. If it floated over a dwelling, or a hotel, or a shop, the population would avoid the place as they would shun a pest-house filled with lepers." [43]

With the condition of affairs thus varying in time and place, Grant as General-in-Chief was reluctant to attempt to formulate set policies cover-ing all possible situations. The suppression of newspapers was one excep-tion. Grant decided, after some Virginia difficulties in this regard, that the power of suspension should lie only at his headquarters. He asked Southern commanders to send him for review copies of papers contain-ing disloyal sentiments, a policy which in Virginia resulted in a minor and quite absurd row between Terry and some publishers over whether the sample copies sent to Washington ought properly to be paid for. Suppressions were infrequent, though; perhaps, as Terry thought, the close scrutiny had some salutary effect on Southern editorial policies.[44]

In the general administration of affairs Grant left as much as possible to the local commanders. It might indeed be comforting to some lieuten-ant or captain commanding a post in backwoods Georgia to know he was

[41]Report of Col. L. H. Whipple to AAAG White River Dist., in *House Reports,* 39th Cong., 1st Sess., No. 30, Pt. 3, pp. 169–70; *Report of the Sec. of War, 1865–66,* p. 22 (1st pagin.).

[42]Foster to AAG Div. Gulf, July 8, 1866, in Sheridan Papers, LC; *Report of the Sec. of War, 1865–66,* pp. 48–49 (1st pagin.).

[43]Sickles to Stanton, private, July 19, 1866, in Stanton Papers, LC.

[44]Gen. T. S. Bowers, AAG HQA, to all So. cmdrs., Feb. 19, 1866, HQA, C, RG108, NA; Terry to AAG Div. Atlantic, March 1, 1866, and to Gen. J. A. Rawlins, C/S HQA, March 19, Dept. Va., 14, RG98, NA.

carrying out minutely detailed instructions he had received from Washington via intermediate headquarters; ultimate responsibility then clearly rested at the highest level. But on the other hand Grant was correct in his belief that, in many matters, it was the commander on the spot who was best qualified to determine the necessary action, though of course such action did run the risk of disapproval at one level of command or the next. In November Grant told General Edward O. C. Ord, recently assigned to the Arkansas command, that no instructions could cover all exceptional and extraordinary situations. Wherever cases arose under the Freedmen's Bureau or Civil Rights acts, those laws had to be the Army's guide. In other circumstances commanders ought to exercise a "wise discretion" and act in concert with the civil officials whenever possible. "In the exercise of the discretionary powers possessed by you, you will wherever it is possible be supported by the General-in-Chief." [45]

This problem of discretion harassed commanding generals when they wrote instructions for their subordinates. In Mississippi, where bureau agents often received instructions directly from department headquarters, one subcommissioner at Pass Christian received a directive to arrest a certain citizen in his area. Even so, "The use of Military power in times of peace must be exceptional," his instructions read, "and the exceptions can only be justified by the strongest circumstances; . . . you, in the duties which devolve upon you in this matter, will be expected to act with such discretion that while a firm obedience of orders is given, yet a proper and just respect for the Civil authorities may be kept in view." [46] A delicate situation arose in Arkansas involving cooperation with the bureau. Some plantation owners had reportedly abducted forty to fifty Negroes from the city workhouse in Nashville and were forcing them to work without a contract and treating them cruelly. General Ord sent a major with a small detachment from Little Rock to accompany a bureau agent and investigate. The troops were to turn over to the agent such Negroes as in the *major's* opinion were wrongfully held. If the *major* thought cruelty had been practiced, he was to inform the local civil authorities and turn the plantation owners over to them. If the *major* thought justice would not be had, he was to bring the men to Little Rock with him. "In the performance of this duty keep your party well under command and in perfect discipline; allow them to use no harsh or insulting language in carrying out your orders, and avoid the

[45]Col. C. B. Comstock, AAG HQA, to Ord, Nov. 24, 1866, HQA, C, RG108, NA.
[46]AAAG to Capt. R. F. Gardner, Sept. 18, 1866, Dept. Miss., 2, RG98, NA.

exercise of unnecessarily harsh or arbitrary measures. If force is necessary, use it with firmness and without hesitation, but as kindly as circumstances will admit." Clearly, then, the discretion lay with the Army officer and not with the bureau agent.[47]

If the presence of military forces with wide discretionary powers was to do more good than harm, the troops would have to be on their best behavior. Sometimes this seemed especially difficult. Eastern Mississippi garrisons gave cause for complaint during the spring of 1866; at Columbus there was so much misconduct by officers—conniving with citizens to swindle the government and one another, for one thing—that the district commander had to order a special inspection. "If you can keep that part of your command in good discipline and subjection, [and] make them attend to their duties and nothing else, you will earn an enviable notoriety," his instructions read. A young lieutenant at Meridian asked headquarters for more troops and received a pointed if grammatically defective reply: "From the conduct of your troops as reported by your letter I think the more you have the worse you would be off. . . . You will have to be exceedingly careful and vigilent [sic] and allow no tamperizing [sic] with your troops by citizens." The harried officer replied defensively that mischievous citizens were inducing his men to desert and steal government property and that he was forced to put some of his men in the city jail for misconduct. He was trying his best to stop the irregularities, he said, but his corrective efforts were hampered by his first sergeant's being drunk more than half the time.[48]

One officer stationed at Victoria, Texas, caused a commotion by his lack of good judgment. He had left a gamecock and two hens under the watchful eye of a local hotel clerk. But the clerk's eye proved more covetous than watchful, and when the officer returned the clerk was gone and the poultry too. The enraged officer went back to camp, ordered his men to arrest the new clerk (who knew nothing about the case) and had him tied up by his thumbs and "subjected to the taunts and insults of a lot of Negroes, whose meanness would more than suffice to sicken the stomach of hell." The poor clerk was released through the intercession of the officer's superior, but the local newspaper editor, for using the objectionable language quoted, found himself under military arrest. Presumably the poultry was gone for good.[49]

[47]AAG to Maj. Jacob Rawles, Nov. 11, 1866, Dept. Ark., 3, RG98, NA.
[48]AAG to Col. G. Zeigler, March 19, 1866, and to Lt. A. Hedburg, April 23, Dept. Miss., 2; Hedburg's reply, April 26, 4MD, 85, RG98, NA.
[49]Galveston *Daily News,* Jan. 29, 1867, quoting the Victoria *Advocate.*

Among the worst cases of misconduct by troops during Reconstruction was the burning of Brenham, Texas, in September of 1866. There had customarily been a ball in town every Friday night, and on this particular Friday, two were held—one for Negroes and one for whites. Several soldiers of the 17th Infantry, a rather rowdy outfit generally, decided to attend the Negro ball. They refused to pay the requested admission price, and the ball subsequently closed for lack of patronage. The soldiers, still seeking excitement, next undertook to referee a street fight between a Negro and a drunken Indian. Who won does not appear, but the referees chastized the Negro and he fled to seek refuge at the white ball. The soldiers chased him and had an encounter with several of the white men present, who feared for the safety of their ladies. One soldier was shot in the scuffle and borne back to camp by his friends. Thinking him mortally wounded, they returned to town and set it afire, though the blaze was brought under control before too much damage was done. The soldiers involved then deserted, fearing that their lives would not be safe near the town.[50]

Most commanders realized that shielding their men from legitimate punishment would merely have worsened civil-military relations. Thus a soldier of the 38th Colored Infantry charged with murderous assault on a local policeman was held by the Army for delivery to the civil authorities under the 33rd Article of War. The municipal courts of New Orleans in late 1866 were allowed to prosecute soldiers in proper cases, whether it was Private James Donnelly of the 6th Cavalry, who let his Irish temper get the better of him while having a night on the town, or a trooper of the 9th Cavalry accused of murder.[51]

During 1866, as during 1865, the presence of colored troops was a sore point in civil-military relations. The first half of the year was especially difficult because of the continuing muster-out of white volunteer regiments and the fact that Congress was slow to pass the new law establishing the size of the regular Army. Maintaining a balance between white and colored troops was therefore difficult. In mid-March Grant sent Sheridan the 17th Infantry in hopes it would permit the re-

[50]Accounts of this espisode differ markedly. The one given here is principally from the report of a military investigating board, file 626G1866, AGO, RG94, NA, and from a brief made by Townsend in the Sheridan Papers, LC. This account places more blame on the soldiers than Sheridan did, but not as much as the official state investigation, which was printed as an appendix to the Journal of the House of Representatives of the Eleventh Legislature of Texas.

[51]AAAG Dist. Tex. to Capt. J. H. Bradford, Dec. 26, 1866, 5MD, 111; AAG to Clerk of N. O. Recorder's Court, Oct. 15, 1866, Dept. Gulf, 258, and to CO 9th Cavalry, Dec. 5, Dept. Gulf, 274, RG98, NA.

lease of all remaining white volunteers. He added, "Unless you think security demands the retention of some of the white Volunteers muster the whole of them out as rapidly as possible. In the case of colored troops muster out such of them as you think can be spared." Ten days later came the further instruction to retain all the colored troops on the Rio Grande frontier for the present; in May the remaining white volunteers in Sheridan's command went out.[52]

The July 1866 law reorganizing the regular Army provided for two regiments of colored cavalry and four of infantry. The 40th Infantry was to be raised on the south Atlantic coast, the 38th Infantry and 10th Cavalry in Sherman's territory, the 9th Cavalry and 39th and 41st Infantry by Sheridan in Louisiana and Texas. Sheridan was supposed to recruit his colored regulars from volunteer regiments in his department, but he found the quality of the personnel to be generally unsatisfactory. The regiments at Greenville, Louisiana, were particularly bad. The issuance of passes was strictly regulated; all "huckster women and strumpets" were driven from the camps and colored women forbidden to enter except for "regularly authorized laundresses and servants." When some men of the 116th Colored Infantry assaulted a discharged Union soldier the damages were assessed against the regiment as a whole.[53]

Sheridan was not the only commander to be troubled by colored troops in 1866. From Arkansas General Reynolds grumbled about them to Sherman and urged that, if any were kept in the service at all, they should be kept together by regiments and not scattered in small detachments. He liked to send small commands roaming through the state periodically but thought it unwise to use colored troops for these patrols. In Georgia, when six men of the 103rd Colored Infantry were charged with assaulting citizens at Macon, General John M. Brannan remanded them to the civil authorities upon muster-out of the regiment; but he did take the precaution of ordering them tried in Savannah rather than Macon. Brannan felt that lax discipline by the officers caused most of the complaints against colored troops. "Use energy," he advised the Macon commander; "arrest and confine both Officers and soldiers, if they do not do their duty and preserve peace, among themselves, and

[52]Grant to Sheridan, March 19 and 29, 1866, and Col. Thomas M. Vincent, AAG USA, to Sheridan, May 18, 1866, in Daniel O. Drennan Papers, LC.
[53]AAG to CO's of colored regts., Oct. 15, 1866, and Gen. G. L. Hartsuff to Gen. J. A. Mower, Nov. 13, Dept. Gulf, 258; AAG to CO 116th Col. Inf., Nov. 19, Dept. Gulf, 274, RG98, NA.

with Citizens." [54] Some colored volunteer regiments remained in the South until late 1866; the Carolinas had a regular infantry regiment until late 1868; and Louisiana and Texas had both infantry and cavalry for an even longer time.

Whatever is said about the relations between Army and populace generally, certain military actions had no justification at all. An example occurred in Galveston in January, 1867. The remains of Confederate General Albert Sidney Johnston, killed at Shiloh in 1862, were to pass through the city on their way to Houston for re-interment. General Charles Griffin, then commanding in Texas, refused to allow any kind of funeral escort or ceremony. The mayor appealed to Sheridan, who replied, "I have too much regard for the memory of the brave men who died to preserve our Government, to authorize Confederate demonstrations over the remains of any one who attempted to destroy it." This haughtiness was rather strange since Sheridan had not interfered with tributes while the remains passed through New Orleans, though conceivably both he and Griffin feared the possibility of uncontrolled Rebel demonstrations. [55] Griffin's stand brought great opprobrium down on his head—"an edict that would stain the escutcheon of a Nero," one paper called it. One of the more fanciful editors saw an allegorical resemblance between the Griffin in the blue uniform and the griffin of mythological fame: "The malignant hatred that can thus reach down into the grave to defile the bones of a dead soldier, the craven fear that invokes authority to protect it from the tears of a mourning people, should belong to something that does not walk in the likeness of mankind." [56] Even Northern papers, like the Alton *Democrat* in Illinois, blasted the general: "Griffin deserves a sword of lath and a crown of guano. If Griffin could be ordered to Fort Laramie and let loose a similar order against the Sioux and Cheyenne, what a crowd of redskins would be killed by the jawbone of an ass!" [57] Gradually the storm abated, and a group of ladies in Matagorda sent Griffin an oval leather medal, three inches by five, with all manner of fancy red and blue ribbons, which they requested him to wear only on the highest state occasions. The inscription was a calculated reference to a famous incident of wartime occupied New Orleans: "That the memory of General Griffin

---

[54] Reynolds to Sherman, March 1, 1866, Dept. Ark., 3; AAG to CO Savannah, April 13, and to CO Macon, Feb. 7, Dept. Ga., 1, RG98, NA.

[55] Galveston *Daily News,* Jan. 29, 1867.

[56] *Ibid.,* quoting the New Orleans *Times* of the twenty-sixth.

[57] Galveston *Daily News,* Feb. 8, 1867, quoting *Democrat* of Jan. 28.

will be embalmed with that of Beast Butler and his spoons." [58] Maybe there was a danger of demonstrations getting out of hand, but interference with funeral tributes was a reprehensible display of authority.

In his July veto of Congress' second attempt to pass a Freedmen's Bureau bill, President Johnson had sounded a prophetic note of warning:

There is danger, too, that conflicts of jurisdiction will frequently arise between the civil courts and these military tribunals, each having concurrent jurisdiction over the person and the cause of action—the one judicature administrative and controlled by civil law, the other by the military. How is the conflict to be settled, and who is to determine between the two tribunals when it arises? In my opinion, it is wise to guard against such conflicts by leaving to the courts and juries the protection of all civil rights and the redress of all civil grievances. [59]

Various officers, both before and after the veto, shared Johnson's opinion. In March, 1866, just after the Virginia legislature had removed distinctions in punishment between whites and Negroes, Terry thought it would be well to give the state courts jurisdiction of all criminal offenses by Negroes—"experimentally." It would have to be done sooner or later, Terry said, and if done while the bureau still existed, individual abuses could be corrected. Early October brought a comprehensive order on courts from General Sickles in the Carolinas. The state courts being open to everyone and giving everyone equal civil rights without regard to color, they were now to try all accused civilians, and the bothersome provost courts were to be closed. But there was still the familiar threat: failure or unwillingness of the civil officials to perform their duties would provoke military action. The general also prohibited corporal punishment, his special intention probably being the abolition of public flogging, which was customary in some localities. This part of the order brought objection from the state officials and Johnson finally ordered it revoked. [60]

Johnson's prophecy was not really such a remarkable one; the collisions he alluded to had occurred before, and, try as it might, the Army could not prevent more of them. Perhaps the most tangled one, involving practically all the relevant elements of congressional legislation, executive policy, and military orders, was a case which made the Christ-

[58]Galveston *Daily News,* Feb. 19, 1867.

[59]*Messages and Papers,* VI, 424.

[60]Terry to AAG Div. Atlantic, March 1, 1866, Dept. Va., 14, RG98, NA; GO 15, Dept. South, Oct. 1, 1866, Orders 959, RG94, NA; *Army and Navy Journal,* IV (Jan. 5, 1867), 317.

mas season of 1866 a very unhappy one at the Galveston headquarters of General Samuel P. Heintzelman. The affair began in late summer when Bureau Agent J. Longworth at Seguin was arrested for swindling, although the acts were allegedly done in his official capacity. In September, under orders from General George Getty, then the senior officer in Texas, Heintzelman ordered the new bureau agent at Seguin, Captain John Craig, to make sure his predecessor was not held in jail and to cancel the bonds Longworth had given for his appearance. Craig seized the bonds, and for this he was himself arrested and jailed until released by military force. The local civil authorities then began legal proceedings against individual military officers. They indicted a young lieutenant— the acting assistant adjutant general who had signed the letter directing Craig to cancel the bonds—for theft, and on December 21 the Galveston County sheriff sought to arrest Heintzelman for ordering the lieutenant to write the letter. The general naturally refused to be arrested.[61]

For all practical purposes Heintzelman's adamance ended the matter because he had military power backing him up and the sheriff could hardly have prevailed against it. But contrary to what might be supposed, possession of superior physical force did not make the Army less concerned over the legal niceties of the case. The day after Christmas Heintzelman wrote the United States district attorney at Houston for advice. His New Year's Day was considerably cheered by a reply, complete with painstakingly copied excerpts from the Supreme Court's opinion in *Ableman vs. Booth* and bolstered by the district attorney's own ornate prose: "In the present case you have acted as an officer of the government of this nation, and it is not meet for you to be pestered and annoyed, even though the mischief-makers should clothe themselves in the counterfeit robes of 'loyalty' and falsely assume the counterfeit robes of 'Civil Authority.' . . . I think your conduct in the matter has been proper and becoming a heroic officer who loves his country and his country's laws." In the covering letter he abandoned the fanciness in favor of blunt humor: "The *rebels* are great sticklers for the constitution and laws just now. They profess to have always loved it, and I think a small dose of it unadulterated, right from the [*sic*] Chief Justice Taney, a 'Southern rights man,' would have a fine effect. It would be good for *Rabies* any how, and that appears the prevailing complaint in Texas just now."[62]

---

[61]AAAG Dist. Tex. to Heintzelman, Sept. 29, 1866, 5MD, 111, RG98, NA; Heintzelman to Benjamin F. Wade, Dec. 21, 1866, and ms Journal, Dec. 8–26, in Heintzelman Papers, LC.
[62]Heintzelman to B. J. Baldwin, Dec. 26, 1866, and reply, Dec. 29, in Heintzelman Papers, LC. Original emphasis.

Upon the attempted arrest of Heintzelman in December, the Army had at first held that Getty's order, under which Heintzelman had acted, enjoyed triple support: Grant's General Orders No. 3 of the preceding January, section 14 of the July Freedmen's Bureau Act, and section 3 of the Civil Rights Act. But because of Grant's October instructions to Sheridan that the presidential peace edict voided No. 3, and because the action against Longworth at Seguin had occurred in the interim between the August proclamation and the date of its official promulgation to the Army, No. 3 was dropped as part of the defense; and the Army ultimately rested its case on the Civil Rights Act. That law contained a protection against state prosecution for acts done in carrying out its provisions or those of any legislation relating to the bureau; and in January, 1867, the new Texas commander, Griffin, wrote to Sheridan's headquarters suggesting the Civil Rights Act as the best defense in all similar matters.[63]

Enforcement of the 1866 reconstruction legislation meant that the soldiers would have to continue to work with federal courts and law officers. The Army was a useful source of information for the courts; and commanders, like General Foster in Florida, regularly brought violations of the Civil Rights Act by sheriffs, coroners, and other officials to the attention of the federal courts.[64] Military assistance to other federal law officers continued, though the War Department took care to keep the Army in the background as much as possible. Typical of this policy were May instructions to the Department of Georgia: the commanding general was to furnish aid to enforce the revenue laws near Atlanta, but he ought not to make any *arrests* for treasury agents except under specific orders from Washington.[65]

Without doubt the greatest political question facing the South in the second half of 1866 was the Fourteenth Amendment—to ratify or not to ratify. The South would likely have been reluctant to accept the amendment anyway, but the fact of Johnson's opposition to it added to the determination to resist. Sickles wrote from Charleston that the President had missed an opportunity to moderate the influence of "Republican doctrinaires" and that the Carolinas would have adopted the amendment had Johnson favored it.[66]

[63]AAAG Dist. Tex. to AAG Dept. Gulf, Dec. 22, 1866, and Griffin to same, Jan. 31, 1867, 5MD, 111, RG98, NA.
[64]Foster to Clerk of U.S.D.C. Nor. Dist. Fla., Oct. 19, 1866, Dept. Fla., 6, RG98, NA.
[65]Files 304T1866 and 305T1866, AGO, and Townsend to Brannan, May 16 and 17, 1866, AGO, 42, RG94, NA.
[66]Sickles to Stanton, private, July 19, 1866, in Stanton Papers, LC.

Tennessee, the only Confederate state to ratify in 1866, did so amidst stormy scenes. The state senate accepted the measure but the other house balked. On July 14 the wires brought Grant a dispatch from Thomas: "Some members of the House of Representatives of the Tennessee General Assembly conduct themselves in a very refractory manner, absenting themselves to prevent a quorum, thus obstructing business. The Governor cannot manage them with the means at his disposal, and has applied to me for military assistance. Shall I furnish it?" This telegram received tardy and inefficient handling in Washington; Grant gave it to Stanton, who did not show it to the President until the Cabinet meeting of the seventeenth. Johnson directed that Thomas' question be answered with an emphatic negative. Before the message could reach Nashville, however, legislative sergeants-at-arms had arrested two members and held them so that a quorum would be present; upon taking the vote the amendment was ratified.[67] Governor "Parson" Brownlow jubilantly wired the Senate about the result, stating that two of "Andrew Johnson's tools" did not vote and adding with typical boorishness, "Give my respects to the dead dog of the White House." [68]

Grant hoped the South would accept the amendment. He told the Arkansas commander in early December he was convinced that if one Southern state adopted it, "Congress would establish a precedent that would induce all others to adopt them [*sic*]." This was doubtless a reference to Congress' readmitting individual states upon ratification of the amendment, but the South was not as convinced of the good intentions of Congress as Grant was. The general considered it scarcely thinkable that the solons would accept anything less than ratification and he feared that delay in accepting the amendment would probably lead to further congressional demands. He declined to discuss the amendment's merits and demerits, considering it "a final solution from which there is no appeal." Grant was so anxious for ratification that he wanted the Army to use its good offices to secure this end. "I hope you will talk to the

[67]*Army and Navy Journal,* III (July 21, 1866), 759; Patton, *Tennessee,* 223–24; Francis F. McKinney, *Education in Violence* (Detroit, 1961), 462–64. McKinney says there was no doubt from the wording of Thomas' telegram that he favored the use of troops to force a quorum. It seems questionable that the telegram indicates this, although in September Johnson told one of Grant's secretaries that he thought Thomas had been in favor of interference. C. B. Comstock ms Journal, Sept. 22, 1866, in Comstock Papers, LC. Many accounts of this incident leave some questions as to whether the actual arrests were made by or in the presence of federal troops. A comparison of Nashville papers of varying political affiliations seems to indicate clearly that no troops were involved. Nashville *Daily Dispatch,* July 15–19, 1866, and Nashville *Republican Banner,* July 19.
[68]Quoted in *Cong. Globe,* 39th Cong., 1st Sess., 3957.

Governor, and such members of the Legislature as you may have influence with, on this subject," he wrote. "It it not proper that officers of the Army should take part in political matters. But this is hardly to be classed as a party matter. It is one of national importance. All parties agree to the fact that we ought to be united and the status of every state definitely settled. They only differ as to the manner of doing this. It ought to be seen that no way will succeed unless agreed to by Congress." [69]

Whether the Arkansas commander tried to exert any influence is not clear, but General Schofield did discuss the amendment with Virginia leaders. Sometime during the winter of 1866–67 he prepared a written argument on the subject, in which he called the measure unjust and unwise. He was especially opposed to the third section, which in his view disqualified from office nearly everyone "whose social position, intellectual attainments and known moral character entitle him to the confidence of the people." Any punishment, he thought, should aim to serve the general good; punishment which proved injurious to the community as a whole he considered a crime. "It is folly," he argued, "to attempt to bring back a revolted people by disfranchising all leaders in whom they trust and confide. These leaders if they will act in good faith can bring their people back to their allegiance. Without them it can not be done during the existing generation." The central question of course was whether the leaders could be trusted, and Schofield believed they could.

The general objected in principle to the federal government's prescribing qualifications for state offices or for voting in state elections. He also believed that section 3 was unfair to Negroes since its effect would be to allow more of the "poor whites" to hold local office, thus putting the Negroes in the hands of their only real enemies in the South. He thought any notion of universal suffrage, without regard to intelligence or other qualifications, was quite absurd. And his experience in postwar North Carolina and Virginia had given him some insight into the Southern attitude of mind: "Theorize as much as we please about the criminality of the late rebellion, it is folly to suppose that the present generation of Southerners can be made to acknowledge or believe that it was anything more than a legitimate war for the settlement of a great political

[69]Grant to [Ord], Dec. 6, 1866, in Horace Porter Papers, LC. This letter is addressed simply "Dear General" and was to have been personally delivered by Porter while on a tour of inspection. A reference to the location of Headquarters, Department of Arkansas shows it was clearly directed to the department commander, who at the time was Ord.

question left unsettled by the framers of the constitution. . . . Let us look at the matter in a practical common sense light, and not demand of men "repentance in sack cloth and ashes" when we know that any show of such repentance would be the purest hypocrisy." In spite of these potent objections, however, Schofield considered the matter "in a practical common sense light" and advised that Virginia accept the amendment to save the state from something worse. But his advice went unheeded and Virginia, along with the rest of Secessia, refused to ratify.[70]

In the North the Fourteenth Amendment was a salient topic in the autumn election campaign of 1866, with the Johnson supporters fulminating against it and the bulk of the Republicans arguing for it. Texas was the only Southern state, except for Tennessee, where direct legislative action was had on the amendment prior to the election; and Texas decisively rejected it. Northerners were thus doubtless influenced by what they assumed would happen when the other states acted on the measure.[71]

During the late summer preparations for the Congressional elections got underway, and many wartime military leaders, now resigned or retired, took an active part. In August the National Union Convention met in Philadelphia to try to form a coalition in support of Johnson; Steedman, the ex-Georgia commander, was chairman of an important committee. He was also present at a Cleveland assembly in September, this time in the company of Custer, who had helped to reconstruct Texas, and Lovell H. Rousseau, a Johnson backer who was then out of the service but who would later exercise command in Louisiana. Pro-Republican conventions also attracted military figures, most of whom had been generals of volunteers during the war but by this time had been mustered out of the service.

The President bore his own share of the campaigning and embarked on a speaking tour through the North. His entourage featured a galaxy of starred gentlemen: the omnipresent Steedman, Custer, and Rousseau; now also George Stoneman, fresh from a year's experience with Tennessee troubles; and the most important one of all—Grant. The "swing

[70]Ms essay entitled "Reconstruction," in John M. Schofield Papers, LC. An attached statement dated at West Point in March, 1880, and signed by Col. William Wherry, who had been an ADC to Schofield, states the essay was written in the winter of 1866–67 and had been in Wherry's possession since. Also included is a shorter essay on general principles of government.

[71]The dates of Southern legislative action on the amendment are conveniently found in McKitrick, *Andrew Johnson and Reconstruction*, 358 n.

around the circle" began calmly enough, but paid Radical hecklers in the larger cities succeeded in arousing the fearsome Presidential wrath. Johnson's tirades evoked continued taunts and the dashing Custer, even though his March testimony before the Reconstruction Committee had been unfavorable to Johnson's policy, now ferociously reproached the insulting mobs from the rear platform of the Presidential train.[72]

The presence of an officer in the President's party did not always mean his approval of Johnson's viewpoint, however. Johnson wanted an impressive escort and amassed as many important dignitaries as he could. Finding that he could not do without a naval delegation, he induced Admirals David G. Farragut and William Radford to go with him. He perhaps hoped that the public would equate "presence" with "active support" especially in the case of Grant. But Grant, while certainly not a presidential opponent of the Thaddeus Stevens stripe, was not, like Steedman and Rousseau, a "Johnson man." Some of Grant's friends were not sure of his views, however, and feared that under pressure Grant might go over to Johnson. Writing to one of Grant's personal secretaries, General James H. Wilson expressed the hope that the general could be kept steady and "true to his principles." "If the general wavers now—it will be as fatal to himself and to the country, as hesitation or indecision would have been in the Wilderness." [73]

Wilson would have been somewhat reassured had he seen a confidential letter from Grant to Sheridan at New Orleans in October. The General-in-Chief expressed the fear that Johnson's rashness was increasing along with the dominance over him by people who had been disloyal during the war. Grant felt the nation was "fast approaching the time when he will want to declare the body itself [Congress] illegal, unconstitutional, and revolutionary." He hoped Southern commanders would make sure that "if a crisis does come, no armed headway can be made against the Union." [74]

Wild rumors intimated that Johnson might attempt some sort of military coup d'etat. Indeed, as early as May an Arkansas planter, having heard rumors brought by arriving steamboat passengers that the Radicals had impeached Johnson, dashed off a letter to the President saying that the thinking people of the state, whom he undertook to represent,

[72]Jay Monaghan, *Custer: The Life of General George Armstrong Custer* (Boston, 1959), 266–79.
[73]Wilson to Orville E. Babcock, Sept. 10, 1866, in Babcock Papers, Newberry Library. Original emphasis.
[74]Grant to Sheridan, Oct. 12, 1866, in Adam Badeau, *Grant in Peace* (Hartford, 1887), 51–52.

hoped Johnson would disperse the Senate by military force if it sought to try him and would then call a national convention "to adjust the pending difficulties." [75] They would have taken considerable adjusting.

Johnson certainly never planned any such revolutionary use of the Army against his Northern opponents, but he would likely have been glad to effect some change in the military high command in order to influence affairs in the South. At least, Grant suspected some such sinister intrigue when Johnson tried to send him to Mexico as a military advisor to the American envoy. Maximilian and the French were certainly a problem that concerned the Army, and Grant would have been glad to see the Mexican difficulty speedily resolved. But he twice declined the mission, claiming that it was essentially a diplomatic one and that as General-in-Chief he ought properly to stay in Washington. At a Cabinet meeting Johnson tried once more to get Grant to agree to go and asked the Attorney General if there were any legal reasons why Grant could not. Grant interjected that as a military officer he would obey "any legal military order" of Johnson's, but since this was a civil duty he positively declined it. "No power on earth," he said as he left the room, "can compel me to it." [76]

Cyrus B. Comstock, of Grant's staff, in explaining the affair to Sheridan called the position designed for Grant "a polite banishment" from the capitol in effect and a very foolish role in reality since the minister could consult or ignore the general, as he chose. Almost certainly, Johnson's purpose was political rather than diplomatic because at the same time he tried to induce Sherman to be "Acting Secretary of War"— though what was ultimately to become of Stanton remained vague. With Grant in Mexico and Sherman in the War Office the Army would have been controlled by a man more openly favorable to Johnson's policy than either Grant or Stanton. But Sherman would not hear of it; hatred of politics plus personal friendship for Grant combined to make him refuse to play the game. Since the ostensible cause of the project had been the necessity of sending some prominent soldier with the minister, Sherman went to Mexico and Grant stayed home. Thus the incident closed, but its political overtones remained. [77]

"Things look squally here" was Comstock's summary of the situation as election day approached and, all things considered, it was an accurate estimate. But November, 1866, was to be only the squall before

---

[75]S. R. Cockrill to Johnson, May 7, 1866, Johnson Papers, LC (Reel 22).
[76]Badeau, *Grant in Peace*, 52–55.
[77]Comstock to Sheridan, Oct. 31, 1866, confidential, in Sheridan Papers, LC. Comstock had wanted the letter destroyed.

the hurricane; the elections were a complete triumph for the anti-Johnson forces who could now override presidential vetoes with impunity and devise what Southern policy they liked. Autumn was also time for annual report-writing by military commanders, and one general offered sage observations in the premises. After summarizing the state of affairs in Mississippi, General Wood added:

But when it is remembered what a terrible social, political, and military convulsion the nation passed through in the war of the rebellion; when it is borne in mind that a vast population of slaves was suddenly emancipated by the violence of war, and that the late slaves now occupy as freed people the very same soil, in the closest juxtaposition to the formerly dominant class, on which the two races lived in the relation of master and slave, it should not perhaps be [a] matter of surprise that so many outrages and crimes occur and go unpunished, but rather [a] matter of marvel that so few occur. Great social and political changes are not made in a day. Time, the potential lethe of deep-rooted, long-standing prejudices, and diffused education, the mighty elevator of the human race, must accomplish the great reforms necessary to the permanent prosperity of the white and colored inhabitants of the southern States.[78]

The next two years were to show that such perspicacity was at a premium in political circles at the North.

---

[78]*Report of the Sec. of War, 1865–66*, p. 54 (1st pagin.).

PART II

UNDER THE RECONSTRUCTION ACTS

Congress, having won its struggle with the President over leadership, now enacted legislation setting forth in vague terms the broad outlines of its reconstruction policy. This the Army began to administer—but with serious doubts concerning its own powers. After five months and several more pieces of legislation the Army's powers were strengthened and clarified; and the soldiers, with more direct control over Southern affairs than ever before or since, continued to administer the congressional policy until the states were readmitted.

5

Getting Started—Again

PROVIDING for "the more efficient government of the Rebel States" was the principal task facing the second session of the Thirty-ninth Congress, which convened on December 3, 1866. A welter of proposals filled the legislative hoppers, but the most important one was that which decrepit old Thaddeus Stevens presented to the House on February 6. A preamble stated that the existing governments in the ten unrepresented Southern states were illegal, had been formed without congressional sanction, and afforded no adequate protection for life and property but rather encouraged lawlessness and crime. The first section divided the South into five military districts. The General-in-Chief (later altered to the President) was to assign to each district a regular Army officer not below the rank of brigadier general and to supply each commanding general with sufficient military force to perform his functions. There followed an enumeration of these functions—"to protect all persons in their rights of person and property, to suppress insurrection, disorder, and violence, and to punish, or cause to be punished, all disturbers of the public peace and criminals." Each commanding general could, at his own discretion, "allow" the existing civil courts to prosecute offenders, or he could establish military commissions if his judgment so dictated. Any attempted interference by the existing state governments with these tribunals, or with military authority generally, was prohibited. In addition, the use of habeas corpus proceedings by federal courts to release persons held in military custody was curtailed.[1]

The bill naturally underwent rigorous debate in both houses, with

[1] *Cong. Globe,* 39th Cong., 2nd Sess., 1037.

much recitation of constitutional principles pro and con. Opponents of the bill claimed the Army in the South already had sufficient authority to protect life and property without the blanket grant of power embodied in the Stevens measure. But New York's Congressman Giles Hotchkiss answered that the present military authority would be sufficient were it not for the limited construction put upon it by Johnson. Referring to the restrictive aspects of the Milligan opinion, he said, "We have got to get rid by our legislation of the effect given by the President to the decision of the Supreme Court." [2]

In attempting to sustain that part of the preamble which pointed out the failure of the civil regimes to safeguard life and property, Congressman Augustus Brandegee of Connecticut asked, "What protection is there to-day to loyalty, black or white, from the Potomac to the Rio Grande? What indemnity have you for the past? What security even for the future? What guarantee against a new rebellion?" [3] He meant the questions to be rhetorical, though the other side naturally attempted to answer them. Better answers, perhaps, were to be found in the reports of military commanders in the South which accompanied the President's annual message of December. Sherman described conditions in Arkansas as very satisfactory; Sheridan reported little serious difficulty in Florida; and Sickles' estimate of the Carolinas, if gloomy on some counts, was hopeful on others. Summing up, Grant opined that "on the whole, the condition of the States . . . may be regarded as good enough to warrant the hope that but a short time will intervene before the bulk of the troops now occupying them can be sent to our growing Territories, where they are so much needed." [4]

One of the main objections to the bill was that it provided no procedure for the South to follow in order to bring military rule to an end. Hence a "plan" of reconstruction was added to the bill before its final passage. After a particular state fulfilled a series of political tasks, including election of a convention, framing of a new constitution, and ratification of the Fourteenth Amendment, Congress might at its discretion readmit the state to representation, and military authority would cease. Another provision central to the exercise of military authority found its way into the bill by amendment: until readmission, all governments that might exist in the South were only provisional "and in all respects subject to the paramount authority of the United States at any time to abolish, modify, control, or supersede" them. The act itself

[2]*Ibid.*, 1098, 1100.
[3]*Ibid.*, 1076.
[4]*Report of the Sec. of War, 1865–66*, p. 17 (1st pagin.).

began this "control" by specifying the voting and office-holding qualifications for elections held under these governments. After passing the House and Senate the bill met the expected presidential veto, which the partisan majority in Congress quickly overcame, and it entered the statute books on March 2, 1867. [5]

Three other significant bills became law on that same day. One was the Army Appropriations Act, which provided funds for maintaining the Army during the following year. The financial provisions of the act were of the commonplace kind that Congress had been passing since the nation began—salaries, repairs for arsenals, medical books for the Surgeon General's library, and so forth. But Section 2 was not at all commonplace. It decreed that the General-in-Chief's headquarters should be fixed at Washington, and that he could not be removed, suspended, or assigned to duty elsewhere except at his own request, unless the Senate gave prior approval. Moreover all orders issued to the Army from the President and Secretary of War had to go through the General-in-Chief; orders not so routed were null and void, and to obey them could lead to imprisonment for two to twenty years.

This section was of doubtful constitutionality for it infringed on the powers vested in the President as Commander-in-Chief, as its opponents pointed out. Little was said in defense of the measure—little was necessary, indeed, since the Radicals had sufficient votes to obviate the need of a campaign to convince doubtful members. The purpose of the provision was only too plain: the Radicals sought to freeze Grant in his position in order to prevent presidential interference with military administration of Congressional Reconstruction.[6] Undoubtedly Congress was influenced by the attempt in the previous autumn to send Grant to Mexico.[7] The success of the congressional scheme, of course, depended

[5]*Messages and Papers,* VI, 489–511; 14 U.S. Statutes at Large 428. The states were not required to incorporate in their constitutions the provision of the act that those who were disqualified from holding office by the Fourteenth Amendment were also disqualified from voting.

[6]14 U.S. Statutes at Large 485. The support for the view that Johnson lost all control over the Army in the South because of this legislation is at best tenuous. The intent, certainly, was to hamstring Johnson by requiring him to send all military orders through Grant, but the complete effectiveness of the measure was never demonstrated. In a practical sense the extent of the law was not revealed because there never was a direct confrontation between Johnson and Grant in which the general positively refused to transmit a direct military order of the President, although at times he declined presidential "requests." And in a legal sense the effect of the measure went undetermined because it was repealed in 1870 without having been ruled upon by the Supreme Court.

[7]*Cong. Globe,* 39th Cong., 2nd Sess., 1353–56.

on Grant's adherence to the Radicals' view of reconstruction. Grant seemed to be moving in their direction, but thus far he had taken no overt action which irrevocably placed him in their camp.

Another part of the bill, equally as irrelevant to an appropriations act as Section 2, disbanded all existing militia organizations in the Southern states to prevent danger of armed interference with the procedures to be taken under the Reconstruction Act. Because these two sections had been attached to a critical piece of legislation, Johnson faced the dilemma of vetoing the entire bill and letting the Army go unpaid, or approving the bill in the face of Section 2. He did about the only thing he could under the circumstances: he signed the bill but sent Congress a written protest against the objectionable provision. Since Johnson had signed the bill no answer to his protest was necessary—and a sound answer would have been hard to devise.

"An Act regulating the Tenure of certain Civil Offices" also became law on the fateful second of March. The most significant provision was that cabinet officers should hold their posts "for and during the term of the President by whom they may have been appointed, and for one month thereafter, subject to the advice and consent of the Senate." [8] When this section is read in conjunction with the Appropriations Act proviso on the high command of the Army, the motives behind the Tenure of Office Act become clear. The Radicals sought to freeze Stanton in the War Office just as they had frozen Grant in the General-in-Chief's position. No other motive is conceivable, for of all the cabinet posts the War Department had most to do with the administration of reconstruction, and of all the cabinet members Stanton was most in harmony with the Radicals. Since the Constitutional provision concerning presidential appointments was silent regarding removals, it was invoked both for and against the bill. But even if found constitutional, the wisdom of the measure remains doubtful. Johnson thought the bill unconstitutional and asked Stanton to help write the veto message; Stanton did so—it was a safe move even though the bill was a protection for him; and the veto fell in Congress, as expected.

The last of the acts of March 2, 1867, was a sweeping retroactive validation of all actions of the President or his subordinates regarding military trials for participation in the rebellion and related offenses. Such actions were made valid just as if each had been done in pursuance of some previously enacted law of Congress and were to be regarded, prima facie, as having been authorized by the President. This was yet another

[8] 14 U.S. Statutes at Large 430.

step in broadening the protection afforded the Army against prosecutions and damage suits, and a greater broadening could hardly have been imagined. This bill, alone among the four, did not receive a veto.[9]

The Reconstruction Act set forth the framework of Congress' Southern policy, but some details still remained to be filled in. Although this first act had made provision for state conventions, it had omitted particulars as to the election of delegates. Therefore on March 23 a Second Reconstruction Act, passed over Johnson's veto, remedied the problem. Each commanding general was to order a registration of voters by September 1, and the oath to be taken upon registration—essentially that the registrant met the qualifications—was prescribed. The conventions were to consist of the same number of delegates as there had been members of the most numerous house of the state legislature in 1860, and the commanding general was to apportion the delegates in proportion to the registration figures. As many three-man boards of registration appointed by the commanding general as necessary were to conduct the registration and superintend the election. The commanding general was to promulgate the election results; and if a majority of the votes cast on the question favored a convention, he was to order the elected delegates, chosen at the same election, to assemble within sixty days.[10]

The power vested in the commanding generals by the March legislation was indeed sweeping. Previously during Reconstruction the Army had been primarily concerned with the detection and suppression of crime and with injustice towards loyal citizens; now, if military establishment of convention districts is a fair measure of authority, the amount of direct military supervision over the political activities of the Southern people was more complete than at any time previously. It was of course necessary that men of the greatest competence and discretion be assigned to exercise this far-reaching power. A general order of March 11 announced the selections. Virginia, the First District, went to Schofield; it was a logical choice, for he had been handling that state well since the preceding August. The Carolinas, the Second District, received General Daniel E. Sickles, who had exercised intermittent command in that area since the end of the war. Sickles was not a West Pointer but had risen to prominent command in the Army of the Potomac during the war. He was an impetuous, volatile individual, though to a lesser extent than Sheridan. Johnson thought him a "conceited cuckold"; if the noun was

[9] 14 U.S. Statutes at Large 432.
[10] 15 U.S. Statutes at Large 2.

ill-chosen, the adjective was not.[11] Carolinians may have feared his rule but nonetheless made sport of his haughtiness. Once, it was told, when Sickles "condescended to ride with ordinary folks" on the Charleston horsecars, he was smoking a cigar. The conductor told him the company rules prohibited smoking. " 'Ah, indeed,' replied the great man, taking out his watch with the utmost nonchalance. 'Indeed! Then you shall consider the rules suspended for the next half hour!' " [12]

The original plan had been to give Georgia, Alabama, and Florida, comprising the Third District, to General Thomas, then in Tennessee. But Thomas requested revocation of the order, which was granted, and General John Pope went in his place. Thomas would have been better from the standpoint of temperament and Reconstruction experience. Pope's ability as a general had come into some question during the war, and his bombastic edicts had gained scoffing celebrity. He was forty-five years old and a West Point graduate of 1842. In speculating on the possible commanders one commentator classified Pope politically as a moderate Republican.[13] Perhaps he fit that description, but he was not long in Atlanta before Southerners became convinced he was a thoroughgoing Radical. Such was also the view of Republican Congressman James G. Blaine, who said Pope's political convictions were "of a very positive character" and "not at all in sympathy with the National Administration." [14]

Arkansas and Mississippi, joined together as the Fourth District, went to General Edward O. C. Ord, who had commanded in the former state since the preceding summer. It was a good choice, for Ord's rule in Arkansas had given little cause for complaint though, to be sure, Arkansas was generally a less troublesome and more easily administered state than some of the others. The same observer who called Pope moderate called Ord conservative and added that Arkansas Unionists regarded him as "a just man, and true to the country." A close personal friend of Grant, he had graduated from West Point in 1839 and had served in the western armies during the war.

Sheridan retained two of the three states of his former command, Texas and Louisiana, now styled the Fifth District. It was perhaps a sound choice from the standpoint of experience, but the turbulent state

[11]GO 10, AGO, March 11, 1867, RG94, NA; ms notebook of Col. W. G. Moore, Johnson's secretary, July 5, 1868, in Johnson Papers, LC (Reel 51).
[12]Milledgeville (Ga.) *Federal Union*, Sept. 10, 1867.
[13]*Army and Navy Journal*, IV (March 30, 1867), 514, quoting Worcester (Mass.) *Spy*.
[14]James G. Blaine, *Twenty Years of Congress* (Norwich, 1886), II, 297 n.

of affairs there required more tact and dexterity than Sheridan was able to muster on most occasions.

It is not possible to determine positively who was responsible for each of the five selections. Welles observed that Johnson was reticent on the matter at Cabinet conclaves between March 2 and 11, and this vexed old "Neptune" because he feared it would result in Grant and Stanton having too great an influence in the appointments. Their positions might reasonably entitle them to some influence, but Welles was becoming increasingly suspicious of Grant and was even more strongly convinced that Stanton was a mischief-maker. The Navy Minister discovered the selections in reading his morning newspaper on the thirteenth and when he saw Sickles' name among them his already black mood grew yet darker. "The slime of the serpent is over them all," he grouchily wrote in his diary. It was one of his more venomous character estimates and was unfair to all of the generals, especially to Ord and Schofield.[15]

Blaine thought Grant had made the selections and that while the President did not "interpose any serious objection," he did not much care for the idea of Pope's going to the Third District in place of Thomas.[16] Had he so chosen, however, Johnson could have sent almost anyone he pleased to the South. The Reconstruction Act made it his duty to assign the commanding generals, although in the law's original form this had been the task of Grant. The customary alignment of territorial commands dictated "military divisions" at the highest level, each of which contained one or more "departments." The divisions went to the highest ranking officers, and the departments were distributed among the next senior generals. From August, 1866, until February, 1868, there were only two divisions, the Missouri (embracing principally the Great Plains) and the Pacific. The rest of the country comprised departments, whose commanders reported directly to Washington without going through any intermediate division headquarters. Thus on March 11, 1867, when the order establishing the five reconstruction districts came forth, Sherman as Lieutenant General commanded the Division of the Missouri and Halleck as the senior major general commanded on the Pacific shore. There was no "Division of the South" as an intermediate headquarters between Washington and the five districts. But had Johnson been determined to moderate or even sabotage the enforcement of the congressional plan, he could have created such a

---

[15]Beale (ed.), *Diary of Gideon Welles,* III, 65.
[16]Blaine, *Twenty Years,* II, 296.

command, given it to Sherman, and put Halleck and Meade (the next major general in rank to Halleck) in command of the two remaining divisions. Nothing in the Reconstruction Act would have prevented this means of putting a pro-Johnson officer in overall command of Secessia. Some such plan might possibly have been under consideration for a time, for the subject of the autonomy of the five district commanders from a higher level of field command came up in one Cabinet meeting. The advisors split on the question and no action was taken on it.[17] In view of his intense dislike of political machinations, Sherman would likely have balked at such a plan in any case.

Johnson would not necessarily have required either a cooperative Sherman or a "Division of the South." He could have achieved the same goal by playing a martial version of musical chairs with the national total of sixteen commands resulting from the creation of the five Southern districts in the order of March 11. Assuming that Sickles, Sheridan, and Pope were the most objectionable of the five commanders, two of them could have been eliminated by the assignment of Hancock, a known Democrat, and Meade, who was a moderate Republican if he was a Republican at all. The third post might have presented some problems at first. Johnson could have refused Thomas' request to stay in Tennessee. Or perhaps one of the brigadiers, Philip St. George Cooke, would have done nicely since one observer said of him, "He is a Conservative; perhaps worse." [18] But before the end of March even this problem could have been handily solved, had Johnson wanted to solve it. On the twenty-eighth William S. Rosecrans resigned his brigadier generalship and on the same day Johnson gave it to Lovell H. Rousseau, a personal friend and a confirmed Democrat who had represented Kentucky in the Thirty-ninth Congress. But Rousseau did not go South. One month after his commission he received an assignment to isolation (the Department

17Thomas and Hyman, *Stanton,* 533, in treating this Cabinet discussion, make it appear that the question was autonomy from the *War Department* and *Headquarters of the Army* rather than autonomy from a higher military field command. There is, of course, a considerable difference between the two, and to misunderstand the problem is to misunderstand the roles of Johnson and the other principals. Thomas and Hyman cite as their references Beale (ed.), *Diary of Gideon Welles,* III, 59–63, and a "memo" of some sort in the Gideon Welles Papers, LC. The *Diary* makes it quite clear that autonomy from the War Department and HQA was not involved at all, and whatever the "memo" may indicate, the LC staff could not locate it in the Welles Papers.

18*Army and Navy Journal,* IV (March 30, 1867), 514, quoting Worcester (Mass.) *Spy.*

of the Columbia at Portland) though he did not actually assume the command until November.[19]

Yet another Machiavellian course was open to Johnson, had he been so inclined. The Reconstruction Act, in requiring that the district commanders be at least brigadiers, had not specified that they be brigadiers in *lineal* rank. Consequently Johnson could have given some Southern posts to colonels and lieutenant colonels who held the specified rank by *brevet*. Among the hundred or more such officers Johnson should have been able to find two or three of his own political persuasion. Such appointments would not have violated Army custom since officers had frequently been assigned to duty according to their brevets. Indeed, during 1869–70 (while Grant was President) one commander in the First District, two in the Fourth, and two in the Fifth were colonels in lineal rank and generals by brevet, and Congress never considered it a violation of the law.

Sickles' case was unique among the district commanders. Until July 28, 1866, he had no rank in the regular Army at all and was being retained in service in his wartime grade, major general of volunteers. On that date he was commissioned colonel of the 42nd Infantry, a regular regiment, and on the day the Reconstruction Act became law he was made major general in the regular Army by brevet. Interestingly, the original text of the Reconstruction Act employed the phrase "an officer of the regular Army not below the rank of brigadier general," but the word "regular" was dropped after Congressman Robert C. Schenck felt it would be maintaining an "unnecessary and invidious distinction" to retain it. But whatever his motives—and searching for the motives that impelled Andrew Johnson is at times like searching for a propulsion mechanism in a fogbank—the President did not attempt to sabotage the Congressional plan by any such devious schemes.

Southerners, however, did mean to prevent execution of the Reconstruction Acts if they could, and they lost no time in making the attempt. No sooner had the commanders established themselves than pleas for injunctions began coming before the Supreme Court. Mississippi tried to induce the Court to prohibit Johnson and General Ord from

[19]Thian, *Military Geography of the U.S.*, 55. One Southern paper, in listing the possible commanders, also included the heads of the various staff departments at Washington, who by that fact held the rank of brigadier general. Galveston *Daily News*, March 7, 1867. Most of these officers having been away from command duty for a decade at least, they would have made improbable reconstruction commanders.

enforcing the acts on the ground they were not the law of the land. But the Court refused, holding that it had no power to prevent the President from enforcing the laws.[20] Georgia tried a slightly different approach and asked for an injunction against Stanton, Grant, and Pope. In arguing against this petition, Attorney General Henry Stanbery claimed that enforcement of the law did not necessarily threaten the existing civil government of Georgia since Pope had not said whether he would enforce it by removing the civil officials or by leaving them alone. It was perhaps a facile argument, but the Court denied Georgia's petition; and in delivering the formal opinion at the following December term, Justice Samuel Nelson branded the matter a "political question" of the kind the Court ought properly to avoid.[21] There was even some talk of Governor Sharkey getting up a case against Ord for treason against the state of Mississippi, but nothing serious ever came of that remarkable idea.[22]

The first general orders issued by the new district commanders set forth the basic guidelines of military policy; details were left to be filled in later as specific problems arose. Some variations in tone and style reflected personal differences, but all of the generals made several things clear. The existing civil governments were provisional and subject to the full control of the military power. Their officials were expected to carry out their duties as before and see that justice was done in all cases. Military interposition was promised in individual instances of abuse of power or neglect to punish crime. General Pope warned the officials in his district to "confine themselves strictly to the performance of their official duties," and not to use their influence to "deter or dissuade" people from actively participating in reconstructing their state under the congressional plan.[23]

Sheridan promised there would be no removals unless local officials hindered reconstruction; Ord and Pope said they would fill existing vacancies by appointment. Ord cautioned the freedmen of Arkansas and Mississippi and told them that their most important duty was to support themselves and that the general prosperity of the community was more a function of zealous labor than of zealous politicking. He urged

[20]*Mississippi vs. Johnson*, 4 Wallace 475 (1867).
[21]*Georgia vs. Stanton*, 6 Wallace 50 (1867).
[22]Galveston *Daily News*, May 1, 1867.
[23]GO 1, 3MD, April 1, 1867, in *House Exec. Docs.*, 40th Cong., 2nd Sess., No. 342, pp. 99–100. This item is a compilation of the principal orders relating to civil affairs issued in the five districts from their inception through early February, 1868. It will be cited in preference to National Archives collections where possible.

them not to frequent the political meeting-house at the expense of the field and promised that registration and elections would be conducted near their homes so that they would not have far to go.[24] All commanders exhorted the people to cooperate. As Sickles told his Carolinians:

The commanding general, desiring to preserve tranquility and order by means and agencies most congenial to the people, solicits the zealous and cordial cooperation of civil officers in the discharge of their duties, and the aid of all good citizens in preventing conduct tending to disturb the peace; and to the end that occasion may seldom arise for the exercise of military authority in matters of ordinary civil administration, the commanding general respectfully and earnestly commends to the people and authorities of North Carolina and South Carolina unreserved obedience to the authority now established, and the diligent, considerate and impartial execution of the laws enacted for their government.[25]

The commanders shortly faced a great variety of problems. Ord found parts of Mississippi and Arkansas infested with horse thieves and had to send his cavalry off to chase them. He made horse stealing a military crime and directed that all suspects, whether arrested by the civil or military power, be held for trial by military commission.[26] Both Ord and Sickles took action to curb the distillation of grain into whiskey. Much of this was in fact moonshining and hence a violation of federal revenue laws; in addition, it caused a considerable food shortage among the poorer people of many areas. Ord directed his local subordinates to break up stills whose operators had not paid the required federal taxes and to sell the property for the benefit of the poor. Sickles was more drastic and flatly prohibited the distillation of whiskey from grain, prescribing military trial for violators. Ord's Arkansans bravely endured the curtailment of their liquor refreshment, but Sickles' Carolinians could not steel themselves to it and so turned to the distillation of fruit as a substitute. Enforcement of Sickles' order caused the price of grain to drop by about half. Later the district commander and Internal Revenue officials, after joint consideration of the matter, decided that the policy could be safely abandoned; and on New Year's Eve— appropriately if unintentionally—the order was revoked.[27]

[24]GO 5, 4MD, April 15, 1867, *ibid.,* 132.
[25]GO 1, 2MD, March 21, 1867, *ibid.,* 35–36.
[26]GO 9, 4MD, May 16, 1867, *ibid.,* 133.
[27]GO 12, 4MD, June 12, 1867, *ibid.,* 133–34; GO 25, 2MD, May 20, 1867, *ibid.,* 45; Canby to E. A. Rollins, Comm. Int. Revenue, Sept. 17, 1867, 2MD, 1, RG98, NA; AGO file 373T1867, and Townsend to Canby, Dec. 5, 1867, AGO, 46, RG94, NA; GO 164, 2MD, Dec. 31, 1867, in *House Exec. Docs.,* 40th Cong., 2nd Sess., No. 342, pp. 82–83.

Another manifestation of Sickles' concern for the hazards of ardent spirits was this edict: "No license for the sale of intoxicating liquors in quantities less than one gallon, or to be drank [*sic*] on the premises shall be granted to any person other than an innkeeper. . . . If any person shall be found drunk on the premises where liquor is sold, the license may be revoked by any magistrate." This last provision placed innkeepers in a delicate position. If they chose to maximize their profits by selling a customer all he demanded, they then had to pray that he would make it to the street before being caught; the only other way of staying within the regulation was to be able to judge accurately each customer's capacity. When Sickles was asked how he defined "innkeeper," he ruled that in addition to paying the required federal internal revenue fee and conforming to any municipal regulations, a person claiming to be an innkeeper had to provide "adequate and substantial conveniences and entertainments for travellers, their beasts and luggage." [28]

The condition of roads and highways was of concern in some areas. In North Carolina many county overseers complained that they could not get the cooperation of people liable for work on roads under state law, and that the Negroes, who as slaves used to maintain them, now refused to work on them even as a means of paying their taxes. The law imposed a fine of one dollar per day on everyone liable to road duty who refused to perform it, but so many people were impoverished and bankrupt that the fine could not be collected. A. J. Willard, a civilian legal advisor to the commanding general, held that post commanders should enforce the local regulations governing road work, and a general order to that effect soon appeared. Local officials were to inform the post commanders of what work needed to be done and which individuals were responsible for it; and if the post commander were satisfied that the estimates were "just and equitable," he could order the individuals to perform the work. Recalcitrant persons could be tried by a post court and sentenced to a fine or hard labor. [29]

It was clear from the Reconstruction Act that the Army was expected to exercise some degree of supervision over the activities of the civil governments, and it was clear from the preliminary orders that the commanders meant to do so. The precise means varied from district to district, with each general prescribing different rules to suit his own ad-

[28]GO 32, 2MD, May 30, 1867, in *House Exec. Docs.*, 40th Cong., 2nd Sess., No. 342, p. 46; AAAG to CO Plymouth, Aug. 14, 1867, 2MD, 1, RG98, NA.
[29]French Strange, Co. Solicitor, to CO Fayetteville, Aug. 22, 1867, file 217S-1867, 2MD; Willard's opinion, Sept. 23, 1867, 2MD, 45, RG98, NA; GO 95, 2MD, Sept. 26, in *House Exec. Docs.*, 40th Cong., 2nd Sess., No. 342, p. 62.

ministrative predilections. Sheridan, for example, issued no detailed orders on the subject but merely devolved the duty of supervision upon his subordinates, to be carried out in their own way along with their purely military duties. The most systematic and thoroughly developed plan was that used in Virginia by General Schofield, who had a penchant for smooth and orderly operations. He divided the state into fifty-five areas and appointed for each area a "military commissioner," ordinarily a captain or lieutenant, who was relieved of other military duties to devote his time to civil affairs. For purposes of Army administration and command the state was already divided into seven subdistricts; therefore, the counties in each subdistrict were grouped together in such a way that each subdistrict had seven or eight military commissioners, each of whom was responsible for one or more counties.

These commissioners received careful instructions. For the purpose of quelling riot or insurrection they were given command of city and county police, and in case of disturbance civil officials had to obey the commissioners' orders. For the purpose of seeing justice done, they had the powers of county justices or city police magistrates, and in carrying out their duties they were to follow the laws of Virginia where those laws did not conflict with federal statutes or military orders. When commissioners took jurisdiction of cases, they were to report promptly to Schofield's headquarters; and where individuals were held for trial, the officers were to send a statement of the case in enough detail to enable Schofield to decide whether a civil or military trial was in order. Civil trial was preferable "where there is satisfactory reason to believe that justice will be done," but once a commissioner had assumed jurisdiction of a case it would remain in his hands until higher headquarters issued orders concerning it. Schofield closed his order with two warnings: disobeying a military commissioner constituted the military equivalent of civil contempt, and the appointment of these commissioners did not excuse the civil authorities from faithfully performing their duties.[30]

General Orlando B. Willcox commanded the Subdistrict of Lynchburg, which embraced thirty-two counties in the Blue Ridge and Appalachian country of southwestern Virginia. He kept a record of the cases brought before his commissioners—nearly three hundred for the period between July, 1867 and May, 1868. The life of a military commissioner was hardly dull, as these random samples from Willcox's records attest:

A petition to prevent the Virginia and Pennsylvania Railroad from

[30]GO 31, 1MD, May 28, 1867, in *House Exec. Docs.*, 40th Cong., 2nd Sess., No. 342, p. 7; Circ. 4, 1MD, June 23, 1867, *ibid.*, 19–21.

changing the site of its Abington Depot until the courts could investigate—military interference refused. A man's complaint that the civil courts had unjustly jailed him for bigamy—case ultimately dismissed by the civil courts for want of prosecution witnesses. The words "This house shall not stand!" found on the door of a new school at Christianburg—investigated, but the culprits not found. A petition from John O'Reily that while he was away in the Union Army during the war some men obtained certain property by deceiving his wife as to the outcome of the war—investigation suspended when O'Reily ran away and joined the Army under an assumed name. A complaint about an officer who assaulted a Negro porter for losing one of his trunks—officer obliged to make redress. A complaint that during an election a deputy sheriff denounced the local board of registration—sheriff not dismissed because the local commissioner thought him a good man. A complaint that 180 armed Negroes were drilling in Pulaski County—investigated and found untrue. A man who bought a supposedly healthy horse which promptly died complained that he would not receive justice in a damage suit against the man who sold it to him—no interference possible until all civil remedies exhausted. A complaint that the Carroll County Almshouse was given to "the most abandoned and dissolute vices"—several officials removed and new ones appointed. A petition from Raleigh W. Dyer, a prewar schoolteacher, for help in collecting $42.50 back pay from the state—no action taken. A complaint about some Washington College [now Washington and Lee University] students who broke the store windows of a known Unionist—investigated, but local officials claimed they could not prevent such things. A complaint from a man who was hit by rotten eggs while carrying the United States flag in a political procession—assailant held pending decision by higher authority on trial.[31]

In April General Sickles issued a broad order on the subject of civil court proceedings. He claimed he was issuing it "to contribute to the permanent welfare and future happiness of the people," although one newspaper, which called Sickles "a man of great political tact, and entirely competent to hold his own in political maneuvring [sic]," claimed the order was meant to increase Sickles' popularity and help him become a United States senator from South Carolina.[32] The order prohibited imprisonment for debt. It forbade taking the property of the defendant in execution of any judgment in a cause arising between

[31]1MD, 339, RG98, NA, *passim*.
[32]Washington correspondence of the Galveston *Daily News*, April 27, 1867.

December, 1860, and May, 1865. With minor exceptions it suspended for one year the sale of property to satisfy liabilities contracted before December, 1860. It forbade the forced sale of property belonging to a person with dependents if such sale would deprive the person of items necessary for the subsistence of his family—a house, twenty acres of land, clothing, tools, and such. The order also abolished the death penalty for burglary and larceny, limiting the sentence to two to ten years in the discretion of the trial court. But it did not interfere with bankruptcy proceedings or with the collection of state or local taxes. An explanatory circular issued shortly thereafter stated that the order would be interpreted and enforced "by the courts" and that it enjoyed the force of an ordinance having the sanction and authority of the United States government.[33]

In the Third District Pope undertook no such broad regulation of commercial law as did Sickles. From Elberton, in northeastern Georgia, he heard that some people in that locale hoped he would use his power to afford greater relief from debt than could be obtained under the state bankruptcy law or under the new government to be formed under the Reconstruction Act and that they consequently desired a continuance of military rule. Pope denied any intention to interfere generally with business relations, though he did reserve the right to interfere in individual cases of manifest injustice. He said he would only issue orders necessary for the execution of the Reconstruction Act, and he did not think himself warranted in making "violent and radical changes in the ordinary course of civil business." The state convention, or subsequent legislation, would have to provide the relief prayed for.[34]

Different commanders handled the matter of local elections in different ways. The Louisiana Legislature had provided for a municipal election in New Orleans on March 11, a date which fell in the interim between the passage of the Reconstruction Act and the appointment of the district commanders. Since violence was feared if the election took place, Sheridan on the ninth assumed the powers of a district commander under the new law to the extent necessary to order the election postponed.[35] In the Third District Pope's first order forbade all elections except those authorized by the Reconstruction Act; and when he discovered that the Alabama town of Tuscumbia had held one, he

[33]GO 10, 2MD, April 11, 1867, in *House Exec. Docs.*, 40th Cong., 2nd Sess., No. 342, pp. 39–40; unnumbered Circ., 2MD, April 27, *ibid.*, 42.
[34]Pope to Amos L. Akerman, Aug. 26, 1867, 3MD, 1, RG98, NA.
[35]GO 13, Dept. Gulf, March 9, 1867, Orders, 890, RG94, NA.

annulled the results and appointed a mayor himself.[36] Ord told his Fourth District inhabitants not to hold any elections but subsequently informed the mayor of West Point, Mississippi, that it was all right to hold purely municipal ones.[37]

A wide array of miscellaneous problems came before the commanding generals. Pope showed his concern for public education in Florida. The state imposed a tax of one dollar on every male Negro between the ages of twenty-one and fifty and an additional dollar on every child attending a state-established school. Pope did not object to the tax, which he felt benefited the Negroes, but he wanted to make sure the money was being honestly and judiciously used; consequently, he directed General John Sprague, commanding in Florida, to investigate the character and conduct of the state superintendent of schools and to suggest a replacement if the incumbent were not a competent administrator.[38] Pope's concern for education extended to the University of Georgia, though in a different way. At the 1867 commencement exercises, one of the students used an oration on "The Vital Principle of Nations" as a vehicle for excoriating the Republican party and its reconstruction ideas. Upon concluding he was greeted with immense applause and a deluge of bouquets. Pope was outraged, and only after earnest entreaties by university dignitaries was he persuaded not to close the school and cut off its appropriation from the state.[39]

Sheridan was on the lookout for fraud in New Orleans. In June of 1867 the city's Common Council, over the mayor's veto, entered into contracts for $108,800 for repairs to city streets and the operation of "street draining machines." Sheridan said it was "believed" the contracts were "fraudulent in design and injurious to the best interests of the city," and so he annulled them. In Virginia the ordinarily mild-mannered Schofield probably bristled at the receipt of a letter from Confederate General Fitzhugh Lee asking if he would object to the staging of musical entertainment to raise money for a monument over the grave of the Confederate cavalry leader "Jeb" Stuart. Schofield did disapprove; since efforts were being made all over the country for the relief of the destitute in the South this goal seemed a more "opportune" one than a monument for Stuart.[40]

[36]GO 1, 3MD, April 1, 1867, in *House Exec. Docs.,* 40th Cong., 2nd Sess., No. 342, pp. 99–100; SO 2, 3MD, April 16, *ibid.,* 121.

[37]GO 5, 4MD, April 15, 1867, *ibid.,* 132; AAG to J. H. Westbrook, April 30, 4MD, 1, RG98, NA.

[38]Pope to Sprague, July 30, 1867, 3MD, 1, RG98, NA.

[39]Augustus L. Hill, *Annals of Athens, Ga., 1801–1901* (n.p., 1906), 325–27.

[40]SO 122, 5MD, Aug. 21, 1867, Orders, 606, RG94, NA; AAG to Fitzhugh Lee, March 21, 1867, 1MD, 1, RG98, NA.

As had happened previously, the Army was still called on sometimes to quell large-scale disturbances of the type which occurred in Mobile in May. A Pennsylvania congressman sought to address a crowd of Negroes but was prevented from doing so by shots fired at the speaker's stand after taunts such as "Give that dog a bone!" failed to silence him. Although violence had been feared before the meeting began, the mayor and chief of police, whether from cowardice, ineptness, or connivance with the rioters, did nothing, and several people were killed. The customary investigations were had; Pope "deposed" the mayor and police chief and later—on the recommendation of General Wager Swayne, commanding in the state—the board of aldermen, the city council, and other officials too.[41]

As a result of the Mobile disturbances Pope issued General Orders No. 25 to educate local officials in their duties. Whenever a "public political meeting" was to be held in a city or town, the mayor and police chief were to be present and to make arrangements that would "render disturbances or riots impractical." This goal was to be facilitated by municipal regulations requiring that advance notice of such meetings be given to the local officials. For those meetings held outside of town limits, the county sheriffs performed the role designated for the municipal authorities. Furthermore, local military commanders were to keep themselves informed of scheduled political meetings and to send "a judicious and careful officer" to observe at each gathering and call for military force if necessary. The edict included a standard threat: "In case of any riot or disturbance, if it cannot be clearly shown that the civil officers above indicated were present, and did actively and faithfully perform their duties, both by word and deed, such officers will be deposed from their offices, and otherwise held responsible by the military authorities to the full extent of the neglect or criminality manifested by them." In his October annual report Pope remarked that this order had been observed throughout the district.[42]

The Mobile riot had caused concern in Washington as well as in Atlanta, and Pope suspected that his removals might meet some objection, especially from Johnson. He wrote a long missive to Grant defending his course and imploring to be left alone; if the President interfered and reinstated the "deposed" officials, it would create so much turmoil that

---

[41]SO 27, 3MD, May 22, 1867, in *Sen. Exec. Docs.,* 40th Cong., 1st Sess., No. 14, p. 131; SO 34, May 31, *ibid.,* 133. This is a compilation of correspondence and other documents relative to the first few months of Congressional Reconstruction. It will be cited in preference to National Archives collections where possible.

[42]GO 25, 3MD, May 29, 1867, *Report of the Sec. of War, 1866–67,* pp. 329–31.

complete martial law and the supersession of all civil power there would be necessary. He concluded plaintively, "The fact that I have made no removals elsewhere, and have interfered not at all with the civil administration in any other place, ought to be good evidence that when I do interpose I do so reluctantly, and only because I think it cannot be avoided, in view of the security of person and property to citizens, for whose safety I am held responsible by the law." This statement sounded impressive, but Pope's memory was short. He *had* made other removals. In April he had "deposed" the probate judge of Sumter County, Alabama, for "intemperance and general worthlessness"; and in May, following an "investigation by a competent officer," he had "deposed" the sheriff and deputy sheriff of Bartow County, Georgia, for "gross neglect of duty." [43]

Stanton had asked Grant to ensure that Southern commanders would be ready to maintain order, and Grant in turn asked the officers concerned to report what precautionary measures had been taken. Pope responded with a copy of his already prepared Orders No. 25; Sickles sent a long letter explaining what he was doing. He had established twenty-one military posts throughout the Carolinas, each consisting of one company with additional reserves at central points. Post commanders kept close watch on law enforcement officers and were empowered to assume command of local police forces if need be. Civil officials had to make detailed reports on commission of crime to Sickles' provost marshal general. And occasionally Sickles found it necessary to remove some official for misconduct or neglect. [44]

After reading the various Army reports on the Mobile affair, Stanton gave more thought to the whole question of keeping the peace. At the end of May he prepared a written opinion for Johnson: the Reconstruction Act gave district commanders the power to remove civil officers; Pope's information warranted such removals in the Mobile case; and since Pope's action was subject to the approval of the President, the Secretary "respectfully recommended" that the action stand. The first draft of this document, in Stanton's hand, contains another suggestion which he left out of subsequent drafts: "In cases of this character it would be more in accordance with military rules if the commanding offi-

[43]Pope to Grant, June 5, 1867, in *Sen. Exec. Docs.,* 40th Cong., 1st Sess., No. 14, pp. 104–105; SO 9, 3MD, April 26, 1867, *ibid.,* 125, and SO 21, 3MD, May 14, *ibid.,* 128.
[44]Maj. G. K. Leet, AAG HQA, to Sheridan, May 22, 1867, in Drennan Papers, LC; Pope to Grant, May 30, 3MD, 1, and Sickles to AAG HQA, June 18, 2MD, 1, RG98, NA.

cer previous to final action upon the removal of any civil officer would report the facts with his recommendation for the antecedent approval [interlineation: 'or disapproval'] of the President." [45] The point of the Secretary's reference to "military rules" is really debatable, but more important are the possible explanations for his omitting the whole sentence. He might have reconsidered because he feared the delays that would ensue if each case were first sent to Washington. If so, it was a weak reason. Any removals would ordinarily be made after the Army had restored order and a further delay would not likely produce much additional harm. More probably Stanton did not want to give Johnson any more opportunity than necessary to obstruct the congressional plan, for the War Minister's support of that plan was increasing.

Unruly civil officials, affrays, unfair court practices, schools, liquor, road improvements—all these had to varying degrees been part of the Army's Southern experience before 1867. And other aspects of the soldiers' task under the Reconstruction Acts would prove familiar, too. Most vexing and delicate were the responsibilities, such as registering voters and organizing elections, which bore directly upon Southern politics. Over such matters the commanding generals had much greater power under the Reconstruction Acts than they did previously. But they were to find that extensive power did not necessarily make the task any easier.

[45]There are three drafts of this document filed under May 30, 1867, in Stanton Papers, LC. The first is in Stanton's distinctive, jerky hand; the others are clerical.

⑥

Registering Voters
And Removing Officials

ONGRESSIONAL Reconstruction required that eligible voters be registered, and this duty gave the Army its greatest headaches during
the summer of 1867. The Reconstruction Acts had prescribed the qualifications for registering, but they had left most other details to the generals, except for stating that local boards of registration should consist
of three loyal citizens. Before much could be done, one paramount
question had to be settled: *exactly* what previous office-holding and wartime activity worked disfranchisement? Congress required a prospective
registrant to swear, among other things, that he had never been "an
executive or judicial officer of any State" before the war and then "engaged in insurrection or rebellion against the United States, or given
aid or comfort to the enemies thereof." It should not have required
much astuteness to have foreseen that the interpretation of those phrases
would cause great trouble, and on March 22 Schofield wrote from
Richmond asking for an official opinion from the Attorney General.
His request was referred upwards through channels, reaching Johnson
on the twenty-eighth. In the most remote part of Secessia General Griffin
also pondered the same question, and he remarked in his request to
Sheridan's headquarters for advice, "Webster distinctly says that Sheriffs
and Constables [*sic*] duties are executive." Sheridan had been wondering
about the troublesome language too, and he telegraphed for an opinion
from Stanbery, as had Schofield. Early in April the Attorney General, at
Johnson's request, began drafting an opinion.[1]

[1]Schofield to AG USA, March 22, 1867, 1MD, 1, and Griffin to Maj. G. A.
Forsyth, April 3, 1867, 5MD, 53, RG98, NA; Sheridan to Grant, April 1, and
Townsend to Grant, April 3, in *Sen. Exec. Docs.,* 40th Cong., No. 14, p. 193.

Stanbery took some time wrestling with the question; meanwhile commanding generals began to formulate the details of registration procedure. Exercising the discretion granted by the silence of the law, each arranged things to please himself. Schofield's system in Virginia, announced on May 13, was more comprehensive than most, but all were similar in broad outline. Schofield established a board of officers to select and recommend members for the local boards of registration; where possible, one member of each local board was to be an officer or bureau agent and the others, two loyal citizens or discharged Union officers. Each county was to have at least one board, though more could be established in counties of large area or population. These local boards would divide the county into registration precincts and determine where the registering would take place. Ten days' public notice in a precinct was required before registration began, and the boards were to sit at least eight hours a day for three consecutive days, excluding Sundays. The local facilities were to be so arranged that everything would be done in an orderly fashion.

Pending Stanbery's opinion Schofield was silent on the grounds for disfranchisement, but on an equally critical issue—the authority of registration officials to challenge someone suspected of being disfranchised—he did elaborate. Each board was to select as challengers three white men and three Negroes who qualified as voters. Each of the six had the privilege and duty of challenging anyone he suspected of being disfranchised under the Reconstruction Act. A person so challenged would then be examined by the three-man board, evidence taken, and witnesses summoned. While Schofield made no direct statement as to whether the board could reject a person who after challenge still insisted on being registered, such power may be inferred from the three designations which could be made after each name recorded on the lists: "registered without challenge," "registered after challenge," and "rejected upon challenge." For each person challenged the grounds therefor were to be entered, and the names of white men and Negroes were to be kept separately. This lists of names were to be publicly posted, and at least two weeks after the registration ended, the local board was to reconvene for additions and corrections. Those who were ill earlier could register; those rejected the first time around could present more evidence; and the name of anyone registered earlier could be stricken if a cause of disfranchisement were discovered in the interim.[2] Schofield sent this plan to Washington for review in April,

[2]SO 16, 1MD, April 2, 1867, in *House Exec. Docs.,* 40th Cong., 2nd Sess., No. 342, p. 24; GO 28, 1MD, May 13, *ibid.,* 5–7.

remarking that he would add instructions on disfranchisement based on Stanbery's opinion when that appeared. He asked for suggestions from Grant and Stanton, but the regulations as issued on May 13, before Stanbery's opinion came out, corresponded to Schofield's first draft.[3]

During April and May other commanders issued similar instructions. Ord drew up a separate order for each county in his district, changing only the names of the counties and the appointees. He always told the recipients to give the "strictest interpretation" to the law pending Stanbery's opinion and to exclude anyone about whom there was any doubt. Then, if anyone so excluded was really entitled to vote under Stanbery's opinion, the local officials would inform the person so that he could register. Ord asked Governor Isaac Murphy of Arkansas for assistance in selecting local board members for that state.[4]

With respect to the Attorney General's opinion, Sheridan's directions were identical to Ord's, though which of the two commanders originated the phraseology is hard to determine. Presumably it did not come down from Washington or it might logically have appeared in the other three districts. Sheridan gave "executive and judicial officers" a lavishly wide interpretation, including everyone from the governor on down to harbor pilots, auctioneers, and sextons of cemeteries. He also prohibited local boards from registering persons they "knew" were disfranchised, but he did not indicate what evidence of disfranchisement a board might safely accept.[5]

On May 8 Sickles released his directive, in which he set the third Monday in July as the beginning of registration but said nothing about disfranchisement or challenging prospective registrants. Two weeks later Pope's plan appeared. His attempt to clarify the language of the law was not really much help: executive and judicial officers, he said, were "all persons whomsoever who have held office under the executive and judicial departments of the State or national government; in other words, all officers not legislative, which last are also excluded by the act." A person whom the local board thought disfranchised could take the oath anyhow, if he insisted, and the case would be "held for adjudication

[3]Schofield to Grant, April 22, 1867, in *Sen. Exec. Docs.,* 40th Cong., 1st Sess., No. 14, pp. 20–23.
[4]For example, SO 21, 4MD, April 24, 1867, *ibid.,* 148; Ord to Murphy, April 15, 4MD, 1, RG98, NA.
[5]SO 15, 5MD, April 10, 1867, in *House Exec. Docs.,* 40th Cong., 2nd Sess., No. 342, p. 163, and SO 23, April 20, *ibid.,* 164; memo on disfranchisement, undated but sent to Grant on April 16, 1867, in *Sen. Exec. Docs.,* 40th Cong., 1st Sess., No. 14, pp. 199–201.

hereafter." Unique to Pope's order, and unfortunate considering all the trouble it later caused, was this proviso: "It is hereby made the duty of all registers, and they will be expected to perform it strictly, to explain to all persons who have not heretofore enjoyed the right of suffrage what are their political rights and privileges, and the necessity of exercising them upon all proper occasions." [6]

Stanbery presented his opinion to the Cabinet in serial form, one installment per session, and during discussion most of the members save Stanton expressed concurrence in his views. Gideon Welles, who thought the whole subject of the law's meaning was academic since the statute was patently unconstitutional, nonetheless commended Stanbery for his mighty effort "to make sense out of nonsense, law out of illegality." [7] The complete draft, dated May 24, was an elaborate and carefully drawn paper. Several main points emerged from the welter of legal verbiage. The act had been vague as to whether a person who had held office before the war and who had then participated in rebellion was disfranchised if he had not taken an oath to support the United States Constitution as part of the requirements of holding his office. Stanbery ruled that the oath was a necessary element in the disfranchisement. As to the offices and positions involved—the "executive and judicial offices" of states—Stanbery held that such persons as governors, lieutenant-governors, auditors, treasurers, and other officials who performed statewide functions at the state capitol were certainly included. Two groups that he claimed were not included were municipal officers of cities and towns, such as aldermen, constables, and mayors, and those persons, sometimes styled "commissioner," whom the state employed to supervise certain services or functions, like road commissioners, superintendents of lunatic asylums, bank examiners, and overseers of the poor. For the moment Stanbery reserved judgment on the status of county and township officers; and it was not until June 12 that a supplementary opinion brought these within the meaning of the phrase "executive and judicial officers of a State," provided they had taken an oath to support the Constitution.

The harried Attorney General next grappled with the problem of what constituted engaging in rebellion. He decided that such actions had to be voluntary and deliberate and, hence, that serving in the Rebel army as a conscript did not qualify. Acts of charity or kindness to individual Rebel soldiers did not qualify either, but participating in organized con-

[6]GO 18, 2MD, May 8, 1867, in *House Exec. Docs.*, 40th Cong., 2nd Sess., No. 342, pp. 42–43; GO 20, 3MD, May 21, *ibid.*, 102–103.
[7]Beale (ed.), *Diary of Gideon Welles*, III, 93–99.

tributions of food or supplies did. As to wartime office-holding, those who in their official capacity furthered the rebellion were proscribed, but those whose duties were essentially keeping order and administering local laws were not. Stanbery also turned to the powers of the local registration boards and ruled that they had no authority to reject a prospective registrant who insisted on taking the oath even if they did think he might really not be eligible to vote. The only remedy was indictment and trial for perjury.[8]

The text of the May opinion was apparently not officially transmitted to Southern commanders, but it was published in the press, and several generals issued additional instructions after its appearance. On June 3 Schofield issued new directions which conformed to most of the salient points of the opinion, except that holding office as town or county coroner, escheator, flour inspector, and a few other such local positions was considered as working disfranchisement. Schofield directed the local boards to register anyone who insisted on registering, even though the board was not satisfied after challenging and examining the person.[9]

On June 1 Pope issued further directions for his district. He failed to clarify the nebulous statement concerning "executive and judicial officers" in his earlier order, and on top of that added an even more opaque one concerning the investigatory powers of the registrars. The procedure he designated was to give the voter a printed certificate of registration, which was in effect an attested copy of the oath. "Upon examination of the act of Congress," Pope told the registrars, "you will find that you are to register the names of the male citizens of the United States, twenty-one years of age and upwards, resident in each county within your district, who shall have taken and subscribed the prescribed oath." That was clear enough—but was this: "If any person shall apply to register whom you consider as excluded by law, you will permit such persons, if they desire it, to take the prescribed oath, and will attest the same. You will then write across the printed certificate the word 'excluded' and note below, in as few words as possible, the character of your objection. A full and accurate list of all persons thus excluded will be made and preserved, and their several applications will be inquired into and adjudicated as specified . . . [in Pope's first set of instructions]." [10] There could clearly be some question whether such a person had been actually registered.

[8]12 Opinions of Attorneys General 141, 182.
[9]GO 34, 1MD, June 3, 1867, in *House Exec. Docs,* 40th Cong., 2nd Sess., No. 342, p. 8.
[10]"Instructions to Registers," June 1, 1867, *ibid.,* 103–104.

Ord devised new instructions too, dated June 10. His local boards could not refuse to register anyone who insisted on taking the oath, but they were expected to keep a record of all doubtful cases and report them to headquarters. While Stanbery's first opinion had been silent on county offices, Ord considered that mayors authorized to act in a judicial capacity, plus sheriffs and coroners, were clearly included within the meaning of "executive and judicial officers of a State." [11] Sheridan did not produce any new edict, but adhered in spite of Stanbery's opinion to his own earlier and harshly proscriptive construction.

On June 15 Ord sent his new regulations to Grant with the remark that he thought he had, "as near as may be [,] covered the intentions of Congress." Grant's reply was grumpy and sullen. He totally disagreed with the idea that local boards had to register everyone who wanted to take the oath, but admitted that Ord was sustained by the Attorney General. He gave his own interpretation of the power of the local boards and then threw on Ord the burden of deciding whether to follow his military superior or the government's chief lawyer: "The law, however, makes district commanders their own interpreters of their power and duty under it; and, in my opinion, the Attorney General or myself can no more than give our opinion as to the meaning of the law; neither can enforce their views against the judgment of those made responsible for the faithful execution of the law, the district commanders." [12] It may be presumed as a general rule that the Attorney General of the United States is more competent to interpret federal law than the General-in-Chief of the Army, and particularly when those two gentlemen are Henry Stanbery and Ulysses Grant. And indeed, in telling Ord that the law made commanding generals their own interpreters of their power and duty under it, Grant was giving unsound legal advice. Whatever may have been the intent of Congress, nothing in the phraseology of the First Reconstruction Act supported Grant's contention. Obviously, if the law *had* vested interpretive powers in the generals, there would have been no reason for Schofield and Sheridan to ask for an opinion from the Attorney General in the first place—and they asked for Stanbery's interpretation rather than Grant's.

Washington can be stifling in the summer, and Grant's letter to Ord was written on the twenty-third of June; but the heat which brought on Grant's petulant tone was probably that generated by events of the preceding ten days. Stanbery's final piece of work on the problems of

[11]Circ. 3, 4MD, June 10, 1867, *ibid.,* 145–46.
[12]Ord to Grant, June 15, 1867, and reply, June 23, *ibid.,* 141–43.

registration was the nineteen-point summary of his May opinion, which he annexed to a general opinion on the power of district commanders dated June 12, 1867. This opinion underwent thorough discussion at a protracted series of Cabinet meetings from the fourteenth through the twentieth, during which Stanton controverted Stanbery's positions at almost every turn. Since district commanders had asked for the opinion, the Cabinet finally advised Johnson to transmit it to them as the government's official interpretation of the law. Thus on the twentieth Assistant Adjutant General Edward D. Townsend addressed a communication to each of the five, embodying the nineteenth-point summary concerning registration; the remainder of the opinion, concerning other powers, was apparently not sent. Townsend's letter began with the statement that the President accepted what followed as "a practical interpretation" of the law and directed that it be sent to the Southern generals "for their information, in order that there may be uniformity in the execution" of the law. The letter closed, "By order of the President." [13]

Sheridan had asked for an opinion, but he did not like the one he received. He wired Grant asking whether Townsend's letter was an order. It did not *look* like one or *read* like one, he said, but he admitted he might be mistaken and asked for enlightenment. Grant lost no time in wiring back: "Enforce your own construction of the military bill until ordered to do otherwise. The opinion of the Attorney General has not been distributed to district commanders in language or manner entitling it to the force of an order. Nor can I suppose that the President intended it to have such force." For the first time Grant had resorted to subterfuge to counter the President's wishes.[14]

This telegraphic exchange was the most perfect humbug imaginable—

[13]Beale (ed.), *Diary of Gideon Welles,* III, 107–14; Townsend to Southern cmdrs., June 20, 1867, in *Sen. Exec. Docs.,* 40th Cong., 1st Sess., 9–12.

[14]Sheridan to Grant and reply, June 28, 1867, in *Sen. Exec. Docs.,* 40th Cong., 1st Sess., No. 14, pp. 236–37. It is only now, in the summer of 1867, that Grant opposes Johnson by devious means; this in contrast to Thomas and Hyman, *Stanton,* 478, 498–99, *et passim,* who date the general's machinations from the spring of 1866. See *supra,* Ch. IV, notes 4, 13, and 22. Grant's advice to Sheridan concerning Stanbery's opinion does not provide a good test of the effectiveness of the March, 1867, legislation on the high command of the Army (see *supra,* preface and Ch. IV, note 6) because it did not culminate in a "direct confrontation" between general and President. Grant *had* transmitted the opinion, and Johnson did not press the matter further. The President apparently felt that informing Southern commanders of the official executive interpretation of the law was the only action required in the circumstances; he certainly never doubted his legal authority to take further steps if necessary, including removal of individual commanders.

yet hardly surprising in view of the sleight-of-hand Sheridan had employed in trying to circumvent Johnson's peace proclamation of the preceding summer. For his own part Grant, after giving Ord poor legal advice five days earlier, now compounded his culpability by action that was ethically questionable. The language of his reply to Sheridan indicates that he undertook to estimate the President's intentions without personally checking with Johnson (and there is no evidence that he actually did so). Moreover, by urging two district commanders—there had been a similar exchange between Grant and Pope—to do what they pleased, he encouraged the very situation it was the stated purpose of the opinions to prevent. Manifestly, uniformity in the administration of policy was impossible if there were no restraint on its administrators.

Gideon Welles made the charitable and correct observation that chief responsibility for the Southern muddle did not rest with the generals. He dutifully confided to his diary what should have been crystalline even to the densest of individuals—the fact that disagreement over the interpretation of the law was a sympton of grave defects in the law itself.[15] That being the malady, the remedy was manifest. Let Congress tell, if it could, in yet a third law what it had really meant in the first two.

By July 13, 1867, both houses had passed the Third Reconstruction Act and sent it to Johnson for the expected veto. The law covered other aspects of the Army's powers and duties, but on the subject of registration it overruled Stanbery on all points. The local boards did have the power to deny registration to anyone they believed disfranchised. They also had the power to make a sweeping revision of the lists, deleting names almost at will "upon being satisfied" that such persons were disfranchised and adding any eligible person not already listed. Not having taken an oath of office was immaterial in determining disfranchisement. And the troublesome phrase "executive and judicial offices" was defined to mean "all civil offices created by law for the administration of any general law of a State, or for the administration of justice. . . ." Just for good measure the Radicals added that no district commander, registering official, or person exercising civil office under military appointment need pay attention to "any opinion of any civil officer of the United States." This, of course, wrote into law what Grant had erroneously supposed was in the First Reconstruction Act. The concluding section was in effect a confession of the solons' inability to write legislation which said what they meant: ". . . all the provisions of this act and of

---

[15]Beale (ed.), *Diary of Gideon Welles,* III, 113.

the acts to which this is supplementary shall be construed liberally, to the end that all the intents thereof may be fully and perfectly carried out." [16]

Johnson's veto was overriden and the law became effective on July 19. Schofield had been following developments closely, and once Congress passed the new law he began harmonizing his decisions with it without waiting for the formality of the veto and the vote to override. On the fifteenth he informed the prewar mayor of Lynchburg, who had been required to take an oath promising not to engage in duels but had not taken one to support the Constitution, that he was disfranchised anyway.[17]

The new law was the final word on registration, and some commanders had to issue new regulations to conform to it. But even so, there never was the desirable degree of uniformity. Registration was supposed to be completed by September, and in some districts it had been started even before final settlement of the question of interpretation; the result was that revision of the lists before the elections posed additional difficulties. At times the line of distinction between acceptance and rejection was fine indeed. Consider two Virginia lads who had worn the gray. Before the war, at the age of sixteen, each had worked in the local post office. The one who had taken an oath so he could "assist his mother in the duties of postmistress" was disfranchised; the one who had taken an oath so he could be a "post office clerk" was not. What difference was there, really?

Fine lines of distinction were also drawn in the Carolinas. Having been a "commissioner of the poor" or a "commissioner of roads" was sufficient to disfranchise, but having been a "warden of the poor," an "overseer of the poor," or a "roadmaster" was not. Similarly it meant exclusion to have been a custom-house officer but not a lighthouse-

---

[16]15 U.S. Statutes at Large 14. Thomas and Hyman, *Stanton*, 546, claim that this law "specifically" made the district commanders independent of the White House and "implicitly recognized the existence in the South of a separate army under Congress's control." This seems a more lavish interpretation than the wording of the act will bear. In the last analysis Johnson never really lost all control of the Southern forces because he retained and exercised his power to remove individual generals from command. Indeed, the First Reconstruction Act itself could be construed to protect this power. It specifically made it the duty of the President to assign the district commanders, and in the absence of a positive statement it would require some straining to hold that this applied to initial appointments only. Thus, it could well be argued that the power to "assign" included the power to "reassign."

[17]*Messages and Papers*, VI, 536–45; ADC to W. D. Branch, July 15, 1867, 1MD, 1, RG98, NA.

keeper. Having raised the Confederate flag over the United States Arsenal at Fayetteville in April, 1861, constituted aiding and abetting the rebellion, but having been a candidate for the Rebel legislature did not. Having "hired horses to Confederate service" removed one's right to vote, but having "hired horses to Confederate soldiers" did not. Among the miscellaneous grounds of challenge which were considered sufficient to cause rejection were "born in Africa," "Insane," "Disfranchised while a citizen of Tennessee; ignores United States government," and "Deserter [from] United States army"; those which were insufficient included "Too old; over 100 years," " 'For seducing a white woman,' (said to be deficient in intellect)"; "convicted of murder and pardoned by the governor," and "Disfranchised by the laws of Tennessee for participating in the rebellion." [18]

All things considered, the Army did try to achieve as efficient and fair a registration as possible. When some Richmond Negroes objected to one of the local officials, Schofield examined the charges and, finding them to be without support, kept the man. Sheridan used Army officers to exercise general supervision over boards of registration. Pope took the opposite view and used blue-clad men as sparingly as possible. He also decided to pay the local registrars per capita so they would have a monetary interest in getting a full registration. The main deficiency, of course, was the difference in interpretation from one command to the next and the fact that local registration boards were largely autonomous. Since the law applied to the entire South, its application ought properly to have been more uniform. Registration was arduous work, but it was completed in time for elections to be held in the autumn.

The other topic which gave all commanders headaches and contributed to the transfer of some was the removal of state officials. The March laws had not specifically granted the power of removal, but since the United States had "the paramount authority . . . at any time to abolish, modify, control, or supersede" the civil governments, the removal power might logically be part of that authority. The commanding generals all thought so, even if some were more certain of it than others, but they exercised it in varying degrees of severity. A corollary problem was that of filling vacancies already existing in civil offices. Since it was not possible to hold local elections before the registration was complete, two alternatives remained: leave the positions vacant or

[18]1MD, 1, June, 1867, RG98, NA, *passim;* unnumbered Circ., 2MD, Oct. 31, 1867, in *House Exec. Docs.,* 40th Cong., 2nd Sess., No. 342, pp. 69–72.

make appointments under military authority. The first course would have been a detriment to the welfare of the people, so the Army chose the latter.

In Virginia General Schofield was loath to turn the civil administration upside down by wholesale removals, and from the time the Reconstruction Act went into effect until the end of July he ousted only four individuals. Two were justices of the peace whom he ordered "suspended," one was a constable whom he had himself appointed, and the other was the superintendent of the Richmond Almshouse, whom he removed and ordered committed for treatment as a lunatic. Until the end of September he made a total of 105 appointments to existing vacancies.[19] Sickles in Charleston thought the Reconstruction Act "would justify the removal of *nearly every Civil officer in these States for disability* [i.e., disqualification under the Fourteenth Amendment]." At the same time he complained that life and property would not be safe if he could not remove civil officers who failed to perform their duty. But in spite of this attitude he exercised the power sparingly, making only a handful of removals and fewer appointments than Schofield.[20]

Pope had a longer casualty list than either Schofield or Sickles because of his remodeling of the city government of Mobile. Between April and the middle of July he "deposed" 31 Alabamans, 2 Georgians, and 1 Floridian. His appointments to fill existing vacancies during the same period were numerous: 123 in Alabama, 26 in Georgia, and 13 in Florida. His appointees included mayors, councilmen, bridgekeepers, justices of the peace, wharfingers, school commissioners, and city physicians.[21]

Pope very nearly removed Governor Charles Jenkins of Georgia in April, 1867, but finally decided not to do so. While Jenkins was in Washington to take part in bringing *Georgia vs. Stanton* before the Supreme Court, he wrote an address to the people of Georgia enumerating all the trials and tribulations the state had gone through since Appomattox. He termed the Reconstruction Act "palpably unconstitutional and grievously oppressive" and recommended what might be labeled passive resistance—strict maintenance of law and order, but refusal to perform the steps indicated in the congressional plan, and "a patient,

[19]*House Exec. Docs.*, 40th Cong., 2nd Sess., No. 342, pp. 25–26; *Report of the Sec. of War, 1866–67*, p. 242.
[20]Sickles to Stanton, June 16, 1867, in Stanton Papers, LC (original emphasis); Sickles to AG USA, cipher telegram, June 14, file 964S1867, AGO, RG94, NA; *Report of the Sec. of War, 1866–67*, p. 312.
[21]*Report of the Sec. of War, 1866–67*, p. 364–74.

manly endurance of military government" until "better counsels shall prevail at the federal capital. . . ." In tone the address was considerably more temperate than newspaper editorials which had been advising the same thing, but Pope took a dim view of it and considered it a direct violation of his inaugural order as district commander which had prohibited civil officers from using their official positions to impede reconstruction.

On April 17 Pope drew up an order "deposing" Jenkins and sent it to Grant with a statement of the case. He claimed Jenkins was exercising a pernicious influence in the state and expressed the determination to stop him before it went too far. "If he is permitted to set authority at defiance, it will be useless to notice such offences committed by the minor officers." Pope said, however, that he would withhold his order until he learned whether Jenkins had been aware of the prohibition on such activity at the time he wrote the address. Pope's inquiry on this point brought from Jenkins a plea of ignorance of the order, a promise to do and say in the future what his official oath required, and a hope that no future controversy would ensue. But the Governor also said, "I supposed I was exercising such freedom in the public expression of opinion relative to public matters as seems still to be accorded to the citizens of this republic, not imagining that it was abridged by the accident of the speaker or writer holding office." Pope would not let this remark pass, and wrote Jenkins a lengthy dissertation on the differences between private and official statements of opinion. Here the matter rested.[22] Pope subsequently tried to work cordially with Jenkins on civil affairs, particularly appointments, but he never had as much success as with Robert Patton of Alabama and David S. Walker of Florida.[23]

In the Fourth District Ord's troubles were not so much with individual civil officers as with the Arkansas Legislature. In April, 1867, that body had adjourned with the intention of reconvening in July to try two state judges. Ord feared the judges would in reality be persecuted for being loyalists and for trying to see that Union men received fair trials in their courts. Consequently he directed Governor Murphy to tell the legislature that its reconvening would be "incompatible" with the Reconstruction Act. At the same time he replaced the Arkansas state treasurer with one of his assistant quartermasters for fear the incumbent would

[22]*Sen. Exec. Docs.,* 40th Cong., 1st Sess., No. 14, pp. 96–104.
[23]Pope to Jenkins, May 3 and June 12, 1867, 3MD, 1, RG98, NA; *Report of the Sec. of War, 1866–67,* p. 334.

recognize the validity of wartime state warrants and would misappropriate state funds.[24]

The problem of removals was most serious in the Fifth District, where people in high places incurred Sheridan's displeasure. Just after the Reconstruction Act became operative he ousted a New Orleans judge, along with the mayor of the city and the state attorney general.[25] He had been displeased with the last two ever since the New Orleans riot of the preceding summer. No sooner had the order for these removals gone out than Sheridan received a despondent letter from Griffin, his chief lieutenant in Texas, complaining of the "irreclaimable character" of many prominent leaders there and urging the immediate removal of Governor James W. Throckmorton. Griffin claimed the governor was disqualified from holding office and was dragging his feet with regard to prosecution of murderers of Union men. The governor did not have a very high opinion of the general, either, and pointedly described him to a friend as "a dog, mangy and full of fleas, and as mean as the meanest radical in Texas, and that is saying as mean a thing of a man as can be said." Griffin felt additional removals would ultimately be necessary but that they could wait for a while if Throckmorton were speedily removed.[26] Sheridan sent Griffin's note on to Grant saying he concurred in Griffin's view and that while he hoped to make few removals, he feared he would have to turn out Louisiana's Governor J. Madison Wells—"he is impeding me as much as he can." But Grant's secret telegram in reply advised against gubernatorial casualties for the moment since the legal basis for the removal power was then "under consideration." So the two unruly governors were temporarily spared.[27]

Wells did not last much longer, however, and the specific controversy which caused his downfall arose over an action of the board of levee commissioners, whose duty it was to supervise flood control in the state and to administer funds earmarked for that purpose. The legislature had set aside $4 million, and a political brawl soon erupted between the governor and the legislature over how this money should be disbursed. "To relieve the State of Louisiana from the incubus of the quarrel," Sheridan abolished the existing board and appointed one of his own.

[24]Ord to Murphy, April 15, 1867, Stanton to Ord, May 10, and reply, May 11, in *Sen. Exec. Docs.,* 40th Cong., 1st Sess., No. 14, pp. 137–39.

[25]GO 5, 5MD, March 27, 1867, *ibid.,* 240.

[26]Griffin to Maj. G. A. Forsyth, March 28, 1867, *ibid.,* 194–95; Throckmorton to B. H. Epperson, Sept. 5, 1867, quoted in Claude Elliott, *Leathercoat* (San Antonio, 1938), 174.

[27]Sheridan to Grant, April 2, 1867, and reply, April 3, in *Sen. Exec. Docs.,* 40th Cong., 1st Sess., No. 14, pp. 194–95.

This action led Wells to appeal to Johnson, who directed that Sheridan suspend proceedings until further notice. Sheridan dutifully issued the necessary order, reprinting verbatim therein the telegram he had received from Stanton, which revealed Wells' action and conveyed the instructions of the President. In the very next paragraph Sheridan played his own trump card and announced the removal of Wells "for having made himself an impediment to the faithful execution of the act of Congress of March 2, 1867, by directly and indirectly impeding the general in command in the execution of the law. . . ." Sheridan's first choice of a successor would have no part of the position, and the general finally gave it to Benjamin F. Flanders, a New Orleans resident of Northern birth who had fled when the war began and returned when federal troops recaptured the city in 1862.[28]

Sheridan's action aroused stormy applause in some quarters and stormy denunciation in others. After seeing a newspaper report alleging that he had favored reprimanding Sheridan, Grant wired his friend an emphatic denial, claiming he was not even in Washington at the time. Georgia's recent reconstructor, James B. Steedman, was on the scene in New Orleans as an observer for Johnson. He thought Sheridan had taken the action deliberately to embarrass Johnson and informed the President that the feeling against Sheridan was being mellowed only by the general want of respect and confidence in Wells. He added that many persons thought Johnson might reinstate Wells, but he advised the President not to do so and to settle instead for a prohibition on such action in the future.[29]

Five days before Steedman wrote, the legal basis for such a prohibition had been provided by the Attorney General, who had been working on the problem of removals since Griffin's request in April to oust Throckmorton. It was another closely-reasoned paper, typical of Stanbery's work, and dealt with many phases of military rule. The Reconstruction Act did not give district commanders the power to alter or change the state governments, said Stanbery; that power was reserved to Congress. The generals might interfere with the criminal jurisdiction of the state when absolutely necessary, as in case of riot, but they could not touch civil matters such as Sickles had dealt with in his code governing commercial relations. The Army could transfer jurisdiction from civil courts to military tribunals when essential, but it could not put a civil judge out of office. A military commission could not punish an offense

[28]SO 34, 5MD, May 3, 1867, and SO 59, June 3, *ibid.*, 165–66.
[29]Grant to Sheridan, June 7, 1867, in Drennan Papers, LC; Steedman to Johnson, June 19, transcript in Sheridan Papers, LC.

committed before the Reconstruction Act was passed nor one triable by a federal court. The commanders were answerable to the President for the manner in which they performed their duties. And as for the vexing question of the removal power, Stanbery argued that only an express and clear statement would have given the Army that authority. Following this exposition came Stanbery's nineteen-point summary of his earlier opinion on registration.[30]

Although only the last part concerning registration was officially transmitted to the commanders, they doubtless knew of the part dealing with their general powers from publication in the press. Sickles asked in vain to be relieved of command and added, "Congress having declared the so-called State governments illegal, the declaration of the Attorney General that military authority has not superseded them prevents the execution of the reconstruction acts, disarms me of means to protect life, property, or the rights of citizens, and menaces all interests in these States with ruin." Sheridan claimed the opinion was causing "defiant opposition" to all his actions and that anarchy would ensue if he could not continue in his own "just course." [31]

It was not long before Congress came to the generals' support with the Third Reconstruction Act of July 19. In addition to clarifying registration questions, as set forth above, the new law overruled Stanbery on the overall powers of the commanders, declaring that the existing state governments were completely subject to the generals' control. The removal power was now expressly granted to the commanders, subject to the approval of the General-in-Chief, who could also remove civil officers on his own initiative. Congress made it the duty of the commanders to remove officials disloyal to the government or who used their positions and influence to hinder congressional reconstruction.[32]

The Third Reconstruction Act was in one sense a climax. Having rejected Johnson's plan of Reconstruction in December, 1865, Congress required fifteen months, until March, 1867, to produce its own replacement plan. Even then, largely because of faulty legislative draftsmanship, the Army was left in the dark for four additional months until the July measure clarified once and for all the extent of its legal power. The Reconstruction Acts taken as a group, and the Third in particular, gave the Army a clearer and greater amount of direct control over every facet of Southern civil affairs than it had possessed prior to the

[30]12 Opinions of Attorneys General 182.
[31]Sickles to AG USA, June 19, 1867, in *Sen. Exec. Docs.*, 40th Cong., 1st Sess., No. 14, p. 59; Sheridan to Grant, June 27, *ibid.*, 236.
[32]15 U.S. Statutes at Large 14.

enactment of the laws, or would possess after the operation of the laws had ceased. Since they were now standing on firmer legal ground, the commanding generals could henceforth devote principal attention to specific applications of their new power.

7

In Pursuance of the
Third Reconstruction Act

FROM their own standpoint the Radicals had now given district commanders all the tools they needed to carry out the policy of Congress. From the standpoint of Southerners the new law merely emboldened the generals to take more outrageous and audacious steps. Whatever the standpoint, the new law did affect the Army's administration of Congress' Southern policy. No sooner had Congress told the generals they had the removal power than Sheridan ousted Governor Throckmorton of Texas for being an "impediment" to reconstruction and replaced him with E. M. Pease, whom Throckmorton had defeated at the last election. This prompted harsh comments from the press:

His Majesty, the King of Louisiana, has issued another imperial edict. . . . This is the second Governor his Majesty has removed, for like cause. History tells of a good many Philips, of one kind and another, whose ambition led them to do a great many foolish things; but this King Philip of Louisiana bids fair to distance them all. He is making history for himself. He is the biggest beggar that ever got on horseback to ride to the—[sic]. A few more General Orders and vermillion edicts, and—so it seems to us—the beggar must be at his destination.[1]

Throckmorton's removal heralded those of various sheriffs and justices in both Texas and Louisiana. In the Third District Pope "deposed" a few more civil officers—a sheriff and two judges in Alabama; in Georgia, seven officials of Cobb and Milton counties for "openly opposing reconstruction," plus a sheriff and justice of the peace from another part of

[1]SO 105, 5MD, July 30, 1867, in *House Exec. Docs.,* 40th Cong., 2nd Sess., No. 342, p. 170; Milledgeville (Ga.) *Federal Union,* Aug. 13, 1867.

the state for "misconduct"; and in Florida, two more for neglect of duty. In Virginia, Schofield removed various local county officials, making a total of six during the latter half of 1867. At the request of the governor he also removed the board of directors of the Eastern Lunatic Asylum for financial untrustworthiness and appointed a group of Army officers to assume temporary control until a new board could be organized in accordance with state law.

The commanders watched closely the activities of the civil courts, and some found it necessary at times to suspend proceedings or otherwise prevent a judgment from being carried out. The special orders emanating from Schofield's headquarters show interference with the civil courts in twenty-one cases between July and December, 1867, as opposed to two cases before the Third Reconstruction Act. In one instance where a court imposed a fine of $2,000 in Confederate currency, Schofield decided $88.80 in United States currency to be the proper equivalent. Sometimes he simply halted all proceedings; at others he ordered the case turned over to a military commission for trial. Schofield, however, was careful in deciding whether to interfere or not, and he always insisted that a person petitioning for military interposition exhaust all possible civil remedies first and show definite proof that the civil authorities were not handling his case fairly. Schofield felt interference should come after the civil courts had shown by their actions that they were not being fair—not because there was a possibility that they might act unfairly. He also disapproved a proposed order of one of his military commissioners requiring magistrates to send the commissioner all the evidence, warrants, and affidavits in criminal proceedings involving freedmen.[2]

In the Second District, even though Sickles had gotten himself deeply involved in matters of business and commerce, there were fewer instances of judgments being set aside in specific cases. The one which caused the greatest objection was Sickles' voiding of an equity proceeding concerning two South Carolina banks. The funds in question having been part of a loan made in early 1865 to help remount some Confederate cavalry, Sickles held that they were United States property. He also set forth, in a complicated and intricate order, the rules and procedures necessary to allow the Bank of Lexington to go into receivership, a case which could as easily have been left to the civil courts; and in another

---

[2]*House Exec. Docs.*, 40th Cong., 2nd Sess., No. 342, pp. 26–34; AAG to Capt. W. A. McNulty, Oct. 14, 1867, and to Capt. D. J. Connolly, Oct. 15, 1MD, 2; AAG to Lt. F. J. Dunn, Feb. 28, 1868, 1MD, 3; file 688S1867, 1MD, and AAG to Lt. L. W. Stevenson, Oct. 2, 1867, 1MD, 2, RG98, NA.

edict he voided a North Carolina statute of March, 1867, concerning the rights and duties of guardians and trustees.[3]

The Army still utilized one of its strongest standard weapons—the threat of trial by military commission. From the imperfect statistics available it would appear that the greatest number of such trials during the first months of administration of Congressional Reconstruction was in the Second District, where 216 took place between March and September, 1867. Seventy were in North Carolina and 146 in South Carolina, and a large share of the offenses were violations of Sickles' orders concerning carrying deadly weapons, selling liquor to soldiers, and the licensing of bars in hotels and inns. Throughout the South the generals desired to keep military trials to a minimum because of the expense to the government and because constant use of military courts would have meant the detailing of large numbers of commissioned officers, who frequently were not available. For the most part military trials occurred primarily in cases of felony and other serious crimes. One of the less serious instances was the military trial of a citizen of Grand Glaze, Arkansas, for insulting the United States flag. He had allegedly pulled it down from in front of a registration office, torn it to shreds, trampled it underfoot, and called it a "damned nigger flag." The commission decided he had not trampled on it or used the word "damned" but found him guilty anyway and sentenced him to forty-five days at hard labor. Of greater consequence was General Pope's trial of one of the men who had been involved in the Mobile riot. The commission found him guilty of disturbing the peace, but not guilty of inciting and engaging in a riot, and fined him $100.[4]

Former Confederate General James Longstreet, now become a Radical sympathizer, wrote to Pope in September asking for military interference in a civil case in Alabama. Pope declined to intervene until more information was presented. He proudly claimed, "I have hitherto refrained from interfering in any manner with the Courts, or with the ordinary course of Executive and Judicial business, in any of the States of this Military District," although he did admit having interfered in individual cases of clearcut injustice. This disclaimer was a manifest falsehood; and if it had been published throughout the district, any knowledgeable man could have utterly refuted it by pointing out what was widely

---

[3]SO 119, 2MD, Aug. 7, 1867, SO 121, Aug. 9, and SO 144, Sept. 5, in *House Exec. Docs.*, 40th Cong., 2nd Sess., No. 342, pp. 89–93.

[4]*Report of the Sec. of War, 1866–67*, pp. 313–16; GCMO 26, 4MD, Nov. 21, 1867, in *House Exec. Docs.*, 40th Cong., 2nd Sess., No. 342, p. 154; GO 44, 3MD, Aug. 1, 1867, *ibid.*, 108.

considered one of Pope's greatest "usurpations" following passage of the Third Reconstruction Act. The offending order was simple enough: all grand and trial juries had to be made up exclusively of registered voters, without racial discrimination. Nobody could serve on a jury without taking an oath that he was duly registered. Little was really wrong with this idea, but even so, Southerners immediately viewed it as an attempt to force Negroes into the jury boxes. As a little backwoods newspaper in southwestern Georgia put it, "Why don't the Yankees at once displace every white man in the South from office, and fill the places with negroes? It's just as well to do it at once, and be done with the matter. A Southern white man has just about as much chance here now as a flea would have in hell—there's no difference, that we can see—if anything, the flea would be better off, until Brownlow [the Radical governor of Tennessee] takes charge, anyhow." [5]

Southerners were correct in their view that Pope had been endeavoring to make Negroes eligible for jury service, for Pope acknowledged this in his own annual report. His reason was easily imaginable and undoubtedly sound: the action was necessary in order to protect the lives and property of Negroes and Union men. Pope believed his order generally achieved its purpose, although one judge in Madison, Georgia, refused to obey it and so was "deposed." Actually Pope was not the first commander to attempt some control of civil juries, nor was his action the most rigorous. On April 27 Texans awoke to find General Griffin had issued a circular requiring that all jurors had to be able to take the "iron-clad" oath of 1862—essentially, that the person had never voluntarily borne arms against the United States or given aid, counsel, or encouragement to anyone who had. Griffin also published the section of the Civil Rights Act prohibiting deprivation of any right secured by the act on grounds of race; the purpose of doing so, the circular announced, was to prevent loyal citizens being excluded from the jury box on the grounds of race. [6]

In denying that his circular was an attempt to force the courts to accept Negro jurors, Griffin said that "the local authorities whose duty it is to impanel juries" would decide whether they would include Negroes or not. He claimed the state law on jury qualifications was still in force "so far as it does not conflict with the civil rights bill." He then al-

[5]Pope to Longstreet, Sept. 19, 1867, 3MD, 1, RG98, NA; GO 53, Aug. 19, 1867, in *House Exec. Docs.*, 40th Cong., 2nd Sess., No. 342, p. 110; undated clipping from *Early County News* in file A1831, BCA, 3MD, RG98, NA.

[6]Circ. 13, Dist. Tex., April 27, 1867, in *Sen. Exec. Docs.*, 40th Cong., 1st Sess., No. 14, pp. 208–10.

luded to one provision of the state law requiring that jurors be house-holders in the county or freeholders in the state, which provision he said excluded nearly every Negro voter. On its face this provision was probably not a violation of the Civil Rights Act, and although Griffin was broadly hinting that it was, he made no definite statement on the point. If the Civil Rights Act really did void this provision, it would have been difficult to exclude Negroes without committing any clearer violation of the federal statute. Griffin accused local officials of trying to make it look as though the circular rendered it impossible to obtain juries at all, and he countered with the contention that an ample number of persons could take the oath.[7] The general's assertion may have been true, but it would nonetheless appear that Griffin was forcing the courts more than he cared to forthrightly admit.

Griffin's circular went up to Grant, who in August decided the other commanders should take similar steps. He did not require that the Texas document be adopted verbatim; each commander was free to make whatever jury order he felt suited his own district. Sickles had in May prescribed that Carolina juries be drawn from those citizens who had paid their taxes. Shortly after Grant's August directive Sickles relinquished command to General E. R. S. Canby, who thought it unwise to extend the jury lists too much because of the almost 50 to 1 preponderance of Negroes in the seaboard counties and on the island plantations. He preferred to defer action until after registration was completed. In September he finally added registration to payment of taxes as a qualification for jury service and abrograted whatever property restrictions existed under state laws.[8]

Juries were not the only area where military interference by General Pope brought the wrath of his subjects down about his ears. His "newspaper order," which preceded the jury edict by seven days, led to an equally intense and more warrantable furor. Pope was convinced that civil functionaries, in order to circumvent his prohibition of using their official influence to hinder reconstruction, were giving their governmental announcements and publications only to papers which opposed the congressional policy. In addition to the obvious financial support, Pope thought this gave official encouragement to such editorial policies. He considered it "simply an evasion" of his earlier order though he added the curious and probably facetious remark that the "evasion" was "per-

[7]Griffin to Sheridan, May 29, 1867, *ibid.,* 209–10.
[8]Grant to Sheridan, Aug. 15 and 16, 1867, in Drennan Papers, LC; GO 32, 2MD, May 30, 1867, in *House Exec. Docs,* 40th Cong., 2nd Sess., No. 342, p. 46; Canby to C/S, Sept. 14, 1867, 2MD, 1, RG98, NA; GO 89, 2MD, Sept. 13, 1867, in *House Exec. Docs.,* 40th Cong., 2nd Sess., No. 342, p. 61.

haps unintentional." He therefore issued General Orders No. 49, directing that all official announcements and advertisements by state and local governmental agencies be made only in papers which did not oppose congressional reconstruction. The protests came thick and fast, centering around the fact that such things as notices of sheriff's sales, settlements of estates, actions of probate court, and other legal announcements were required by state law to be given to papers in the local area in order to make valid the legal actions involved. One letter from Athens, Georgia, which brought Pope's order to Johnson's attention and which argued against it on the legal ground stated, also bared the political question involved: "All conservative newspapers in the Counties and outside of the Cities and all papers friendly to you and your policy must fall under those orders unless they are revoked in some way." Johnson sent this letter across to the War Office with the pencilled scribble, "The Special attention of the Secretary of War is called to this letter." From there it went to Atlanta for Pope's explanation. Georgia's Governor Jenkins had also protested to Pope on legal grounds. All the governor received in reply was the rather lame, general statement that the Army was supreme over the civil government, but Pope did offer Washington further explanation in his annual report. He claimed the disloyal papers had cowed the loyal ones for the past six or eight years by violence and intimidation and were now undertaking to hinder reconstruction by heaping imprecations and abuse upon people who accepted offices as military appointees. Since the smaller papers were heavily dependent on the patronage of official advertisements, Pope felt compelled to take action. In an era when editors could handle their political opponents roughly without much fear of legal retribution, action such as Pope's constituted an abridgement of freedom of speech; yet in one fashion or another Pope always ignored or danced around such accusations.[9] But no matter how he explained it, since the alternative of publishing nothing at all on the country's most important political topic was an unreasonable one, Pope was still saying to the newspapers of three states, in effect, "Publish pro-Radical editorials or perish."

Pope's August attitude towards the press was all the more remarkable in view of an earlier episode. On May 19, 1867, the commander at Mobile, General O. L. Shepherd, issued some regulations for the preservation of peace and order which said, "Severe responsibility will attach to the publication of articles commending or exciting riot, or

[9] GO 49, 3MD, Aug. 12, 1867, in *House Exec. Docs.*, 40th Cong., 2nd Sess., No. 342, p. 109; George S. Housten to Johnson, file 60H1867, 3MD, RG98, NA; Pope to Jenkins, Sept. 3, 1867, and Pope's report, *Report of the Sec. of War, 1866–67*, pp. 326–29.

violence to individuals, to the public use of incendiary language and to the occurrence of disorder in rooms of public entertainment." The Alabama commander, General Wager Swayne, sanctioned this order. On the thirtieth the Mobile *Nationalist* printed a letter to the editor, signed only with initials but from internal evidence apparently written by a Negro or a white Radical. The writer commented on recent disturbances in the city and after objecting to the practice of firing pistols in the air offered this advice to the Negroes: "I beg you, therefore, on all future occasions of that kind, not to waste a single shot until you see your enemy, then be sure he is your enemy, and if you should put him to flight, never waste the balance of your ammunition, lest he should rally, and again assault you. But don't forget my first advice: don't shoot your pistol until it is absolutely necessary, and then be sure you shoot your enemy." The accompanying editorial comment approved the advice. Shepherd thought this article violated his order and he had his provost marshal post a guard over the paper's editorial offices to prevent any further publication until proofsheets were submitted to Shepherd's headquarters. The news reached Atlanta almost immediately, and Pope telegraphed Shepherd the next day to remove the guard.

Not satisfied with the sufficiency of this step, Pope decided to give Shepherd a reprimand in general orders—a penalty not often invoked and one quite unpleasant to the officer receiving it: "The interference of the post commander at Mobile with a newspaper of that city is unauthorized and entirely disapproved. He will at once undo whatever action he has taken." But General Orders No. 28 said more: "It is the duty of the military authorities in this district to secure to the people the utmost freedom of speech and of the press consistent with law; not to restrict either. No satisfactory execution of the late acts of Congress is practicable unless this freedom is secured and its exercise protected by the usual legal means. No officer or soldier in this command will hereafter interfere with newspapers or speakers on any pretext whatever." The same Southerners who lauded these words in June would justifiably think them hypocritical, or at least strange, when recalled in August. At summer's end they pointed out to Pope the inconsistency between No. 28 and No. 49, but that officer in his annual report to Grant blithely passed over the point without explaining his singular notion that they were not inconsistent at all.[10]

Pope was the only commander under the Reconstruction Acts to at-

[10] File 23S1867, 3MD, RG98, NA; GO 28, 3MD, June 3, 1867, *Report of the Sec. of War, 1866–67,* pp. 326–27.

tempt a general regulation of the press. Some indeed, like Ord, strove mightily to avoid giving the impression of interference with free speech. The Camden *Constitutional Eagle* had been treating its Arkansas readers to anti-military effusions for most of the summer. In July it found fault with the sentence a military commission gave two men convicted of larceny, observing, "A military commission of regular officers, or in other words a drum head court martial of drunken blue coats and shoulder straps [,] know about as much of law, evidence, justice, and right, as the whipper-in of a nobleman's hounds in England. What a sweet security the citizens 'so-called' have in these dismal military districts. God help us for we cannot help ourselves." The Arkansas commander, General C. H. Smith, and the commanding general himself, styled "King Ord," came in for abuse when part of the Arkansas Legislature gathered at Little Rock "and enquired of the sub-majesty there located [presumably Smith], if they would be allowed to make more laws and do other things in the name of the State of Arkansas, and were briefly answered that they had better go home." The editor looked with apprehension to the day when Ord would distribute all the offices in the state to his Radical "hirelings", but advised his readers not to complain. "Bow down your neck to the yoke, but let no unmanly accession come from you, for a fearful day of retribution is close at hand, and those who now rule with a rod of iron, may soon be glad to grasp a straw for safety. Be firm." The article over which the local command at Camden finally lost its patience appeared in August, and it was admittedly a rather personal one. The editor complained about the soldiers coming to town "and getting so inebriated as to be totally indifferent as to decency, propriety, or anything else, and as the[y] swagger and stagger towards camps [*sic*], use such profane and obscene language, and make such obscene exhibitions of themselves as would make the most obdurate Negro blush, if such a thing was possible, to say nothing of respectable ladies and children."

Several nights later Captain George Peirce led some of his men on a raid on the paper's offices during which they thoroughly wrecked the place and did $1,000 damage. To the mayor's complaint the post commander, Colonel C. C. Gilbert, answered that the paper had "unnecessarily exasperated the soldiers." Gilbert thought the paper "well out of the way," as he made clear in a letter to Ord's headquarters: "The censures of the press directed against the servants of the people may be endured; but Gen. Ord and the military force detailed to enable him to perform his duties are not the servants of the people of Arkansas but rather their masters, and it is felt to be a great piece of impertinence for a newspaper in this State to comment upon the Military under any circumstances whatever." Ord might have been peeved at the *Constitutional Eagle* too, but that did not muffle the explosion when he read Gilbert's letter, for Gilbert promptly received a sample of his commanding general's talent for crusty rebukes: "Your assertion that the Military forces are not the servants of the people of Arkansas, but rather their masters, is unjust both to the people and the military, and unfounded in fact. The Military forces are the servants of the laws, and the laws are for the benefit of the people." The sting got worse as the general continued, "so that instead of presuming to violate these laws to gratify private revenge, troops are placed in Arkansas to ensure their execution equally upon, and for the benefit of all. The assumption that a party of soldiers could at their own option forcibly destroy a citizen's private property and commit a gross violation of the public peace would not be tolerated under a 'Napoleon.' " Ord had Peirce court-martialed; the sentence required him to pay the damages and forfeit his pay for a year, and moved his name fifty positions lower on the list of captains of infantry. Ord wanted the money withheld to be turned over to the editor, but Grant refused to approve this in spite of the fact that the 32nd Article of War allowed it. He also perversely refused to approve Ord's perfectly reasonable request that Gilbert be sent elsewhere.[11]

Southern public reaction to the extensive military rule imposed under the Reconstruction Acts varied greatly. Few openly advocated resistance *vi et armis;* most favored either the passive resistance of Georgia's Governor Jenkins on the ground that military rule would be better than Negro-white radical rule, or sullen acceptance of the inevitable. It was common for editors to argue against military government on constitutional grounds and with appeals to traditional republican principles of government. There was nothing at all remarkable about this, for consciousness of constitutional arguments typified the mid-nineteenth century. Nor did the South need to feel embarrassed in using such arguments after losing a war which it had begun to break up the Union. For differ as they might over secession and the nature of the Union, the North and South nevertheless shared certain governmental prin-

[11]Clippings, ms transcripts of articles, some undated, and correspondence in files 1234M1867 and 1615M1867, AGO; Townsend to Ord, Dec. 2, 1867, AGO, 46, RG94, NA. On the other hand, Ord did arrest a Vicksburg editor, William McCardle, for publishing inflammatory articles. The case ultimately found its way to the Supreme Court as *Ex parte McCardle,* 7 Wallace 506 (1869). The chief significance of the matter was that it provided an opportunity for Congress to restrict the appellate jurisdiction of the Supreme Court to avoid the danger of the Court declaring the Reconstruction Acts unconstitutional.

ciples in a common heritage, and subordination of the military power to the civil government was one of them. Also, in using constitutional arguments the South was playing the game to its own strength and the North's weakness, for the charge that reconstruction was unconstitutional was the South's strongest weapon.

But while Southerners were eager to find fault with military government in theory—and at times in practice too—they were usually willing to express gratitude when the Army did something to benefit them. This dichotomy was clear from two articles in the same issue of the Galveston *Daily News*. Sheridan had authorized Griffin to make whatever changes in the Galveston police force were necessary to ensure the suppression of disturbances. Griffin thereupon recommended several men to Mayor J. E. Haviland as new appointees. Haviland appointed nine of them; but the others had not been residents of the city for a year, as municipal law required, and the Negroes Griffin had recommended could not read or write. The mayor asked Griffin to recommend some others instead, but the general simply removed Haviland and appointed a mayor of his own. The newspaper complained and said Griffin probably had his reasons, "But it will be hard to convince a great many of the people that the removal was not the result of the idea that the toadyism of the city towards the military authority was less perfect than was considered desirable, and that because this could not be commanded it was determined to make the community bow to the brazen image of force." On the same day the paper commended two of Griffin's recomendees for catching some robbers: "Keep up the practice—rid the city of thieves, and in this way restore order, peace, and security, and we don't care whether you're Gen. Griffin's or anybody else's police—we will stand up for you, lead pencil in hand, as a terror to those who would deter you." [12]

The Third Reconstruction Act put the commanding generals beyond the reach of interference from Southerners, and it gave Grant an increased role in Southern affairs; but it did not put the commanders beyond the reach of the President's authority to remove them. By late summer of 1867 Johnson decided he did want to make some changes. His first move, however, was to rid the War Department of Stanton. The President had long been distrustful of his War Minister but had been extraordinarily slow in determining to oust him, much to the annoyance

[12]AAG to Griffin, May 21, 1867, 5MD, 1, RG98, NA; Galveston *Daily News,* June 11 and 12, 1867.

of Welles and others who were fully convinced of Stanton's pernicious influence. For all of Stanton's good qualities, there were still incidents that pointed to the necessity of his dismissal. A telegram from New Orleans had encountered avoidable delays at the War Office, with unhappy results. During Cabinet meetings Stanton had often been evasive on issues directly relating to the Army's affairs. He would not tell Johnson straight out whether he favored a written protest to the unconstitutional riders on the Army Appropriations Act. Neither would he express an opinion on whether Stanbery should resist Mississippi's plea for a Supreme Court injunction against enforcement of the Reconstruction Act. He had also leaked details of Cabinet proceedings to the press after enjoining the strictest secrecy on his colleagues. The areas of dissatisfaction did not always center around Southern policy; Stanton had at times displayed ignorance of military movements against the Indians on the frontier.[13]

By August 1 Johnson decided he could put up with Stanton no longer. He sent for Grant, told him that he planned to remove Stanton and that he wished the general to be acting secretary. Grant opposed the plan but grudgingly consented to perform whatever "public duty" might be asked of him. On the fifth Johnson sent his famous note to Stanton— "Public considerations of a high character constrain me to say that your resignation as Secretary of War will be acepted"—and Stanton returned his impudent answer—"public considerations of high character, which alone have induced me to remain at the head of this Department, constrain me not to resign the office of Secretary of War before the next meeting of Congress." Johnson had a second interview with Grant on the morning of Sunday the eleventh and again asked him to accept the temporary appointment. Again Grant said he would obey orders. The interview ended and Johnson asked his secretary to bring the letter already prepared suspending Stanton. The Tenure of Office Act occasioned some question as to whether it was more desirable to "suspend" the minister or "remove" him; but this question was not immediately settled, and the President went off to church with Seward.[14]

[13]Even after making allowances for his personal dislike of Stanton, and for some habitual overstatement of his dislikes, the best running evaluation of Stanton by a contemporary is that of Gideon Welles; cf. Beale (ed.), *Diary of Gideon Welles*, II, 295, 355, and III, *passim*. Some idea of Johnson's attitude may be had from the notes of his private secretary, Col. W. G. Moore, in Johnson Papers, LC (Reels 49, 50). Excerpts from these were edited and published by St. George L. Sioussat as "Notes of Col. W. G. Moore, Private Secretary to President Johnson, 1866–1868," *American Historical Review*, XIX (Oct. 1913), 98–132, hereinafter cited as "Moore's Notes."

[14]"Moore's Notes," 107–109, give the chronology of events. Johnson to Stanton and reply, Aug. 5, 1867, in *Messages and Papers*, VI, 584.

Next day the official letters went out to Stanton and Grant, and when the general received his, he notified the suspended secretary that he intended to accept the ad-interim appointment. Grant's attitude towards the whole affair was constantly changing, as the circumstances of his note to Stanton show. The original draft was so phrased that it appeared Grant was reluctant to accept the post and did so only under great duress. But Grant himself scratched these phrases out before the note was recopied and sent to Stanton. The displaced minister naturally protested before finally giving up the office to Grant, and the key statement in Stanton's reply was his denial that Johnson had a right "under the Constitution and laws of the United States, without the advice and consent of the Senate and without legal cause" to suspend him. Stanton thus made his position quite a foolish one by taking refuge in the Tenure of Office Act, which he had himself thought unconstitutional.[15]

From Johnson's point of view the choice of Grant was an excellent one, provided Grant could be brought to the full support of the President in his struggle with Congress and kept on the President's side. Grant, after all, was the most popular man in the country, and his presence on Johnson's team would add much-needed prestige. It was not perfectly clear in August, 1867, whose side Grant was on, for in public Grant wore a mask of circumspection on political issues. Practically his only direct action indicating some leanings towards the Radicals was his blatant circumvention of Stanbery's opinion on registration. A few additional events indicated his sentiments. In June General John A. Rawlins delivered a major political address at Galena, Illinois, which approved every tenet of radicalism including the necessity of Negro suffrage. Many contemporaries jumped to the conclusion that this speech represented Grant's views because Rawlins was Grant's chief of staff and because Galena was Grant's home town. Rawlins may have been merely speaking for himself, but even so it seems likely that Grant received regular and personal exposure to such thinking. At about the same time as Rawlins' speech Grant gave testimony to the House Judiciary Committee which was more favorable to the congressional conduct of reconstruction than the presidential.[16]

Johnson at the time was also circumspect about his feelings towards

[15]"Moore's Notes," 109; Johnson to Stanton, to Grant, and Stanton's reply, all Aug. 12, 1867, in *Messages and Papers*, VI, 583–84; photographic reproduction of the original draft of Grant to Stanton, Aug. 12, in Badeau, *Grant in Peace*, 91–93. Thomas and Hyman, *Stanton*, 551, quote the original draft as if it were the one actually sent. Some correspondence concerning Stanton's suspension is in *House Exec. Docs.*, 40th Cong., 2nd Sess., No. 57, pp. 1–3, which is a jumbled assortment of papers on various aspects of Reconstruction.

[16]*Army and Navy Journal*, IV (July 13 and 27, 1867), 742, 786.

Grant, but in August, 1868, a year after he had appointed Grant to Stanton's job and after an irreparable break between President and General, Johnson reminisced: "Grant was untrue. He meant well for the first two years [of my term], and much that I did that was denounced was through his advice. He was the strongest man of all in the support of my policy for a long while, and did the best he could for nearly two years in strengthening my hands against the adversaries of constitutional government. But Grant saw the Radical handwriting on the wall, and heeded it. I did not see it, or, if seeing it, did not heed it." [17]

Commenting on Stanton's suspension, the *Army and Navy Journal* believed that Johnson had really meant to oust Sheridan but had settled on Stanton as a substitute object of his wrath when friends cautioned him not to remove as popular a commander as "Little Phil." The *Journal* concluded, "Sheridan's course provoked in great part the cabinet plans and policies which Stanton resisted; it was around Sheridan that the storm began to break, but Stanton caught the lightning." [18] Johnson, however, was well stocked with lightning bolts, and as soon as Grant was in the War Office he began visiting them upon selected district commanders. Sheridan was the first to be struck. On August 17 Johnson drafted an order removing Sheridan and sent it to Grant, with a note that the General-in-Chief could make any suggestions he pleased before issuing it. Grant sent a written protest, but after a brief conversation on the nineteenth he acquiesced in the removal and issued Johnson's order supplanting Sheridan with George H. Thomas. Grant added a proviso of his own: Thomas was to continue in force whatever military orders existed in the Fifth District at the time of his assuming command unless Grant authorized him to annul or modify them.[19] This was a remarkable order from a purely military standpoint for at such top echelons a commanding general may properly expect to be able to exercise his own discretion. It was also a dramatic reversal of Grant's June statement to Ord that district commanders could exercise their own judgment regardless of his opinions as General-in-Chief. If Grant were basing his new stand on the powers granted him in the Third Reconstruction Act, passed after his message to Ord, it was too expansive an interpretation, for the law gave him some special authority only as to

[17]Johnson to B. C. Truman, Aug. 3, 1868, in "Anecdotes of Andrew Johnson," *Century Magazine*, LXXXV (Jan., 1913), 435–40.
[18]*Army and Navy Journal*, IV (Aug. 17, 1867), 827.
[19]Johnson to Grant and reply, Aug. 17, 1867, and same to same, Aug. 19, in *House Exec. Docs.*, 40th Cong., 2nd Sess., No. 57, pp. 3–6; GO 77, AGO, Aug. 19, RG94, NA; "Moore's Notes," 110.

Union generals (clockwise from the top)—GEORGE STONEMAN, CHARLES R. WOODS, JOSEPH A. MOWER, THOMAS J. WOOD, JAMES B. STEEDMAN, LOVELL ROUSSEAU, EDWARD D. TOWNSEND, HENRY W. SLOCUM; (center) JOHN M. SCHOFIELD.

DANIEL E. SICKLES   QUINCY A. GILLMORE

PHILIP SHERIDAN

EDWARD R. S. CANBY   JOHN POPE

CHRISTOPHER AUGUR   ALVAN C. GILLEM

EDWARD O. C. ORD

WILLIAM H. EMORY   JOSEPH J. REYNOLDS

ALFRED H. TERRY   GEORGE G. MEADE

WILLIAM T. SHERMAN

GEORGE H. THOMAS   WINFIELD S. HANCOCK

The military commission in action, receiving testimony concerning the New Orleans riot of summer, 1866, in which 153 Negroes and 20 whites were killed or wounded. (From *Harper's Weekly*)

Richmond ladies snubbing a Union soldier on their way to receive U.S. government rations, 1865. (From *Harper's Weekly*)

Contemporary cartoon illustrating one interpretation of President Johnson's attitude toward the Negroes. The caption read, OTHELLO: Dost thou mock me? IAGO: I mock you! No, by Heaven: Would you would bear your fortunes like a man. (From *Harper's Weekly*)

Two examples of barracks for the army of occupation during Reconstruction: in New Orleans (top) and in Atlanta.

removals, while his interdict covered every facet of military activity. But then again, Grant had already misinterpreted one law that summer. The best explanation seems to be that Grant wanted to make certain that Sheridan's vigorous interpretation of the laws would be continued and that he was not certain Thomas would adopt that policy.

Thomas, much to his happiness, was promptly excused from having to play the rugged sort of political football which the New Orleans command required. On August 22 he wrote Grant pleading poor health and suggesting Winfield Scott Hancock instead, who was then off on the Plains fighting Indians. Johnson considered this suggestion an act of Providence for he had wanted to send Hancock in the first place but had chosen Thomas because the Radicals would offer less objection. On the twenty-sixth Grant sent the President another written protest, which Johnson thought an insubordinate political essay. After another two-day pause Johnson sent for Grant, they discussed the question, Grant asked permission to withdraw the letter, and Johnson assented. The order which went out appointing Hancock was almost a duplicate of the first one appointing Thomas, and it contained the same restricting provision.[20] From a political standpoint Grant doubtless thought it more necessary this time, since Hancock was strongly Democratic in his political leanings.

The reaction to Sheridan's removal was quick; the Radicals stormed and ranted, while the conservatives chortled gleefully. Welles was happy for once and mused, it "will break no bones." Horace Porter, one of Grant's aides, wrote his wife, "Sheridan is relieved! We are dreadfully sorry. The General had a hard fight for him, but no go." Many papers immediately published the Grant-Johnson correspondence, and in doing so the *Army and Navy Journal* said of Grant's productions, "every word is golden." [21] Nobody could find fault with Sheridan's record as a soldier, but there are quite different skills involved in commanding a division of cavalry in the field and in supervising civil affairs in as turbulent a district as Louisiana and Texas. Sheridan had an inordinate idea of his own adroitness, a penchant for feeling himself a martyr, and a considerable disdain for the people he was sent to govern. The winter before his relief he had poured out his feelings to a close friend:

They are mad at me in Washington because they imagine I have been a head devil in all their affairs, but I have not, I have only helped along. . . .

---

[20]"Moore's Notes," 110–12; GO 81, AGO, Aug. 27, 1867, RG94, NA.
[21]Beale (ed.), *Diary of Gideon Welles*, III, 176; Porter to wife, Aug. 22, 1867, in Horace Porter Papers, LC; *Army and Navy Journal*, V (Aug. 31, 1867), 21.

While I may not be liked I am respected and feared and scarcely anyone will complain that I am not fair and just. If I am disliked it is because I cannot and will not cater to rebel sentiment and be an instrument to advance the merits of political parties or particular reconstruction schemes. I do not permit anyone to approach me on politics, but go on minding my own business and my legitimate military duties as though I did not care whether the Southern States were readmitted tomorrow or kept out for twenty years. . . . The more I see of this people [sic] the less I see to admire. Their social standard would be called ill-breeding in the North except in the case of a few families who have seen enough of the world to keep up with the times. . . . I can assure you Newhall that my position has not been a sinacure one [sic] and that I believe I have done as well if not better than almost any other man that could be put here.[22]

In his annual report following his relief he complained about "the highest authority in the nation" charging him with being "tyrannical and a partisan," and in retaliation he scored Johnson's "apparently open sympathy" with the officials he had removed. The same attitude colored his memoirs: "It was, therefore, my determination to see to the law's zealous execution in my district, though I felt certain that the President would endeavor to embarrass me by every means in his power, not only on account of his pronounced personal hostility, but also because of his determination not to execute but to obstruct the measures enacted by Congress." [23] It was a rather shallow analysis.

The next bolt of presidential lightning struck in Charleston, at General Sickles' headquarters. Sickles had requested his own relief in June, following Stanbery's opinion on the powers of district commanders, and had also demanded a court of inquiry on his conduct. Stanton laid the matter before Johnson but the exact nature of his recommendation is hazy. On one copy of Sickles' telegram is an endorsement in which Stanton urged the general's retention and the granting of a court of inquiry; on another copy, endorsed "Respectfully submitted to the President for his instructions with the recommendation that Major General Sickles be retained in command of the Second Military District," the part after "instructions" is crossed out.[24] Whatever Stanton may have decided to recommend, Johnson left Sickles in Charleston and refused the court of inquiry.[25] It was not long, however, before Sickles got into the trouble which resulted in his removal. In his April, 1867, code on commercial and business law Sickles had ordered, "Judgments or

[22]Sheridan to F. C. Newhall, Nov. 20, 1866, Sheridan Papers, LC.

[23]*Report of the Sec. of War, 1866–67,* p. 380; Philip H. Sheridan, *Personal Memoirs of Philip H. Sheridan* (New York, 1888), II, 253.

[24]Sickles to AG USA, June 19, 1867. The first copy is in file 752M1867, AGO, RG94, NA, the other is in Stanton Papers, LC.

[25]Townsend to Sickles, June 21, 1867, AGO, 45, RG94, NA.

decrees, for the payment of money, on causes of action arising between the 19th of December, 1860, and the 15th of May, 1865, shall not be enforced by execution against the property or person of the defendant." During the summer the federal district court in North Carolina heard a case falling under this order, and when the marshal tried to execute the judgment the local post commander prevented it. Sickles upheld the officer and prohibited further attempts to carry out the court's orders.[26]

The court's complaint to Washington necessitated a decision whether or not to support Sickles, and while the matter was under consideration Grant oscillated from one position to another. At a Cabinet meeting on August 13 he was firmly convinced Sickles was in error and promised to so instruct him. On the twenty-third he told the Cabinet he had ordered Sickles not to obstruct the court but then had countermanded this directive until more information could be obtained. This led to a spirited discussion between Grant and the assistant attorney general, who had been preparing a written opinion on the question, from which the lawyer emerged victorious in spite of Grant's "arrogance and intentional insult." [27] That had been on Friday; Grant spent the weekend sulking and wrote a Saturday letter to Sickles: Johnson and all the Cabinet except himself were adamant that Sickles was wrong, and his own view was that federal courts should only be meddled with if they were clearly acting so as to hinder reconstruction. The Attorney General was hostile to the Reconstruction Acts and thus "representations may be unintentionally biased"; consequently Grant hesitated to revoke Sickles' order.[28] The Cabinet met again on August 27 and Grant suggested Canby as the best replacement if Sickles were to be relieved; three more days were sufficient for him to come full circle to his original position of the thirteenth—now Sickles was clearly wrong.[29] Johnson had already determined on his own to relieve Sickles several days before, and on September 5 Canby announced his assumption of command. The new general allowed the court to proceed unhindered and to be on the safe side he asked his civilian legal advisor for an opinion on the whole subject; when rendered, it held that the Army could not interfere with federal courts.[30]

Sickles did not take his relief with very good grace, and he promptly

[26]GO 10, 2MD, April 11, 1867, in *House Exec. Docs.,* 40th Cong., 2nd Sess., No. 342, pp. 39–40; William A. Dunning, *Essays on the Civil War and Reconstruction and Related Topics* (New York, 1898), 167.

[27]Beale (ed.), *Diary of Gideon Welles,* III, 170, 182–83.

[28]Grant to Sickles, Aug. 24, 1867, HQA, C, RG108, NA.

[29]Beale (ed.), *Diary of Gideon Welles,* III, 187, 190.

[30]Opinion of A. J. Willard, Dec. 17, 1867, 2MD, 45, RG98, NA.

demanded a court of inquiry for the second time. He was ruffled by seeing in print a report by the assistant attorney general which found fault with his conduct of affairs in the Carolinas and called him "a contumacious and unfaithful executive agent." Johnson refused his demand for an official investigation, remarking that the removal had been considered "conducive to the public interests" and that every- thing which had happened since merely confirmed the correctness of his relief.[31] Sickles was in many respects a paradoxical figure. He thrived on controversy and political bickering, as his record before and during the war demonstrates. He did make an effort to achieve harmony with the civilian governors, as his correspondence with them shows, but he could not fully suppress a petulant insistence that he was always right. He interpreted generously the limits of his own legal authority, but he seemed to have used some moderation in its employment. He involved himself much too deeply in detailed matters of general civil law, and in areas thereof which his colleagues generally avoided when possible. It was the application of his expansive notion of his own power to such an area which ultimately brought him to grief.[32]

Many people supposed that after Sickles, Pope would be next "Vice- roy General" to be toppled, and Johnson had indeed been wary about his appointment in the first place. He received more than one complaint about Pope but took no immediate action; when some Alabamans visited him in August, 1867, to urge Pope's ouster, the President merely said he would "make a note of the grievances." As summer turned to autumn there were rumors that Pope would be replaced by General Wager Swayne, his chief lieutenant in Alabama, and after the relief of Sheridan and Sickles, Pope wrote to Grant about his own future. Grant replied that he had heard nothing officially but that he meant to back up the Atlanta commander if Johnson showed a determination to "depose" him. Pope was safe for a while, however, and he finished out the year before being ordered away from Atlanta.[33]

The displacement of Sickles and Sheridan had both favorable and unfavorable results. Sickles' deep involvement in matters of commercial law left a residue of problems for Canby to wrestle with. He modified some of the provisions of Sickles' April code so that it no longer ob-

[31]Sickles to AG USA, Sept. 11, 1867, file 964S1867, AGO; Townsend to Sickles, Oct. 14, AGO, 46, RG94, NA.

[32]His civil correspondence is in 2MD, 1, *passim*, RG98, NA. For alternate appraisals of Sickles see Simkins and Woody, *South Carolina*, 65–66, and John G. deRoulhac Hamilton, *Reconstruction in North Carolina* (New York, 1914), 233.

[33]Milledgeville (Ga.) *Federal Union*, Aug. 6, 1867; Grant to Pope, Sept. 9, 1867, HQA, C, RG108, NA.

structed proceedings in the federal courts, and in certain other respects. He also revoked some of Sickles' regulations on liquor. In September he suspended the collection of state taxes in three circumstances: when the tax was on property sold or transactions made before the passage of the act establishing the tax; when the tax discriminated in commercial transactions in favor of residents and against foreign citizens and residents of other states, thus interfering with the congressional power to regulate commerce; and when the tax was to pay off obligations incurred in support of the rebellion. The provisional government of South Carolina promptly got into financial difficulty, however, and Canby therefore continued in force an intricate tax law passed in December, 1866—but with so many modifications and amendments that his order formed a booklet instead of the usual single-sheet broadside.[34]

Provost courts had been more frequently used in the Carolinas than elsewhere because of the predilection of several commanders in that area for them, and while Sickles had hoped to be able to do away with them, some still remained when Canby took over. South Carolina's Governor James L. Orr wrote to the new general complaining about frequent usurpation by the provost courts and also about their partiality towards Negroes even where the civil courts had shown a disposition to be fair. Orr referred to one instance in which a white man prosecuted a Negro for larceny in the state courts. Upon his acquittal the Negro sued the white man for slander and malicious prosecution in the provost court and was awarded $1,000. Orr thought, and reasonably so, that the Negro ought properly to have been referred to the state court since it had done him justice the first time. Canby had just issued a temporary set of rules which put a $300 ceiling on suits triable by provost courts, and in February, 1868, he introduced additional restrictions.[35]

Canby was especially careful to see that trials by military commission did not result in injustice, and he often wrote lengthy essays when reviewing their proceedings. In one case a Negro, Henderson Cooper, had been sentenced to death for rape by a North Carolina court before the war ended. He escaped and hid in Washington until October, 1866, when North Carolina authorities brought him back. Without granting a new trial, they re-sentenced him to hang in April, 1867. Sickles had annulled these proceedings and convened the military commission, which

[34]GO 164, 2MD, Dec. 31, 1867, in *House Exec. Docs.*, 40th Cong., 2nd Sess., No. 342, pp. 82–84; GO 92, Sept. 21, *ibid.*, 61; GO 139, Dec. 3, *ibid.*, 76–80.
[35]Orr to Canby, Oct 5, 1867, file 221S1867, 2MD, and reply, Oct. 9, 2MD, 2, RG98, NA; Circ., 2MD, Sept. 30 in *House Exec. Docs.* 40th Cong., 2nd Sess., No. 342, p. 62; GO 18, Feb. 6, 1868, *ibid.*, 99.

also sentenced Cooper to hang. In reviewing the case Canby agreed that the original sentence could not be executed once the war had ended. But he did not think a military commission could try Cooper because there had been no federal military control at the time and place of the offense. "The jurisdiction of military tribunals," he said, "is determined and limited by the period and the territorial extent of the military occupation." Thus he remanded Cooper to the civil authorities for trial under a new indictment, since he did not want to allow the man to escape scot free.[36] Canby also took the unusual step of authorizing post commanders to release on bail people held for military trial in noncapital cases. The amount was governed by the state law on similar cases, and the bond had to authorize the Army to seize and sell the necessary amount of the property of the principal and the surety in case of default.[37]

Canby did not make a large number of removals, but his ouster of Judge A. P. Aldrich of South Carolina caused a considerable stir. Aldrich refused to obey Canby's order requiring juries to be drawn from the voter lists and told his court that the Reconstruction Acts were unconstitutional and that Congress' course was "fast reducing the country to the condition of party vassalage." When Canby removed him, Aldrich told his court he felt no personal mortification, adding,

But it almost breaks my heart to witness the humiliation of this proud old State we all love so well, in my poor person. Be of good cheer; it is only for a time. I see the dawn of a brighter day. The great heart of the American people beats true to constitutional liberty. The time is at hand when we will be relieved from the tyranny and insolence of military despotism . . . if God spares my life, I will yet preside in this court, a South Carolina judge, whose ermine is unstained. . . . Mr. Sheriff, let the court stand adjourned while the voice of justice is stifled.

The press naturally assailed Canby, but Aldrich was not reinstated.[38]

Fifth District Southerners thought they saw the dawn of a brighter day too when Sheridan gave place to Hancock. But Hancock was in Kansas at the time of his appointment in August of 1867 and did not assume command at New Orleans until late November. In the interim the

[36]GO 125, 2MD, Nov. 20, 1867, in *House Exec. Docs.*, 40th Cong., 2nd Sess., No. 342, p. 73. Result of the new trial could not be ascertained.
[37]GO 105, 2MD, Oct. 21, 1867, *ibid.*, 66–67. Before the order went out the whole subject received careful attention by the Judge Advocate General and Canby's own judge advocate because bail had been theretofore practically unknown to military law. Cf. papers in file 1169M1867, AGO, RG94, NA.
[38]*Report of the Sec. of War, 1866–67*, p. 304–307.

command devolved on the senior officer present, General Joseph A. Mower, a forty-year-old New Englander without West Point training whose military service began with action as a private in the Mexican War. Mower's Civil War service had been in the western armies; he had marched with Sherman to the sea as a division commander and had been one of Slocum's chief subordinates in the Army of Georgia. During the short time he was in command in Louisiana and Texas some people felt he was even more extreme than Sheridan, particularly on the question of removals. In three months he turned out eighteen officials of varying significance, from police constables to the lieutenant governor of Louisiana. The latter, along with the treasurer, auditor, secretary of state, and school superintendent, had escaped Sheridan's ire at the time of his ouster of Governor Wells; Mower thought them all "impediments" to reconstruction but did not specify wherein they were so. Mower's zeal elicited adverse commentary even from areas outside his command. Rural Alabamans in the southeastern part of the state read about Mower in the "Texas Correspondence" column of their little newspaper: "Sheridan only removed State and county officers by sections. Mower took them by battallions [*sic*]. If he had placed Confederates in arms, *hors du combat,* at the rate at which he has decapitated civil officers, the war would not have lasted one year, before the last 'rebel' would have been consigned to the bone yard." [39]

At length Hancock arrived, and on November 29, 1867, his inaugural order appeared. Like so many that had gone before, it was a dissertation on the general's theory of civil-military relations. Hancock said he was "solemnly impressed" with the idea that when peace existed, and the civil officials were performing their duties, "the military power should cease to lead, and the civil administration resume its natural and rightful dominion." Trial by jury, freedom of the press, habeas corpus and other principles—which "still are the lawful inheritance of this people, and ever should be"—Hancock meant to preserve. But while he indicated his desire to support the existing civil government, he also made it clear that forcible resistance to law would be "instantly suppressed by arms." Hancock drew up this order while en route to New Orleans, and Johnson knew in advance what its tenor would be, for Hancock had told him.[40] The President was pleased with it; the Radicals were not; and when Hancock began to carry out his expressed theories, storm clouds

[39]Eufaula (Ala.) *News,* Dec. 24, 1867.
[40]GO 40, 5MD, Nov. 29, 1867, in *House Exec. Docs.,* 40th Cong., 2nd Sess., No. 342, pp. 161–62; Cornelia Hancock, *Reminiscenses of Winfield Scott Hancock* (New York, 1887), 123–24.

began once more to gather, and the Gulf Coast prepared to receive the forthcoming hurricane.

The personnel changes which Johnson made in the summer of 1867 were of great significance to his relations with Congress. Neither the 1867 enactment on the command of the Army, nor the Third Reconstruction Act, nor the two taken together completely removed Johnson's control over the commanders because he never lost his power to replace them or to reverse their individual actions. And it may be that part of the President's motive for ousting Sheridan and Sickles was to demonstrate to Congress that he was still Commander-in-Chief. Stanton's case was different, however, because that involved the Tenure of Office Act, and it was Stanton's suspension which set in motion the train of events that culminated in the President's impeachment. The replacement of Sheridan and Sickles, although it outraged the Radicals, was not an impeachable offense; and Johnson was not formally charged with that during the trial. Indeed, Johnson was not charged with violating the 1867 enactment or the Third Reconstruction Act, and if he could have ousted Stanton without violating the Tenure of Office Act (or seeming to, at least) there would have been no grounds for impeachment. Johnson's actions of the summer thus increased the political excitement in Washington during the fall and winter of 1867–68. Washington was not the only politically exciting place in the nation, however, for Southerners were holding critical elections under the watchful eyes of the commanding generals.

8

An Autumn, Winter, and Spring of Discontent

THE most important Southern events as the autumn of 1867 approached were the elections to determine whether constitutional conventions should be held and, simultaneously, to choose convention delegates in case the decision were affirmative. Naturally the Army would have to keep itself ready to maintain order if need be; that was standard procedure. But a duty of vastly greater significance also fell to the generals—determination of the election districts and apportionment of delegates. Congress had merely said that each convention should contain the same number of delegates as the most numerous house of the state legislature in 1860 and that seats should be apportioned according to registration figures. Beyond this the generals could do what they pleased. By drawing lines on the state map in particular ways, they could gerrymander the districts and thus make possible a convention of practically any political persuasion they chose. It was a fearsome amount of political power for military officers to have. It was more, indeed, than they had ever exercised over Southerners before, and it was more than some of them could exercise fairly.

Without much question the most reprehensible arrangement of districts was that inflicted upon Georgia by General Pope. In that state the whites clung to a slender majority in voter registration: 95,214 as against 93,457 Negro. But the election districts in which Negro registration predominated controlled 104 out of the 169 seats in the convention.[1] In effect, then, Pope gave the Negroes and their white allies a vastly greater potential for controlling the convention than their registered voting strength warranted. He gave these interests such an ad-

[1] *Report of the Sec. of War, 1866–67,* pp. 358–62.

vantage, indeed, that the convention could not have had a conservative majority even if every white man in the state had so voted. The obvious results of Pope's decision could have been offset only if conservative whites captured many Negro districts, an achievement that was hardly likely unless large numbers of Negroes could be kept away from the polls.

It is true that Pope did not actually delineate new districts especially for the convention; he merely adopted for this purpose the state senatorial districts as already established by state law. He claimed he did so because these districts were familiar to the people and would cause less confusion.[2] This was really a weak argument. It is hardly credible that the average Georgian had committed the boundaries of forty-four senatorial districts to memory; and anyhow, it is difficult to see why a farmer in Decatur, say, would really need to know what district Valdosta, 200 miles downstate, was in. The only information he required—Pope's order handily provided it—concerned the boundaries of his own district, and surely anyone intelligent enough to vote or campaign for office could adjust to a possible change in boundary lines.

As the election turned out, the disparity in composition of the convention was even greater than 104 to 65. There were only 12 conservatives as opposed to 37 Negroes and 111 white scalawags or radical sympathizers—a "conglomeration of scullions, boot-blacks, and black-legs, with a smart sprinkling of wandering Yankees in search of adventures," as one paper called the group.[3] This disparity resulted in part from the fact that numerous registered white voters decided to stay home, either as part of a move by the conservatives to defeat the convention by registering but not voting, or because they felt that Pope's decision on districts lost them the election before it had ever taken place. It was hardly strange that, after seeing what Pope's system would lead to, some whites should take this "stay home" attitude—or that others should resort to violence and intimidation in an effort to keep Negroes away from the polls.

Alabama and Florida complained about Pope's districting too, but those states did not have as strong a case as Georgia. They had Negro majorities, and while there was a disparity in the control of seats, it was not as outrageous as in Georgia. Pope silenced his critics by saying, in

---

[2]Pope to Grant, Sept. 20, 1867, 3MD, 1, RG98, NA.
[3]C. Mildred Thompson, *Reconstruction in Georgia* (New York, 1915), 189; Milledgeville (Ga.) *Federal Union,* Dec. 31, 1867.

effect, "You do it better, if you can." [4] Actually, in the case of Georgia, it would have been possible with a little enterprise and a little care to have divided up the state in such a way that districts with a white majority would have controlled eighty-seven seats and Negro districts eighty-two.[5] Such a distribution would have been a more reasonable reflection of comparative voting strength; it would have made the election a more accurate test of strength and attitudes; and it would have shown Southerners that the Army was trying to be fair.

There is no definite proof that Pope was deliberately helping the Radicals with his Georgia districting; he did, to be sure, use the senatorial districts in the other two states as well. Perhaps he decided to adopt the senatorial districts before he realized what that method would produce in Georgia, although his own statements of self-defense gave no such inference. As he claimed, no method could please everyone; but it is not difficult to feel some sympathy for the white Georgians who denounced Pope as a partisan zealot. From the standpoint of the framers of congressional Reconstruction, Pope in this matter was a great success. As a statesman he was a failure.

The other commanders escaped, largely though not entirely, from the opprobrium Pope brought on himself because their districting orders did not display as much that could be construed as partisan sleight-of-hand. They apportioned delegates to each county individually according to total registration figures and lumped counties together in cases where there were a few extra seats left over after each county had received the number of delegates its registration total entitled it to have.

The generals did attempt to set ground rules which would ensure fair elections. The local commanders were to keep their troops ready for any emergency duty occasioned by riot or disorder, but troops were not to be located at or near the vicinity of the polling places. Keeping order was the responsibility of the civil authorities in the first instance, with the Army providing second-line support. The Army desired to make sure that everything ran smoothly but did not want it to appear that people were balloting at the point of bayonets. Sale of liquor was suspended during the elections, and detailed regulations prescribed the method of handling ballots and record books. In Virginia, Schofield even

---

[4]File 142F1868, 3MD, and Pope to Grant, Nov. 12, 1867, 3MD, 1, RG98, NA.
[5]I spent the better part of three winter afternoons achieving the distribution indicated. Pope's districts all comprised three counties each; some of mine have two and others four, but the proper ratio of 1 delegate for 1,116 voters was maintained as nearly as possible without splitting counties, or as nearly as Pope did.

showed concern for the political rights of people who were in jail and directed that they be escorted to the polls by constables, allowed to vote, and then returned.[6]

When, after the election in Virginia ended, some conservative candidates charged Colonel Thomas B. Rose, the superintendent of election for Richmond, with misconduct, Schofield ordered a court of inquiry. Rose supposedly had been drunk on duty, used insulting language, driven whites away from the polls, and prohibited conservative partisans from addressing the Negroes while allowing radical ones to do as they pleased. It was a significant case because the protests had been made not only to Schofield but to Johnson as well; the complainants told the President there was a great conspiracy against him by the Freedmen's Bureau in Virginia under Colonel Orlando Brown, who was supposedly under the domination and influence of radical Senator Henry Wilson. Brown and Rose, the Virginians believed, wanted the Radicals to carry the election at all hazards and acted accordingly. The court of inquiry on Rose sat for a month under the presidency of General George Stoneman, the second senior officer in the state. It finally concluded that Rose had used his authority as election supervisor in an arbitrary and unwarranted fashion and that his conduct and language were unbecoming an officer, but it absolved him of any political partisanship and of anything "tending to subordinate the white to the colored voters."[7]

Louisiana held its election in late September, followed by Alabama, Virginia, and Georgia in October, and in November by the others except Texas. This state did not hold its election until February, 1868; registration had been complicated there because of territorial extent and transportation difficulties. Some conventions were thus in session during November and December, and it appeared that congressional Reconstruction was progressing apace.

Before the winter of 1867–68 was over three more commanding generals had given way to new men. Johnson's displeasure with Pope increased during the fall, and by December he was determined to "depose" him. Pope had barraged Grant with blustery and pompous letters

[6]GO 65, 1MD, Sept. 12, 1867, and GO 68, Oct. 4, in *House Exec. Docs.*, 40th Cong., 2nd Sess., No. 342, pp. 11–14; GO 99, 2MD, Oct. 16, and GO 101, Oct. 18, *ibid.*, 63–66; GO 59, 3MD, Aug. 31, GO 69, Sept. 19, and GO 74, Oct. 5, *ibid.*, 111–16; GO 31, 4MD, Sept. 26, *ibid.*, 137–38; SO 119, 5MD, Aug. 17, and SO 213, Dec. 18, *ibid.*, 171–72; AAG to Lt. T. E. Merritt, Oct. 19, 1MD, 2, RG98, NA.

[7]Correspondence in files 128E1867, 408G1867, and 417G1867, 1MD; proceedings of the court of inquiry in file 344L1867, 1MD, RG98, NA.

on Southern affairs, and Grant, as War Minister ad-interim, had passed some of these around at Cabinet.[8] The commentary they evoked was generally more unfavorable than favorable; at one point Welles made mocking note of Pope's complaint that certain "pestilent fellows" were interfering with him by anti-Radical speeches and editorials. It was rumored that in November he had written an unofficial letter on Alabama affairs to his chief lieutenant there, General Swayne, in which he said, "I speak not more for the interest of Alabama than for the interests of the political party upon whose retension [*sic*] of power for several years to come the success of reconstruction depends." Another report was that Johnson had relieved him upon becoming convinced that he had manipulated the Alabama registration so as to give the state to the Radicals.[9]

For whatever specific reasons, the order appeared on December 28; Pope went to Detroit to command the Department of the Lakes, and George G. Meade, then at Philadelphia, went to Atlanta.[10] The change elicited a variety of reactions in the South. In an article headed "God Bless Andrew Johnson!" one Georgia paper foresaw a better future under Meade: "we may hope to escape from Negro bondage; with him it is not a crime to be white." On the other hand, former Governor Joseph Brown of Georgia absolved Pope of the charge of having gerrymandered the state in favor of the Negroes and said, "A majority of the thinking men in Georgia would have preferred his rule for years to the chances of a better." And the president of the National Bank of Georgia felt that many whites hated to see Pope leave because he had been using his influence to induce the convention to frame a liberal, moderate constitution which would be acceptable to both the people and Congress.[11] Such may actually have been the case, for the Georgia document was in fact more moderate than those of some other states; but even so, if Pope's districting had been more reasonable in the first place the convention might have framed a good constitution without any influence from him being needed.

[8]Cf. Pope to Grant, June 25, Aug. 17, Sept. 23, and Oct. 22 and 28, 1867, 3MD, 1, RG98, NA.

[9]Beale (ed.), *Diary of Gideon Welles*, III, 174; Milledgeville (Ga.) *Federal Union*, Dec. 17, 1867 and Jan. 14, 1868.

[10]GO 104, AGO, Dec. 28, 1867, RG94, NA.

[11]Milledgeville (Ga.) *Federal Union*, Jan. 7, 1868; Huntsville (Ala.) *Advocate*, Jan. 31 and 10, 1868. Pope had been in Detroit scarcely two weeks when he was already writing Grant "unofficially" that he wanted to go back to Atlanta more than anything. There is no evidence that Grant tried to arrange it. Pope to Grant, Feb. 19, 1868, in C. B. Comstock Papers, LC.

Appointment of the new commander aroused much speculation as to the course he would pursue. Second-hand information from Meade's friends—hardly an oracular source—had it that Johnson advised Meade to adopt a policy similar to Hancock's but that the advice would be ignored. Some people, of course, feared he would be as radical as Pope; but if such were his intention, a personal letter from him to a Radical senator gave no indication of it: "It is not at all improbable that placed suddenly in so arduous and embarrassing a position, I may make errors of judgment, to the regret and disappointment of former friends, and all I can say is that it is my intention, under the light I can get, to discharge my duty conscientiously and do only what I think is right." [12] The closing remarks of his speech to the Georgia convention seem a clearer indication of his intentions: "It is not my duty to dictate, to recommend, or to advice [sic]—but I feel justified in counselling moderation, and earnestly hoping that wisdom, calmness, and reason will govern your proceedings, again I thank you most sincerely for your courtesy." [13]

In short order Meade began receiving petitions for the modification of some of Pope's decrees, particularly the "jury edict" and the "newspaper order." With respect to the first he took no action, hoping instead that the conventions would "arrange this matter satisfactorily." He did revise the policy on newspapers, however, by making ineligible for official announcements only those papers which, by threatening military appointees with violence or prosecution after Army control ceased, deliberately interfered with military government. Thus, while Pope had in effect proscribed opposition of whatever kind, Meade allowed editorial fault-finding provided it was not violent, incendiary, or threatening.[14]

Both Pope and Meade were rather sparing in their use of military commissions. The case under Meade's administration which caused the greatest uproar was that resulting from the "Ashburn murder." George W. Ashburn was the political leader of the Negroes around Columbus, in western Georgia, and had been a member of the constitutional convention. On the night of March 30, 1868, he was assassinated by a group of twenty to thirty disguised men, supposed by some to be members of the Ku Klux Klan. His personal reputation (not at all good) immediately led to many conjectures about his murder; he was widely branded as a "fomentor of strife and a man of discord," and it was alleged he was

[12]Huntsville (Ala.) *Advocate,* Jan. 7, 1868; Meade to Henry Wilson, Jan. 9, in Wilson Papers, LC.
[13]Huntsville *Advocate,* Jan. 14, 1868.
[14]AAG to James C. Henry, Jan. 30, 1868, 3MD, 3, RG98, NA; GO 22, 3MD, Feb. 2, 1868, in *House Exec. Docs.,* 40th Cong., 2nd Sess., No. 342, p. 131.

"in angry collision" with members of his own party. Meade ordered a full investigation under the direction of Captain William Mills, the post commander. At first Mills received assistance from the civil authorities, but they soon began to dawdle; for this lack of enthusiasm Meade removed them, and Mills continued the investigation himself with the help of some private detectives hired through the War Department.[15]

By May, Mills had rounded up several suspects; but since they would not talk, they were sent to Fort Pulaski at Savannah, where they did reveal their knowledge. This fact immediately led to charges that the Army had used torture to get the information out of them. The Atlanta *Constitution* reported that "the dungeons of Fort Pulaski have reverberated with the half stifled groans and screams of victims tortured by a contrivance brought there for the purpose, in order 'to make them tell the truth' or, in other words, give such testimony as was desired by the prosecutors." The description of the "contrivance" came from a man who claimed to have overheard Meade explain its workings at an entertainment in the Atlanta home of a man who had helped the government with the case. Meade, he alleged, described it as a box large enough to hold the victim and fitted with compression screws so that the person could be crushed enough "to squeeze the breath out of him." An apparatus was connected to it by pipes so that jets of steam would add to the unpleasantness of suffocation. Meade sent an officer out to track down the article's author and his source of information; the result was the publication of a rather strange explanation. At the entertainment Meade had been talking to a lady and her little girl when he described the device; but, added the man who overheard him, "General Meade denies making such statements as actual facts, and as I have no intention to call his veracity in question, I am forced to conclude that what I took for serious statements of facts was mere badinage, playfully addressed to the little child with whom he was sporting at the time, and that I was thus misled in the premises." [16]

It was a remarkable story all round, and much conflicting testimony shrouded the details of what exactly happened at Fort Pulaski. Meade himself admitted that, in prosecuting the case, "arbitrary measures" were used "which in a different condition of society and under a well-ordered government might seem to deserve reprobation. . . ." But he thought the evidence would "fully convince any candid and impartial judge" that his

[15]File 293C1868, 3MD, RG98, NA; Meade's report of July, 1868, *Army and Navy Journal*, VI (Sept. 19, 1868), 70; Milledgeville (Ga.) *Federal Union*, Apr. 7, 1868.
[16]Atlanta *Constitution*, July 16, 1868; Macon (Ga.) *Daily Telegraph*, July 18.

course was the only possible one. The military commission began trying the case late in June, 1868; but the proceedings were never completed because the law declaring Georgia entitled to readmission, passed in July, had the effect of terminating the commission's jurisdiction. The Army turned the prisoners over to the civil officials, but no new trial took place.[17]

The Ashburn case, if badly handled in some respects, was an exceptional one, and Meade pointed with some satisfaction to the fact that during the eight months following his assumption of command only thirty-two people were tried by military commission in the three states combined. Of these only fifteen were convicted, and of the fifteen sentences, four were disapproved and eight others remitted.[18] Meade always sought to be fair. In March, 1868, some Alabama youths caught a disreputable fellow—"a pest of society, a perjured blasphemer, expelled from the pulpit for stealing money committed to his charge, an inhuman thief against whom it is in evidence that he stole the coffin of a dead Federal soldier"—stealing wood from land belonging to the father of one of the boys. The youths handled him roughly and ran him off the property but did not seriously hurt him. For this a military commission gave them two years hard labor at the Dry Tortugas, which because of conditions there was a very severe sentence. Meade approved the proceedings but shortly remitted the sentence.[19]

In discussing this affair one Alabama paper referred to an earlier case, under Pope, in which an Army officer had been given a much lighter sentence for a worse offense. A citizen had a disagreement with the officer, during which he called the Yankee a "paltroon [sic], liar, and puppy"—among other things. The officer had the man arrested, and while he was in military custody a further altercation broke out; the officer shot the man in the neck and he died three weeks later following a badly-performed operation which he had been advised not to have. Before the man died, a court-martial convicted the officer on the absurd charge of "conduct prejudicial to good order and military discipline" and sentenced him to be suspended from rank and command for six months, made him forfeit his pay for the same time, and had him reprimanded in general orders by the commanding general. Pope thought

---

[17]File 318D1868, 3MD, RG98, NA; *Report of the Sec. of War, 1867–68,* p. 79. The commission's proceedings appeared daily in the *Constitution* during the trial, and on July 29 that paper printed a statement from the prisoners concerning their treatment. They described some harsh measures, but not the steam cabinet.
[18]*Report of the Sec. of War, 1867–68,* p. 80.
[19]Montgomery (Ala.) *Daily Mail,* May 6, 1868; GO 72, 3MD, April 27, and GO 80, May 20, Orders, 598, RG94, NA.

this result wholly inadequate to the offense; and when the victim died, he ordered a new trial. This time the officer was convicted of manslaughter and assault with intent to kill, but he still received only a $300 fine and six months in jail.[20]

Comparison of the two cases afforded Southerners just grounds for complaint. One newspaper said it dared not publish what it really thought for fear of violating an order Meade had issued against incendiary articles—"The lips of our Alabama journals are pinned together by the bayonet, and our hands are fastened in iron cuffs." But the editors did venture an opinion: "Is this justice? Will the people of the North permit such oppression? Will they look calmly on and see military officers, in the name of law and liberty, violating both; and crushing down to the dust that feeling of nationality which has been struggling to rise, with all the weight of calumny, injustice and oppression which has been heaped upon its back? We tell the people of the North that such transactions as Alabama is witnessing at the hands of those who represent the Government would make a Hell of Heaven." The Alabama commander wanted the paper suppressed, but Meade did not think the article warranted that action.[21]

Meade had hoped to avoid serious trouble over the question of removals of high state officials, but no sooner had he arrived in his district than he came into conflict with Georgia's Governor Jenkins. The crisis arose over funds for the state convention: the treasurer would not appropriate the money without the governor's approval, and Jenkins would not approve. The only way Meade saw to break the deadlock was to oust both of them, which he did, replacing Jenkins with General Thomas H. Ruger and the treasurer with another Army officer. Johnson was "mortified and chagrined," but took no action.[22]

The same orders which sent Meade to Atlanta in place of Pope also changed the commander of the Fourth District. Johnson had apparently not been unhappy with Ord's administration of Arkansas and Mississippi, but for several months at the end of 1867 Ord had been urging Washington to relieve him. The reasons which impelled him were not fully clear; Grant thought he was by nature the kind of person who was never happy if he stayed too long in the same place. Writing to his friend

[20]Montgomery (Ala.) *Daily Mail*, May 6, 1868; GO 107, 3MD, Dec. 26, 1867, Orders, 598, RG94, NA; Pope to Townsend, Oct. 1, 1867, and to Grant, Nov 5, 3MD, 1, RG98, NA.
[21]Montgomery (Ala.) *Daily Mail*, May 6, 1868; file 330A1868, 3MD, RG98, NA; GO 51, April 4, Orders, 598, RG94, NA.
[22]GO 8, 3MD, Jan. 13, 1868, in *House Exec. Docs.*, 40th Cong., 2nd Sess., No. 342, p. 128; Beale (ed.), *Diary of Gideon Welles*, III, 256.

Sherman from San Francisco in 1870, Ord provided a bit of enlightenment. He said he had become convinced in 1867 that Stanton had partially succeeded in making Grant think he was "trying to run an independent concern" in his district. Whatever an "independent concern" might
have been, it was clear that Ord felt Stanton had exercised some pernicious influence against him.[23]

As happened to almost every Southern commander, both political parties found fault with Ord at one time or another, and conflicting charges
were regularly leveled at him. Radicals claimed he had appointed rebels
to his Mississippi registration boards and that he was not providing the
amount of direct aid necessary to establish a Republican party there; in
Arkansas it was supposed he had been giving guidance to members of
the Union League. Without trying to defend Ord, one editor offered the
moderate evaluation that he "does not think it becomes him to play the
tyrant, because he is 'invested with a little brief authority,' but remem-
bers that the time will soon come when public opinion will call him to
strict accountability, unless the country, under the misrule of malignan-
cy, goes with railroad speed to the devil." [24]

Grant's recommendation was that General Irvin McDowell, then at
San Francisco, trade places with Ord. Johnson assented after getting an
evasive reply to his question of whether McDowell could not replace
Pope just as easily as Ord, thus leaving the latter at Vicksburg.[25] Ord
departed the South in January, 1868; but McDowell did not arrive to
assume command until June, and General Alvan C. Gillem, Ord's chief
subordinate in Mississippi, served as the interim district commander.
The order had no sooner gone out than the Southern press began speculating about the motives behind the choice of McDowell. The most
interesting analysis was that Johnson was trying to hamper Grant's
chances of getting the 1868 presidential nomination by making a diver-
sion in favor of Salmon Chase—this interpretation based on McDowell's
supposed personal and political intimacy with the Chief Justice.[26] It
seems clear, though, that whatever brilliant stroke Johnson might have
thought he was delivering in the appointment of McDowell, the new
commander was originally Grant's own choice.

[23]GO 104, AGO, Dec. 28, 1867, RG94, NA; Beale (ed.), *Diary of Gideon
Welles,* III, 245, 249; Ord to Sherman, June 17, 1870, in Sherman Papers, LC.
[24]Galveston *Daily News,* June 12, 1867; *North Arkansas Times,* Jan. 18, 1868
and July 20, 1867 (quoting the Memphis *Appeal*). James W. Garner, *Reconstruction in Mississippi* (New York, 1901), 181–82, paints Ord as severe and more on
the pro-Radical side. For additional evidence on Ord's political views see Thomas
and Hyman, *Stanton,* 558.
[25]Beale (ed.), *Diary of Gideon Welles,* III, 245, 249.
[26]Milledgeville (Ga.) *Federal Union,* Jan. 14, 1868.

The Fifth District command by all odds caused more difficulty than any other; and only three months after the departure of Pope and Ord, General Hancock, himself just recently appointed to New Orleans, was gone as well. The appearance in late November, 1867, of his first general order, the celebrated No. 40, had evoked much comment. It had "the trumpet tone of the Declaration of Independence and of Jackson's celebrated proclamations," extolled one editor. A Washington correspondent reported, "The President's delight at the tone and spirit of General Orders, No. 40, can find no expression in words." [27] Johnson may have been at a loss for words but the Radicals were not. Senator Oliver P. Morton of Indiana blasted it in a public speech and predicted that if Hancock had changed sides and now supported the philosophy against which he fought, "his laurels would wither like the tender flowers beneath the simoon of the desert." Some newspaper correspondents also came to believe that Hancock was fully committed to Johnson's view of reconstruction, but said so in less complimentary phrases: "Hancock has gone over to Johnson body and brains, the former [being] the better part of him. He is a good looking man, with a large endowment of small vanities and enough ambition to make him generally discontented with himself." [28]

Congressional displeasure with Hancock found expression in actions as well as words. No sooner had No. 40 appeared than Johnson sent it to Congress in a special message urging that Hancock be commended for issuing it. But the reaction was not quite what Johnson had in mind. Senator John M. Thayer introduced a bill to reduce the number of major-generals by eliminating the junior one; that was Hancock. It was a crude, boorish insult to an officer whose war record was good and whose popularity was considerable, but it was hardly remarkable in view of the low level to which partisan politics had sunk by that time. Thayer did not press the bill, perhaps because it was meant only as a psychological weapon, or perhaps because it might have backfired and created an adverse effect on public opinion. [29]

Congress may have thought Hancock's first order and subsequent course in the Fifth District were in blatant defiance of its desires as expressed in the Reconstruction Acts, but that hardly makes them so.

[27]Galveston *Daily News,* Dec. 3, 1867. The reference to Jackson's proclamations is not clear. It could mean his 1832 nullification edits, or, since New Orleans was involved, the ones he issued there in 1815.

[28]Huntsville (Ala.) *Advocate,* Jan. 3, 1868 and April 7 (quoting the Cleveland *Leader,* a Radical sheet.)

[29]*Cong. Globe,* 40th Cong., 2nd Sess., 491. The bill also required the muster-out of the junior brigadier general, who was Rousseau. While this provision may have been deliberate too, the chief target was clearly Hancock.

Everything Hancock did was well within the discretionary authority left to him by the laws, and in interpreting them for himself he was doing what the third one said he ought to do. Hancock's glowing statements about principles of liberty in No. 40 made that order seem to stand apart from some that other generals had issued, but there was not really a great deal of difference. Even the Third Reconstruction Act, which clearly made the Army paramount, had not legislated the civil governments out of existence. To have done so would have been the sheerest folly, for it would have thrown the entire burden of civil administration on the Army. The generals could still decide for themselves how much use to make of the civil institutions. Their policy, subject always to individual variances from one general to the next, was usually to allow the civil functionaries to carry out their ordinary duties with military support in cases of resistance and military supersedure in cases of malfeasance or injustice. This was essentially what Hancock's inaugural order had said he too would do.

Registration lists had to be revised before the elections to ratify the new constitutions, and Hancock used this opportunity to annul Sheridan's instructions to the registrars, under which many persons were disfranchised. Hancock said that he did not subscribe to the interpretation of the law which Sheridan had given in the earlier rules, that they were no longer mandatory, and that the registrars were their own interpreters of the law.[30] If they were their own interpreters of the law, then they were their own judges of who could and who could not vote, which was precisely what the July law had said.

The problem of removals had gotten Sheridan in trouble, and the same problem led to the relief of Hancock. In ordering Hancock to New Orleans and Canby to Charleston, Johnson had told them to exercise freely all the powers conferred on them by law. Shortly thereafter Grant sent out some directions of his own. He told the commanders not to appoint anyone to civil office who had been removed by themselves or their predecessors. This order cut into the discretion ordinarily accorded to officers at such high levels of command, but the July law had given Grant the same authority in cases of removals that the district commanders had, and he was quite within his rights. The *Army and Navy Journal* regarded Grant's order as a counterweight to Johnson's instructions and as a precaution against Hancock's reinstating people Sheridan had ousted.[31] It is hard to see any other interpretation. Shortly after

[30]GO 3, 5MD, Jan. 11, 1868, in *House Exec. Docs.*, 40th Cong., 2nd Sess., No. 342, pp. 185–87.
[31]SO 429, AGO, Aug. 29, 1867, RG94, NA; *Army and Navy Journal*, V (Sept. 7, 1867), 37.

Hancock arrived in New Orleans he began reinstating some of the people Mower had removed because he felt no evidence had been presented to support the charges made. He made it clear, however, that the cases would be reconsidered if substantiable charges were presented.[32] Whether this action violated Grant's order is debatable since Hancock felt the removals had been unwarranted in the first place. Grant in any case did not feel it was a violation and did not order Hancock to reverse his action.

The real crisis came in January of 1868, just when the Senate's consideration of Stanton's suspension was causing a commotion in Washington. The New Orleans aldermen desired to hold an election for recorder in one of the city wards. Hancock called the attention of the mayor to the Reconstruction Acts and to an order Sheridan had issued a year previously prohibiting local elections until the provisions of the Reconstruction Acts were complied with. The aldermen decided to go ahead with the election, and Hancock removed those who thus voted to defy him. After a lengthy exchange of letters and telegrams Grant ordered Hancock to reinstate the aldermen, which he did. Because the legal status of the office of recorder was in considerable doubt, it is hard to determine whether Hancock or Grant was more in the right. Hancock thought the aldermen had no authority under Louisiana law to order the election; Grant disagreed. Hancock believed the action of Mower in ousting the city council of Jefferson for a similar offense, which action Grant had upheld, was a parallel case; Grant insisted it was not. Whatever the case, Grant's position was certainly a foolish one because it amounted to his telling Hancock to ignore an order Sheridan had issued, in spite of his own directive, when Hancock assumed the command, to continue Sheridan's orders in effect. The New Orleans aldermen's case was not the only one in which Grant overruled Hancock. Hancock removed the New Orleans street commissioner after an investigation had disclosed evidence of fraud and corruption, but Grant ordered a reinstatement.[33]

Without doubt Grant had the power to take the steps he did; the real question was the advisability of his doing so. It certainly embarrassed Hancock before the eyes of the people he had been sent to govern. The fact that Hancock was on the Democratic side of the political ledger naturally led to the belief that Grant was acting from a purely partisan standpoint, whether at the instigation of others or on his own initiative. Hancock himself felt that the interference from Washington was purposeful and wrote a friend, "I hope to be relieved here soon. The Presi-

[32]SO 200, 5MD, Dec. 2, 1867, in *House Exec. Docs.,* 40th Cong., 2nd Sess., No. 342, p. 179; SO 202, Dec. 4, *ibid.,* 180; SO 214, Dec. 19, *ibid.,* 184.
[33]Orders and correspondence in *Report of the Sec. of War, 1867–68,* pp. 222–34.

dent is no longer able to protect me. So that I may expect one humiliation after another, until I am forced to resign." [34] He applied for relief at the end of February, and in March Johnson sent him to the newly re-created Atlantic Division. The most frequent charge against Hancock was that his leniency, as foreshadowed in General Orders No. 40, greatly increased lawlessness and violence, the clear implication being that Sheridan would have been more vigorous in keeping desperadoes in line.[35] But if Hancock's alleged leniency emboldened criminals—and that assertion would be difficult to prove—Grant's action in reversing Hancock when he did use his authority likely had the same effect.

The winter of 1867–68 was a winter of discontent in Washington as well as in the South. Grant had spent the autumn and early winter in the War Office, while congressmen spent the time considering what they would do about Stanton's suspension and what punishment they would visit upon Johnson when they returned to Washington. After Congress met, the President in accordance with the Tenure of Office Act submitted a written report explaining why he had suspended Stanton. On January 11, a Saturday, before the Senate had acted, Grant told Johnson he would return the War Department to the President's control if the Senate refused to concur in Stanton's suspension and if he felt unwilling to resist the Senate. On Monday the thirteenth the Senate refused to concur and sent official notification of that fact to Johnson. That night Grant also learned of the Senate's action and early on the fourteenth he went to the War Department, locked the door, gave the key to General Townsend (the Assistant Adjutant General), went back to his own office, and wrote Johnson a note to the effect that the Senate's action had terminated his functions as Secretary ad-interim. Grant thus set the stage for Stanton's repossession of the War Office, and the latter promptly took over. Johnson was indignant at Grant's action, called him to a Cabinet meeting that same day, and forced him to admit, in spite of the general's somewhat unskillful dodging, that he had violated their "understanding" of Saturday.[36]

On the morning of the fifteenth Grant called on Johnson, this time

---

[34]Quoted in *The Civil Record of Major General Winfield S. Hancock During His Administration in Louisiana and Texas,* 30, a campaign pamphlet apparently published before the 1880 presidential nominating convention.

[35]Gov. E. M. Pease to Hancock, Jan. 17, 1868, *Report of the Sec. of War, 1867–68,* pp. 268–71.

[36]The two best chronologies of events during January and February are found in "Moore's Notes," 114–22, and Beale (ed.), *Diary of Gideon Welles,* III, 252–99. See also Thomas and Hyman, *Stanton,* 567–71.

in company with Sherman. As the two officers left, Grant turned and suggested that Johnson should issue an order "that we of the army are not bound to obey the orders of Mr. Stanton as Secretary of War." Johnson said he might do that.[37] The scene was a remarkable sequel to Grant's actions of the previous day and must indicate some regret over his haste in yielding the office to Stanton. On the nineteenth Johnson gave the suggested order to Grant verbally; on the twenty-fourth Grant requested that the order be put in writing. Four days later Grant repeated the request, and Johnson sent back written instructions not to obey any order from Stanton unless Grant knew the order had presidential approval. Considering that Grant had asked for these instructions in the first place, his reply to Johnson was rather strange: since Stanton had received no presidential order limiting his authority, Grant would assume that all of Stanton's orders had presidential sanction.[38]

On the night of the fifteenth Sherman, temporarily absent from his regular post at St. Louis, wrote despondently to his wife, "The whole matter is resolved into a war between parties and neither cares nor seems to care a damn for the service or the country. . . . I want to get out of this political maelstrom. Having no aspirations myself, I am made the depository of the secrets and plans of all, and unless I get away I may be embroiled between the factions. . . ." [39] Sherman was trying valiantly to "get away," but he was not having very much success. Though Johnson continually sought his aid, Sherman turned down the ad-interim Secretaryship, the command of a renewed Military Division of the Atlantic (which finally went to Hancock), and the brevet rank of General.[40] He would gladly have seen Stanton out of the War Office for good except that his dislike of politics restrained him from taking a more active role.

For all his unwillingness to play on Johnson's team, Sherman was able to maintain personal cordiality with him during that stormy January, but the President's relations with Grant soon broke down. On January 28

[37]William T. Sherman, *Memoirs of General William T. Sherman* (New York, 2nd ed., 1887), II, 423. This is not likely a case of Sherman's memory failing him after twenty years because Washington papers reported the substance of the conversation within days after it occurred. See Washington *Evening Star*, Jan. 23, 1868.
[38]Grant-Johnson exchange, Jan. 24–30, 1868, in *Messages and Papers*, VI, 613–15. Thomas and Hyman, *Stanton*, 573, give an erroneous impression of this exchange. They do not mention that Grant suggested the order to begin with, and thus it appears that Johnson was purposefully making Grant and the Army choose between insubordination to the President or to Stanton.
[39]Howe (ed.), *Home Letters*, 366.
[40]Sherman, *Memoirs*, II, 420–34.

Grant wrote the President, objecting to "the many and gross misrepresentations, affecting my personal honor, circulated through the press for the last fortnight, purporting to come from the President, of conversations which occurred either with the President privately in his office, or in cabinet meeting. What is written admits of no misunderstanding." By making Grant confess in the presence of the Cabinet that he had violated their "understanding," Johnson had Grant cornered in an ethically uncomfortable position. Grant's letter was almost a challenge, and it is hardly surprising that the President should seize the apparent opportunity to bring the popular general down another notch or two. For the next several days letters went back and forth between the White House and Army Headquarters.[41]

On paper the President had the better of the contest because his position was stronger and his evidence better. But on the public's scoreboard, Grant was successfully able to make himself appear the victim of a deliberate character assassination. All he had to do was deny Johnson's version, and public opinion, already on his side, would do the rest. When the letters became public, as they immediately did, Grant's popularity rose higher and Johnson's plummeted to the greatest depths yet. Politically the episode placed Grant more solidly on the Radical team and affected the chances of both protagonists for the 1868 presidential nominations. Grant became more appealing to the Republicans and Johnson even less so to the Democrats.[42]

With Grant now fully alienated, Johnson was still looking for someone to supplant Stanton. The President was now convinced the best

[41]The full exchange is printed as *House Exec. Docs.*, 40th Cong. 2nd Sess., No. 149.

[42]The Johnson-Grant quarrel presents difficult problems in the analysis of evidence. The dispute centered around the two men's conversation of January 11, to which there were no witnesses, and the Cabinet meeting of January 14, where the witnesses favored Johnson. Consequently Grant's version rests solely upon his own word, but this has not deterred some historians from accepting his story completely; see Thomas and Hyman, *Stanton*, 567–70, and William B. Hesseltine, *Ulysses S. Grant, Politician* (New York, 1935), 103–11. As to the newspaper accounts, they were naturally inspired by the White House, but there is no certain way of knowing the extent to which the editors may have embellished whatever Johnson may actually have told them. Historians have usually assumed that because Johnson was hoping for the presidential nomination and did not want to have to face Grant, the President's motives for defaming Grant were stronger than Grant's motives for making himself appear a martyr. But without denying that Johnson wanted another term, it would seem to be an equally reasonable assumption that if Grant were seeking the presidency in 1868 the pose of a martyr would be very helpful to him. Grant may indeed have sincerely felt his honor impugned, as the standard version holds, but this need not have precluded his determining to turn the affair to his own political gain.

procedure would be to use Stanton's certain refusal to yield as a means of having the Tenure of Office Act ruled on by the Supreme Court. After toying with several possible replacements, varying from the chief clerk of the War Department to General George B. McClellan, he finally settled on the most unimaginable choice of all—sixty-three-year-old Adjutant General Lorenzo Thomas. Had Thomas been a vigorous and sharp-witted individual Johnson's play might have worked. On February 21 Johnson signed the order removing Stanton and appointing Thomas; the white-haired general went to the War Office and demanded that Stanton yield. The Secretary said he would think about it. That night Thomas went off to a masquerade ball where he boasted that come the morrow he would return, batter the door down if necessary, and evict the trespasser. The morrow came, and with it an officer sent by Stanton to arrest Thomas. The general finally got himself released, but by the time he arrived at the War Department his ardor for door-battering had entirely disappeared. After Thomas directed some portentous threats at Stanton, the smooth-talking Secretary lulled the general into submission with sympathy and the offer of some whiskey to make up for the breakfast Thomas' arrest had caused him to miss.[43]

Johnson was foiled again, but his appointment of Thomas gave the House the opportunity to do precisely what it had wanted to do for a good while—impeach him. The vote came on February 24, and from then until the end of May, when the trial concluded, the country barely endured the turmoil. Newspapers had a field day manufacturing ominous headlines out of rumors: "WAR! WAR!! WAR!!! — THE PRESIDENT IM-PEACHED! — THE FIRST GUN FIRED! — THREE WOMEN MURDERED! — THIRTEEN KILLED! — THIRTY-SEVEN WOUNDED! — ANDREW JOHNSON A PRISONER! — GENERAL THOMAS KILLED! — STANTON'S LEG BROKEN! — WAR DEPARTMENT BURNED! — SHERMAN WITH THE PRESIDENT! — GRANT DECLARES HIMSELF DICTATOR! — SECRETARY SEWARD RE-SIGNS! — GENERAL WAR INEVITABLE!" [44] There was much wild specula-tion that Johnson would use military force against Congress during the trial; but Johnson had no such intention, and even if he had, he would have been hard pressed to find cooperative officers. His transfer of Hancock from Louisiana to the Atlantic Division in March was in part meant to

---

[43]E. D. Townsend, *Anecdotes of the Civil War in the United States* (New York, 1884), 124–36, is an eye-witness account of some of these scenes. See also "Moore's Notes," 119–21, and Thomas and Hyman, *Stanton,* 581–91.

[44]Extra edition of the Houston *Telegraph,* Feb. 25, 1868, quoted by W. A. Russ, "Was There Danger of a Second Civil War During Reconstruction?" *Missis-sippi Valley Historical Review,* XXV (June, 1938), 39–58.

have an influence on the trial, but it is hard to imagine Hancock as a party to a coup d'etat.[45]

In the hope that the Senate would convict Johnson and oust him from the Executive Mansion, Stanton clung to the War Department during the trial. That was unfortunate, for his administrative talents were not in evidence during the trial and he caused the Army some financial embarrassment. While Washington was reeling with political tumult the Southern states were making progress in reconstructing themselves and were in the midst of elections to ratify the new state constitutions. These elections cost money; and in May, during the heat of the trial, Meade found himself running short of funds to administer civil affairs in his district. A supplementary appropriations bill had been introduced, but nobody could think about much besides the trial and the bill could make little headway. Meade therefore sent his paymaster, Major Edwin Judd, to Washington to see important legislators and in general to lobby on the bill's behalf. Judd performed his role well and sent back to Atlanta a stream of messages describing affairs. He often saw General Benjamin Brice, the Paymaster General, who told him that Stanton had not signed any requisitions for the last two weeks in spite of all Brice's urging. The result was that the financial affairs of the department fell behind, and Brice's supply of available funds steadily diminished. It was rumored that Stanton was merely waiting for the end of the trial when he would resign, and that was precisely what occurred.[46] After the Senate failed to convict the President, Stanton resigned and Johnson brought General Schofield from Richmond to fill the post.

While the country fixed its attention on the impeachment proceedings, Southerners held elections on their new state constitutions. The Army set

[45]*Ibid.*, 49–55; Gaillard Hunt, "The President's Defense," *Century Magazine,* LXXXV (January, 1913), 422–34; "Moore's Notes," 128. In their discussion of the War Office crisis, Thomas and Hyman, *Stanton,* 577, refer to a "law" which they state "put into Grant's hands all the executive authority [over the Army in the South] that the reconstruction acts had heretofore entrusted to the White House." They give no clear date for the "law" but apparently consider that it was passed around February, 1868, and they state that it was vetoed by Johnson and repassed. There is no such veto message in *Messages and Papers,* VI; there is no such law in U.S. Statutes at Large; nor has any evidence been found in the *Cong. Globe* that such a "law" was formally proposed. It would therefore seem that this "law", the passage of which would support the Thomas-Hyman thesis that Congress stripped Johnson of his control over the Army in the South and made the Army a legislative agency, was at best a contemplated measure of which nothing ever came.

[46]Judd to Meade, May 4–14, 1868, files 87J1868 and 96–98J1868, 3MD, RG98, NA.

the ground rules for these contests, as it had for the 1867 ones, and maintained order where necessary. The troops, ordinarily concentrated at a few key posts in each state, were fragmented into small detachments and widely dispersed during the elections. These detachments were under strict orders to give no appearance of being present to "overawe" the voters; in Louisiana troops were kept away from the polls and in their quarters but ready to move at any hour of the day or night. There were complaints of misconduct nevertheless. The chief registrar and superintendent of election at the little central Georgia town of Perry, a totally illiterate Negro, had a friend write to ask for a new detachment of troops "who have not been tampered with by those opposed to the Government." He claimed he could not rely on the detachment already there because the sergeant in charge was too drunk to look after his men, who were actively electioneering. The post commander at Macon sent a lieutenant out to take command, which apparently halted the troubles, but nobody seemed concerned that the superintendent of election could neither read nor write. From Thomaston, not far away, came a letter from a Negro candidate for the state legislature who claimed the guards there were all Democrats. He said that when he heard a man misrepresenting the constitution to a Negro, he attempted to present the opposite view but that a corporal had made him stop. When he asked the corporal to make the white men stop haranguing the Negroes, the corporal had refused. Then after the election, when it was announced the constitution had been defeated in that county, a "jollification" was held at the corner store during which the corporal sat on the counter praising the Democrats and damning the Radicals. The Army was always careful to investigate such charges, and in this case most of them were found to be without foundation.[47] The fact that political complaints were investigated, and the fact that partisans of one side were so concerned that the soldiers might be partisans of the other, would seem to be additional evidence of the moral and psychological impact which the blue and gold uniform possessed.

General Pope in his first order on registration in 1867 had directed the officials to instruct voters in their political rights. Unfortunately some of them made better partisan zealots than political science teachers, and this caused Meade some trouble during the spring elections of 1868. When he dismissed one registration clerk for making political speeches, the victim pleaded, "During the administration of General Pope I

[47]AAAG to Capt. N. B. McLaughlin and to CO New Orleans, Apr. 16, 1868, Dept. Gulf, 274; files 77C1868, Dist. Ga., and 214G1868, 3MD, RG98. NA.

made reconstruction speeches with his knowledge and consent and in my effort last evening supposed that the defense of the reconstruction policy would meet the approval of Head Quarters." Meade reinstated him but only after making him promise to keep quiet in the future. The commanding general dismissed the superintendent of registration for Georgia and replaced him with an Army officer when it was discovered the incumbent was writing "personal" letters on politics to his official subordinates. Meade would not entertain the man's plea that his official and private actions were separable. "Old Snapping Turtle" was also sensitive to charges that he himself was favoring one party or the other and took offense when Foster Blodgett, a leading Radical organizer in Georgia, wrote to his party colleagues in Washington that the Democrats were putting great pressure on Meade to arrange things in their favor. The general demanded an explanation, and heard in reply that Blodgett got the information by eavesdropping on a conversation during a train ride to Augusta. Not unlikely, Blodgett had written to Washington in hopes that Meade could be influenced to stack the cards in the Radicals' favor.[48]

The Army was particularly sensitive to any charges of political skulduggery emanating from Alabama because that state's constitution had been rejected. In sending Meade a report on affairs, General Julius Hayden attributed the numerous complaints to the fact that "these Head Quarters ceased to be a political Club House on the 15th day of last January, and the officer in temporary command of the Sub District, did not feel it right or proper that he should become the 'whipper in' of a political party, or permit the Registration and appointments to be managed by those who had hertofore [sic] controlled the affair." The worst case of political meddling by an officer in Alabama was that of Captain J. B. Callis of the 45th Infantry, formerly a bureau agent in the Huntsville area. He became "demoralized by the scramble for office" and without resigning his commission had his name put on the list of registered voters. Then he undertook to get himself nominated for Congress, proclaiming in glowing words what he would do if elected—"I care not whether a man come from the icy North, or be bronzed by a torrid sun, so he be a man, I shall earnestly labor for his rights as a man." But the party chose another, and Callis was outraged. He used his influence with the Negroes to alienate them from the white Unionists, telling them that if they voted for the man who beat him for the nomination 10,000 Dutch

[48]Files A2917, BCA, 3MD, and 250D1868, 3MD; AAG to Blodgett, March 2, 1868, 3MD, 2, and file 79B1868, 3MD, RG98, NA.

and Irish immigrants would come in to take their jobs. Meade took the only possible action—he ordered Callis to report in arrest to his regimental commander at Nashville.[49]

In some states the reconstructionists had very narrow electoral escapes. Congress had provided that a majority of the registered voters had to affirm the new constitutions to make them effective. In Alabama the white conservatives used this provision to frustrate the Radicals by urging those opposed to the constitution to stay home and not vote at all. This strategem was successful, for only some 6,000 whites voted, and although the constitution received an affirmative majority of the votes cast, the figure did not constitute a majority of the registered voters. Consequently, by the rules set forth by Congress the Alabama document was defeated. Meade reported in March that the constitution had been lost "on its merits" and that while there were doubtless some irregularities, most charges of fraud would prove "illusory." [50] But the Radicals, who two years earlier had been anxious to keep the Southern states out of the Union, were now anxious to restore them to the fold in order that Southern Republican votes could help win the 1868 presidential election. So they ignored both their own rules and Meade's report and decided to accept the Alabama document. During the crisis, in order to eliminate such problems in the future, they also passed a Fourth Reconstruction Act providing that a majority of the votes cast was sufficient to ratify a constitution. This law had passed the House in December, 1867, and was debated and finally passed by the Senate between the date of the Alabama election and Meade's report of the result. During the debate Senator Roscoe Conkling cited the uncertain Alabama situation as a reason for passing the bill, and some congressmen may have based affirmative votes on the final decision to admit Alabama upon the belief that this Fourth Reconstruction Act was retroactive. Others probably relied on the provision of the Second Reconstruction Act stating that Congress should be "satisfied" that the constitution met the approval of a majority of the qualified voters of the state.[51]

In Arkansas the constitution was saved only by the action of General Gillem. The margin in favor of the constitution was merely 1,316, and

---

[49]Hayden to Meade, March 18, 1868, file 219A1868, 3MD; AAG to AAG Dept. Cumberland, Feb. 5, 1868, 3MD, 2, and files 14W1868 and 103B1868, 3MD, RG98, NA.

[50]Meade to Grant, March 9 and 12, 1868, *Report of the Sec. of War, 1867–68*, pp. 97–98.

[51]*Cong. Globe*, 40th Cong., 2nd Sess., 266, 1313, 2057–58; 15 U.S. Statutes at Large 41. On the whole question of the election and readmission see Fleming, *Alabama*, 538–52.

in Pulaski County the total vote exceeded the registration by 1,195. Clearly something was amiss, but because the election officials had been inefficient in keeping records it was not possible to determine exactly how many of the votes cast were fraudulent. There were several possible courses for Gillem to follow. He could annul the election all over the state, he could simply void the election in Pulaski County, or he could declare the constitution ratified anyhow and leave the next step to Congress. The first one would have required another election, with renewed political turbulence and delay in readmittance of the state. Because Pulaski voted overwhelmingly in favor of the constitution, the second would have so altered the total returns that the constitution would have been lost. So Gillem took the third course.[52] Congress accepted the constitution, fraud and all, and in June, 1868, declared Arkansas entitled to representation, along with Georgia, Louisiana, Florida, Alabama, and the Carolinas, in all of which the process of ratification had been completed. No election had yet been held in Texas or Virginia, and in Mississippi the constitution had been so thoroughly overwhelmed that even the Radicals could not think of a plausible justification for accepting it.

Upon the readmission of these states the Army lost the special authority over them given by the Reconstruction Acts. The legislatures and governors chosen at the recent elections took office, and although the commanding generals proclaimed a curtailment of military power, the troops located in the seven states were concentrated at a few posts rather than being withdrawn entirely. Canby merely proclaimed his power was "remitted to the civil authorities"; Meade told his troops to "abstain in the future, upon any pretext whatever," from interference in civil affairs.[53] But General Robert C. Buchanan, commanding the Fifth District after Hancock's departure, felt like congratulating Louisianans on having delivered themselves from his rule. "Peace and quiet marked the late election, showing the softening influences of mutual forbearance. Should such forbearance animate the councils of the State, the era of kind feeling will return, and the highest prosperity of the people will be attained. That this may be the result under the guidance of a merciful Providence, is his [Buchanan's] devout and earnest prayer. May her restoration to the benefits of our beloved Union mark the commencement of a new era of prosperity and happiness for her people."[54] Louisiana was to need

[52]*Report of the Sec. of War, 1867–68*, pp. 531–36.
[53]GO 145, 2MD, July 24, 1868, Orders, 595; GO 101, 3MD, July 14, Orders, 598, RG94, NA.
[54]SO 154, 5MD, July 13, 1868, Orders, 606, RG94, NA.

the guidance of a merciful Providence, for it experienced fully as much tumult in the 1870's as in the 1860's.

The readmission of these states occasioned a reorganization of Southern commands. The Second and Third Military Districts were combined as the Department of the South under Meade. Virginia's military status remained the same except that, Schofield having been called to Washington to take the War portfolio, the Richmond command fell to General George Stoneman, whose first experience with such problems had been in Tennessee in 1866. Mississippi was left by itself as the Fourth District under Gillem. Reynolds as the Fifth District commander now had only Texas to worry about—which was ample—Arkansas and its southern neighbor having been joined together as the Department of Louisiana under Johnson's friend, General Lovell H. Rousseau.[55] The Union had been partially restored—but there was still more to do.

[55]GO 55, AGO, July 28, 1868, RG94, NA.

The Three Laggards—and Georgia in Limbo

C ONGRESS had been anxious to get the Southern states readmitted because of the forthcoming Presidential election; and that event was uppermost in many minds, North and South, during the last half of 1868. Of the military men who were prominent as possible candidates of both parties, the front-runners were Hancock for the Democrats and Grant for the Republicans. Hancock was an attractive figure to any party because of his war record and especially to the Democrats because of his troubles in the Fifth District. Some Southerners hoped he would be nominated. One Arkansas editor thought Hancock would prove an exception to the general (if doubtful) rule that military men do not make good presidents. Calling him the best friend the South had had since the war ended, he offered Hancock as a man behind whom "peace Demoncrats" and moderate Republicans could rally and unite. In comparing the "massive logic and eminent statesmanship" Hancock had shown in a letter to the Texas governor with the "puerile productions" of Grant, another editor advised the Democrats to go with Hancock, "None would be more acceptable to the white men of the South." He was not acceptable to everyone, however, and the cheering first of Jeff Davis and then of Hancock by a processing of New Orleans firemen elicited this expression of scorn: "Tastes differ, but few men who won distinction in the Union army would consider themselves honored in sharing the appaluse or a multititude with the man who was responsible for the horrors of Libby and Andersonville." [1] Hancock may have wanted the

[1] Batesville *North Arkansas Times,* May 30, 1868; Milledgeville (Ga.) *Federal Union,* April 21, 1868; Meridan (Miss.) *Chronicle,* March 13, 1868.

Democratic nomination, yet when friends urged him before he left New Orleans to put himself forward, he would take no action himself; thus everything in his behalf had to be done by others. He was a leading contender at the Democratic convention, but after he reached his highest total of 144½ votes on the eighteenth ballot, some parliamentary maneuvering turned the tide in favor of Horatio Seymour. Hancock was annoyed and did not actively support the campaign.[2]

Grant was the most popular man in the country, and he was easily the most sensible choice for the Republicans, especially after his break with Johnson. For some time there had been doubt of Grant's willingness to run. In September of 1867 Sherman, his closest Army friend, doubted that Grant, "or any real military man," for that matter, wanted to be President. "All see that, however pure or exalted their past reputations may have been, it don't shield them from the lies and aspersions of a besotted press. . . . Grant writes me in the most unreserved confidence, and never has said a word that looks like wanting the office of President." [3] As time went on Grant's willingness became more apparent. But his abilities were another question. One Mississippi editor was certain that "with such a standard-bearer as this the foes of the nation will be routed and driven to the wall." An Alabaman's prose was even more elegant: "To-day he stands calm and serene, a rock amid the political ocean, a beacon to the whole land, giving assurance of hope, confidence and safety." [4]

Others were not so sure. Grant was habitually reticent in public, which led some people to doubt his political views and ability. One Southerner was able to arrive at an explanation, however: "It seems that letter writers and radical pimps are unable to get any expression of public policy from General Grant. They are hardly rewarded by even a grunt. Certainly not by a significant grunt. Perhaps they go unrewarded, for the same reason that the fellow could not get any whiskey out of the bottle. It was empty! and besides, had never contained any. They are pumping at a dry well. They ought to desist." Grant's sojourn in the Cabinet brought him under the cold, Puritanical surveillance of New Englander Gideon Welles, who was more successful at getting "expres-

---

[2]Hancock, *Reminiscences,* 135; Charles H. Coleman, *The Election of 1868* (New York, 1933), 207, 382.

[3]Sherman to John Sherman, Sept. 12, 1867, in Thorndike (ed.), *Sherman Letters,* 295.

[4]Meridian (Miss.) *Chronicle,* March 10, 1868; Huntsville (Ala.) *Advocate,* March 20, 1868.

sions of public policy" out of him. The Navy Minister was somewhat astonished at the things Grant would say, however, and after deciding that the general was less intelligent and more devious than he had previously supposed, concluded, "He is a political ignoramus." [5]

Nevertheless Grant was the choice of the Republican convention in May and of the country in November and was inaugurated President on March 4, 1869. Several changes in Army commands resulted. Sherman, of course, became General-in-Chief, replacing Grant; and Sheridan became Lieutenant General, replacing Sherman. Sheridan's promotion was pure favoritism on the part of Grant and caused some dissension, for Halleck and Meade outranked him. Even more dissension, though in other quarters, stemmed from Grant's desire to send Sheridan back to New Orleans in command of the department embracing Louisiana and Arkansas. He so ordered on the day after his inauguration, but shortly decided to revoke the action and instead sent Sheridan to Sherman's old post on the Plains, which was more appropriate to his new rank. Louisiana had been bothering Grant since the first of the year. General Rousseau had died just after New Year's—"He had been imprudent in the amount he ate during the holidays," according to Horace Porter, one of Grant's aides, who was touring the area at the time. Porter continued, "Now is the time to send some good man to command this department. Buchanan will *not do* to leave here a month. Reynolds would be immensely better. His heart is in the right place, but his best friends in Texas think he is possessed of very little administrative ability." [6] In the "new deal" following the inauguration, Louisiana and Arkansas went to General Mower, who had temporarily commanded at New Orleans after Sheridan's relief in 1867. Mississippi, the remnant of the old Fourth District, went to General Adelbert Ames, replacing Gillem. Texas, the remnant of the Fifth, went (Porter's report notwithstanding) to Reynolds, whose tenure there had been temporarily interrupted by the assignment of Canby for a few months late in 1868. The Department of the South, comprising the entire array of seaboard states from North Carolina to Alabama, received Terry in place of Meade. The Fifth District was for some reason left by itself as an independent command, while the Fourth and the Department of the South were grouped together under Halleck as the Division of the South. Virginia continued to be

[5]Eufaula (Ala.) *News,* Dec. 24, 1867; Beale (ed.), *Diary of Gideon Welles,* III, 176–81.

[6]Porter to Grant, Jan. 8, 1869, in Porter Papers, LC. This copy is a typescript in which the comment on Buchanan and the adverse opinion of Reynolds are pencilled out. The original does not appear.

the First District, under Canby in place of Stoneman, and became part of the Division of the Atlantic.[7]

For the two additional years that the Reconstruction Acts remained in force in part of Secessia, the Army continued to enforce policy much as it had during 1867–68. Scouring the countryside for lawbreakers took up much of its time and energy, and this proved an especially arduous duty for the Texas troops. The fact that Texas was still basically a frontier state, with a defense perimeter extending some 1,300 miles, increased the tendency toward crime and violence and made things doubly difficult for the Army. The northeastern corner of the state was particularly turbulent, and in June, 1868, Reynolds asked for an additional regiment of infantry to be concentrated at Marshall for further orders.[8] Cavalry would have been far better because the desperadoes were all well-mounted and organized, and transportation facilities were not the best. But the frontier posts had priority on the cavalry, and so the interior had to be content with a preponderance of infantry.

In apprehending criminals the standard practice, as it had been before, was to send out small details to accompany sheriffs and marshals in making arrests or to have the Army act on its own where the civil authorities were unable or reluctant to do so. In some instances, however, it was necessary to establish small temporary posts or camps in troubled locations. In August a county judge complained about the notorious Bickerstaff gang, operating in the country around Sulphur Springs, and cited one instance in which they whipped a Negro and allowed him to escape to the nearest Army post so that when troops came after them they could set an ambush. Reynolds detached a captain with his company of the 6th Cavalry from Fort Griffin and sent him to Fort Richardson to pick up some reinforcements. From there the combined command of one hundred men was to go to Sulphur Springs and remain in the field in that area until the Bickerstaff gang was broken up or captured. They were not to take lives unless armed resistance was offered first, and they were to turn over their captives to the nearest post commander.[9] In October the Sulphur Springs commander reported that he believed the troops would have to remain six months to pacify the area completely and that quarters would have to be built for a more secure defense. There appeared to be some political motive behind the

[7]GO 10, AGO, March 5, 1869, and GO 18, March 16, RG94, NA. The reader is again reminded of Appendix A for assistance in unraveling the confused chain of command in this period.
[8]File 849M1868, AGO, RG94, NA.
[9]File 1210M1869, AGO, RG94, NA.

lawlessness because most of the population was organized into "Ku Klux clubs" which regularly attended the political "barbecues" sponsored by county Democratic organizations. The Army could not pinpoint a specific political motive, but supposed it to be the systematic intimidation and murder of Union men and Negroes.[10]

These gangs of outlaw Texans were bolder than random assaults on individual settlers and Negroes would indicate. Perhaps the most audacious exploit was an assault on the Jefferson jail. In October, 1868, G. W. Smith and some friends got into a "shooting affair" with some other men near Jefferson. They gave themselves up to the Army and asked for military protection to prevent reprisals. When the civil authorities at Jefferson asked to have custody of Smith, promising to keep him under close guard, the Army remanded him and he was put in the town jail. The mayor declined additional military help, although fourteen soldiers were on guard in and around the jail on the night of October 4, when a gang of about 125 men appeared, overpowered the guards without firing a shot, and murdered Smith in his cell. Two Negroes also in the jail were taken outside and shot.

When Reynolds received the report he endorsed it "disposition and conduct of troops unsatisfactory," ordered more men to the area, and began rounding up suspects with a view to military trial. The first arrests came in December, and by April, 1868, thirty-five men were in custody. The trials were delayed in the hopes of finding all the persons implicated, and this brought about the usual newspaper charges of oppression and mistreatment of prisoners, which upon investigation proved exaggerated. The military commission finally convened in May, and upon readmission of the state in 1870 those prisoners remaining in confinement were released.[11]

Canby took over the Texas command just before Christmas in 1868, and he shortly issued a comprehensive order on civil affairs. He scattered his troops into twenty-eight posts, most consisting of both infantry and cavalry. The details were not unlike those previously formulated in the Atlantic states. The post commanders had the powers of county justices and could issue orders to sheriffs and marshals when necessary. They were to act in accordance with the laws of Texas as much as possible, and as an afterthought Canby published relevant excerpts from the state

[10]Report of Col. W. B. Pease, 17th Inf., Oct. 2, 1868, file 1091M1869, AGO, and Reynolds to AG USA, Oct. 22, file 1434M1868, AGO, both enclosed with file 31I1869, AGO, RG94, NA.
[11]Files 558M1869 and 1091M1869, AGO, enclosed with 31I1869, AGO, RG94, NA.

code for their guidance. The general instructions were now standard from years of use: require and allow the civil officials to do as much as possible; interfere when they become powerless, lackadaisical, or prejudiced. As much as possible the colored regiments were distributed among the frontier posts since white troops were more desirable for the administration of civil affairs.[12]

Because each of these posts was responsible for a large amount of territory, small detachments were often in the field for a considerable time at some distance from the main base. In March, 1869, the lieutenant commanding a small outpost of the 6th Cavalry at Pilot Grove complained that he had not enough men or fresh horses to break up the gangs terrorizing the area and that when the terms of service of some of his men expired in a few weeks, he would not even have enough men to hold the camp in case of a strong attack. The district commander sent his report to Washington as a graphic example of Texas troubles, where it received Sherman's scribbled endorsement, "Gen. Reynolds must take care of this. W.T.S." Canby's system was not perfect, but it did improve conditions somewhat. Constant vigilance by the Army steadily reduced the number of murders in the state even though between January and October, 1869, 384 were reported.[13]

Trial by military commission continued as one of the tools the Army used in achieving law and order. Virginia and Georgia did not witness as many as did Mississippi and Texas; in the latter state fifty-nine cases came before military commissions between October, 1868, and September, 1869, resulting in twenty-one convictions and thirty-eight acquittals. Most of the Texas trials were for murder or other forms of aggravated assault; in Mississippi the offenses varied more, including malfeasance in office by a bureau agent.[14] The most sensational case was probably that of Mississippian E. M. Yerger, editor of the Jackson *News*. The acting mayor of Jackson, appointed by military authority, had been trying to collect Yerger's long overdue city tax. Yerger regarded this as a great impertinence, for which he determined to hold the mayor personally responsible, and he became even more outraged when the mayor refused his challenges to fight. At their next meeting, in the street, Yerger insulted the mayor and stabbed him to death when the latter, unarmed, turned to leave. Since Yerger's family was an influential one, he was able to walk away unmolested. The Army arrested him

---

[12]GO 4, 5MD, Jan. 16, 1869, and GO 5, Jan. 20, Orders, 607, RG94, NA.
[13]File 345M1869, AGO, RG94, NA; *Report of the Sec. of War, 1868–69*, p. 145.
[14]*Report of the Sec. of War, 1868–69*, p. 145. The orders announcing the results of trials are in Orders, 600, 601B, 606, and 607, RG94, NA.

and tried him by military commission; he appealed in vain to the federal circuit court for a writ of habeas corpus. He then appealed to the Supreme Court, but the case was postponed so often that Mississippi had been readmitted by the time a decision was made. In February, 1870, the War Department ordered him turned over to the state authorities on a charge of murder. The records do not indicate the ultimate result.[15]

During the last years under the Reconstruction Acts military aid in enforcement of the federal revenue laws was needed, as it had been during the whole postwar period. There had always been periodic complaints from Army officers that the revenue agents were misusing troops sent for their assistance; one cavalry captain complained that a detachment of his company at Cummings, Georgia, was "not there for the interest of the public, but as a convenience for a party of irresponsible vagabonds connected with the Internal Revenue Department." Upon investigation it turned out that the assessor was using the troops for personal orderlies, and the detachment was removed. Because of these complaints the War Department was always careful to tell Southern commanders to furnish only such aid as in their judgment the best interests of the military service would justify.[16] The customary procedure was for the agent to make an official request for aid through channels, whereupon a small detachment, either of cavalry or mounted infantry, would be sent.

Removals and appointments continued to harass the Army during 1868 and 1869. Following the earlier difficulties over removals made in haste and without sufficient evidence the generals proceeded with caution; in Texas the district commander warned his subordinates that full reports were necessary on all suggested removals and that the removal power was a nondelegable authority vested in himself.[17] In Virginia a military commissioner, Colonel T. M. Anderson, found fault with Governor H. H. Wells. Four Negroes had robbed a store and murdered the disabled Union soldier who owned it. The Freedmen's Bureau allowed the civil courts to try them, and they were sentenced to hang. Wells reprieved them repeatedly, until upon the fifth reprieve the exasperated Anderson wrote to headquarters, "I am forced to the conclusion that he is actuated by political considerations and is endeavoring by thus interrupting the course of justice to curry favor with the ignorant and

[15]Garner, *Mississippi*, 170; correspondence during June, 1869, 4MD, 2, RG98, NA; Townsend to Capt. W. Atwood, Feb. 27, 1870, AGO, 51, RG94, NA.

[16]File 85M1868, 3MD, RG98, NA; Townsend to Canby, Feb. 1, 1869, AGO, 49, RG94, NA.

[17]AAG to CO Brenham, June 9, 1869, 5MD, 54, RG98, NA.

execrable class to which these men belong." Anderson wanted the culprits executed by military authority and Wells ousted; but General Stoneman felt that Anderson's letter violated military propriety, and so Wells stayed in office.[18]

The removal question in Mississippi was made more complex by that state's having three different commanders between the summers of 1868 and 1869. Alvan C. Gillem, who held sway temporarily until Irvin McDowell arrived in June, 1868, made some removals, but they had not been too numerous and had generally involved lesser offices. McDowell no sooner got to Vicksburg than he ousted Governor Benjamin Humphreys, the state attorney general, and the secretary of state for allegedly having opposed ratification of the state constitution. He gave the governorship to one of his subordinates, General Adelbert Ames.

Within a month McDowell himself was gone and Gillem was again in command. Some Mississippi Republicans who were not pleased with Gillem's rule told Congress that his administration had been injurious to the loyal people and that he was not "the right kind of a man there." They complained that he had not taken sufficient precautions to prevent fraud in the spring elections of 1868 and that he was generally opposed to reconstruction under the congressional plan.[19] Since he had given a favorable decision in the very doubtful case of the Arkansas constitution, it is hard to see the truth of the latter charge, but the Washington Republicans seemed convinced. Mississippi spokesmen also convinced Congress that all state offices were in the hands of rebels. The result was twofold. In February, 1869, Congress legislated out of office every civil functionary in Mississippi, Texas, and Virginia who could not take the iron-clad oath of 1862, except those whose political disabilities Congress had removed by special legislation; and just days after his presidential inauguration in March, Grant replaced Gillem with Ames, who now functioned both as governor and commanding general.[20]

The vast turnover in offices which Congress decreed in early 1869 had been considered in mid-1867 as well, but Schofield and other commanders had successfully sidetracked it by pointing out the difficulty they would have in finding enough new men to fill the places. The situation was no better in 1869, but Congress was determined, and the policy had to be enforced. A letter concerning appointments in De Soto

[18]File 265A1868, 1MD, and AAG to Anderson, Aug. 18, 1868, 1MD, 2, RG98, NA.
[19]Garner, *Mississippi,* 213–15. A collage of testimony of Mississippi affairs is *House Mis. Docs.,* 40th Cong., 3rd Sess., No. 53, esp. pp. 20–26, 59–69.
[20]Garner, *Mississippi,* 228–30; 15 U.S. Statutes at Large 344; SO 55, AGO, March 9, 1869, RG94, NA.

County left no doubt where Ames' sympathies lay: "The Commanding General had a conversation with Judge Ballard with reference to this matter and desires that you consult with him and other Republicans of the county and arrange a list of officers to be appointed to fill the existing vacancies. It is the intention of the Commanding General that the colored element be represented." [21]

As General-in-Chief, Sherman now possessed the power over appointments and removals under the Third Reconstruction Act which had formerly been Grant's. With Mississippi in the hands of a person as interested in politics as Ames, Sherman watched things closely, but at first he was loath to interfere. S. G. French, representing the state board of levee commissioners, wrote protesting Ames' dissolution of the board. French claimed that in chartering it the state had created a private corporation which was thus beyond the Army's power. But Sherman just scribbled on the back of the letter, "File away." As the summer of 1869 wore on, Sherman became more concerned. In August Ames removed a judge and several other officials for no apparent reason, and in the circumstances the general's action had strong partisan overtones. The Adjutant General conveyed Sherman's feelings about the matter, saying that the General-in-Chief had deliberately not acted in earlier cases because he felt Ames, as the commander on the spot, was the one to decide who would make the best office-holders. "But if you have made removals now, on the very eve of an election in the seeming interest of one of the parties to the contest, it is his [Sherman's] clear conviction that it will as surely defeat that Party as any single act would do. It may be too late now to interfere, but the General desires that his opinion should be made known to you, and be a matter of record." Sherman had seen the report of Ames's action in his morning newspaper, and just before leaving for Philadelphia he gave Townsend a rough draft of the letter, the last sentence of which displayed with typical bluntness what he suspected Ames was attempting: "I don't care which party succeeds, provided the election be honest and fair." [22]

Sherman's wariness about Ames proved to be well-founded. Just after cautioning Ames on ill-advised removals he received a report from a Holly Springs resident. What he thought of the opening line—"Knowing the frankness of your youth, and trusting the justice of your manhood, I pen you this letter"—and the ensuing laudations of his boldness during

[21]AAAG to Hon. J. W. Vance, July 6, 1869, 4MD, 27, RG98, NA.

[22]French to Sherman, June 8 and 9, 1869, in Sherman Papers, LC; file 516A1869, AGO, and Townsend to Ames, Aug. 13, 1869, AGO, 49, RG94, NA.

the war is anyone's guess. But he probably scowled when he read that Ames was doing everything he could to proscribe the moderate Republicans and to openly ally himself with the extremists. "In this he sinks the character of the Ruler in that of the Partisan," said the writer, "and we fear a fair election cannot be had in November next." Sherman next received an "unofficial" letter from Ames himself. Claiming "honesty of purpose" in performing a task that was "certainly not very pleasant," he said, "A living sense of duty forces me to act for the regeneration of the state—the protection of *all* and the advantages to flow therefrom. What do I get in return—the hatred of the democracy—the evil instead of the good wishes of friends—and the consciousness of doing right." Ames was aware that he had been charged with political aspirations, and he took great pains to deny them. There were rumors that he wanted to represent Mississippi in the Senate, but he said, "A moment's reflection should show that I could not leave a lifelong position in a profession I love for a temporary honor the very holding of which might reflect discredit upon me." [23] In 1870, however, the Mississippi legislature did elect him to the Senate, and (whether with or without any "reflection") he accepted the post, potential discredit and all.

The appointment question was fully as acute in Virginia as in Mississippi. A special board of officers grappled with the problem. It first met in Richmond and "after consulting with such trustworthy citizens as were accessible" made recommendations to the commanding general. It then toured through the state, following an itinerary published in advance. At Lynchburg it held daily sessions, listened patiently to everyone who came before it, and then met behind closed doors to evaluate the applications and petitions it had gathered. It ultimately was able to make recommendations for 1,351 offices, thus leaving 3,205 posts for which no "suitable persons" could be found. Several factors made "suitable persons" scarce. The offices sometimes were a distraction from the holder's ordinary business and offered little in the way of compensation. Perhaps more important was the social and political ostracism applied to native Southerners who accepted the posts. By October there were still 2,814 vacancies in the state, but General Canby reported that most counties had enough judges available to hold regular court sessions.[24]

Congressional Reconstruction came to an end in Texas, Virginia, and Mississippi through the same process as in the other states. Elections

[23]H. W. Walton to Sherman, Aug. 16, 1869, and Ames to Sherman, Aug. 17, in Sherman Papers, LC.
[24]Report of the board, March 7, 1869, 1MD, 237, RG98, NA; *Report of the Sec. of War, 1868–69*, pp. 111–12.

were held to ratify new constitutions and choose officers; these actions along with ratification of the Fourteenth Amendment—and as an added punishment for these three states the Fifteenth as well—resulted in re-admittance to Congress. The Army found itself called upon to maintain the peace at polling time, as it had done before. The mayor of Alexandria, Virginia, for instance, feared his police force was too weak; and he wrote to the local commander, "If you had under your immediate command a squad of 10 to 15 cavalry men, their *presence* might prevent any outbreak, as you know *some* of our people have rather a dread of *U.S.* boys." The Virginia election was generally peaceful and showed about an 80 per cent turnout of registered voters.[25] The Mississippi commander also received such requests, and after borrowing some spare troops from Louisiana he sent small detachments to numerous places in the state. In Texas the commander scattered his men to selected county seats at the rate of ten or fifteen each. He was careful to warn the troops to stay close enough to the polls to prevent disturbance but far enough away to avoid giving the appearance of influencing voters.[26] In all three states the final steps of reconstruction were completed by early 1870, and the civil authorities assumed full control of affairs.

Georgia had the most difficult time of all getting completely back into the Union. In the summer of 1868 Congress agreed to the state's readmission, and in the last days of that session the Georgia members of the House took their seats. The state legislature, however, did not elect the senators in time for them to be seated before Congress adjourned. Upon the organization of the state legislature General Meade remanded his authority to the civil officials, and it appeared that military rule had finally come to an end. But there were indications that all was still not peaceful. In September a disturbance occurred at a Republican political meeting in Camilla, in the southwestern part of the state. Several hundred Negroes, some armed, marched on the town to attend the gathering. The sheriff met them at the town limits and told them they could not enter the town armed; when the white candidates with them avowed their peaceful purpose, the sheriff went back to the settlement

[25]Files 921M1869 and 937M1869, AGO, RG94, NA; *Report of the Sec. of War, 1868–69*, p. 112. Original emphasis.

[26]Ames to Mower, Oct. 8, 1869, 4MD, 27, RG98, NA; GO 185, 5MD, Oct. 18, Orders, 607, RG94, NA. *Sen. Exec. Docs.*, 41st Cong., 2nd Sess., No. 13, is a rather jumbled assemblage of documentary material, primarily correspondence, relative to these elections.

but warned the residents to be ready in case he needed them. Upon their arrival in town the Negroes encountered a drunken white man who ordered them to leave; when they would not, he fired on them. In the ensuing melee, which lasted only a few minutes, nine Negroes were killed and thirty wounded. There were no troops in the vicinity because, as Meade later explained, it was a remote area and the necessity for their presence could not have been anticipated from prior experience.[27]

Also in September the composition of the Georgia Legislature caused additional unrest. When it was first organized earlier in the summer, there was some question of the eligibility of certain members under the Fourteenth Amendment. Georgia Radicals importuned Meade to take some action, since in July he still exercised his authority under the Reconstrution Act. In a similar case in Louisiana several members of the Reconstruction and Judiciary committees had given it as their opinion that the legislature itself was the judge of the qualifications of its members, and the War Department sent this opinion for Meade's guidance in the case of Georgia. Meade required the legislature to investigate, and he accepted that body's report that nobody was ineligible, although Governor Rufus Bullock implored him to eject those who had been challenged.[28] The dissension thus begun in July further increased in September when the legislature undertook to expel its Negro members and replace them with white men of doubtful eligibility. By September, however, military power had ended and there was nothing the Army could do.

So the Georgia question came before Congress in December, 1868, and the reaction was speedy. No Georgians were admitted, even though the House members had been seated at the previous session. A committee took evidence on Georgia affairs, which were painted in grim colors. One witness claimed that during 1868 there had been at least 600 attempts on the lives of freedmen in a single congressional district. The Freedmen's Bureau, on the other hand, reported only 336 for the entire state.[29] However exaggerated these reports may have been, conditions in the state were clearly not good. From numerous locales came requests for troops to keep the peace. A resident of Warren County wrote the governor, "If the troops were required to patrol the county and would be diligent and let the people know that assassination and all other

---

[27]Report of military investigation, in *Army and Navy Journal*, VI (Oct. 17, 1868), 132; Meade to Gov. Rufus Bullock, Oct. 3, 1868, Dept. South, 242, RG98, NA.

[28]*Report of the Sec. of War, 1867–68*, pp. 108–14.

[29]*House Misc. Docs.*, 40th Cong., 3rd Sess., No. 52, pp. 91–98, 124–39.

outrages had to be stopped, or some one would have to suffer, quite a different state of affairs would exist, but without Military Law I fear nothing of any good will be accomplished but things made worse." [30]

In May, 1869, Senator Henry Wilson wrote President Grant pleading for military action to stop the "political murders" in Georgia, claiming that martial law was necessary in "the worst of all the States, for the security of the friends of the country." Grant turned this over to Sherman, who sent it to General Terry, now commanding the Department of the South, for a report. In August, Terry sent in a very gloomy analysis of the situation. He contended that in many parts of the state there was, for practical purposes, no government; that the civil officers were either afraid to do their duty or were in league with desperadoes and criminals; and that "numerous insurrectionary organizations known as 'Ku-Klux Klans' " were able to commit crime with impunity thanks to their disguises. He believed the only way to restore order in Georgia was to place it once more under the operation of the Reconstruction Acts, with a military commander to exercise all the powers conferred thereby. He was positive that this could legally be done because, to his mind, the reconstruction of the state had not been completed. The fact that the legislature which ratified the Fourteenth Amendment contained ineligible members made its acts void, and the fact that Georgia's senators had never been seated meant that the last step in reconstruction had not been effected.[31]

[30]John Neal to Bullock, June 17, 1869, file 1155S1869, AGO, RG94, NA. For some unapparent reason Bullock did not want this letter published. *House Exec. Docs.*, 41st Cong., 2nd Sess., No. 288, is a compilation of reports and affidavits on Georgia affairs in the second half of 1869.

[31]Terry's report, Aug. 14, 1869, *Report of the Sec. of War, 1868–69*, pp. 89–95. On Sept. 5 Terry requested return of this report for the correction of what he called a "serious error." At that moment it was in the hands of the Attorney General; Sherman retrieved it and sent it back to Terry on the nineteenth. Terry returned a corrected copy on Oct. 9. File 1156S1869, AGO, and Gen. J. C. Kelton, AAG USA, to Terry, Sept. 16, 1869, AGO, 49, RG94, NA. The nature of the error was not disclosed in the correspondence and the manuscript of the original report could not be found. However, the text of the original report was copied into Terry's headquarters letterbook (Dept. South, 242, RG98, NA), and the following paragraph has been crossed out: "The point has been made that the oath prescribed for officers of the United States commonly called the 'test oath' should have been administered to all the members of the legislature. I will not say that the formal administration of that oath was *necessary*, but I do contend that the end sought to be attained by the administration of that oath should in some way have been reached; that in some way the eligibility or ineligibility of members elect should have been determined by the District Commander [Meade]; that the administration of the oath would have been a *proper* method of ascertaining the facts" [original emphasis]. This paragraph does not appear in the

Many congressmen had perhaps wanted to do exactly what Terry suggested, but they made their decisions slowly, and not until December 22, 1869, did the law finally go into effect. It directed the governor to assemble the people whom Meade had in June of 1868 declared elected to the legislature. Everyone claiming a seat in the body had to take either the 1862 iron-clad oath, or else an oath that Congress had removed his political disabilities. After the oath-taking the legislature could then organize itself and elect its officers. Exclusion of any duly elected members on the ground of race was prohibited. The legislature was not required to re-ratify the Fourteenth Amendment, but ratification of the Fifteenth was demanded before senators and congressmen would be seated. The crucial provision concerning the legal authority for the Army's subsequent actions was Section 7: "Upon the application of the governor of Georgia, the President of the United States shall employ such military or naval forces of the United States as may be necessary to enforce and execute the preceding provisions of this act." [32] No reference whatever was made to the Reconstruction Acts, and nothing was said about the Army resuming the control over Georgia it had exercised between March, 1867, and July, 1868.

Bullock, however, was a determined man, and he urged Grant to make Georgia a military district under Terry's command. From telegraphic exchanges immediately following passage of the act, it may be deduced that pressure in favor of Terry's appointment must have been exerted even before the act became law, that the pressure was coming not only from Bullock but from other Republicans, and that Terry, in spite of preliminary hesitation, soon gave in to their desires. On December 23 Terry wired Bullock at Willard's Hotel in Washington. If he thought it would do any good, the general said, he would be glad to be assigned. But he believed it was now too late, for he anticipated Georgia's readmission within six weeks. A simultaneous wire to Sherman was more desperate: "I beg that this [assignment] may not be done till I can be heard. The matter will be decided tonight." Sherman's reply came back on Christmas Eve. He said Grant had already decided to appoint Terry before the latter's telegram arrived, "and though he [Grant] feels disposed to comply with any request you should make, still he thinks

---

printed version of the report and should be inserted following the words "having taken effect" in the middle of the first paragraph on p. 94. The only apparent reason for striking out the paragraph would seem to be the conflict between the first clause of Terry's second sentence and the disqualification clause of the Fourteenth Amendment. By striking the whole paragraph the implied criticism of Meade was also removed.

[32] 16 U.S. Statutes at Large 59.

you better than any other officer can execute the delicate responsibilities of the office. I concur in this and hope you will cheerfully conform." He added that the job would "require less labor on your part than at first appears." As if to help Terry along he also offered the suggestion, "Do not remove any officer, but let matters continue as at present until a necessity arises." This was an afterthought on Sherman's part, which he added to the message when the draft copy was already in the hands of the telegraph operator. Also on Christmas Eve Terry again wired Bullock. "My despatches to you and to General Sherman clearly express my own judgment. Still I am not disposed to insist on my own conclusions. If our friends, including yourself, Senator Morton, Senator Thayer, and General Butler, are clearly of the opinion that I am wrong I will withdraw my opposition to the course of action which you propose, in which case you are at liberty to show this to General Sherman and to the President." [33]

Whoever "this" may have been shown to, the order appointing Terry went out on Christmas Eve. It was a simple one: "Brevet Major General A. H. Terry, in addition to his duties as commander of the department of the South, is, by order of the President of the United States, appointed to exercise the duties of commanding general of the district of Georgia, as defined by the act of Congress approved December 22, 1869." The last clause was remarkable in that the law cited did not even establish such a command, much less specify any duties. A week later Terry wired Sherman that he had assumed command of Georgia as a district and that he was now convinced the action had been necessary. He added, "I think that I should be clothed with the powers given by the reconstruction acts. I would suggest that the orders proposed in my report of August 14th be issued. I think that the knowledge that I have those powers would go far to prevent the necessity for their use." The War Department promptly obliged. What Terry had suggested in his August report was simple: revocation by Washington of the order by which Meade had turned over the state to the civil authorities in July, 1868. This was done, and Terry specifically received the powers vested in dis-

[33] Terry to Bullock, Dec. 23 and 24, 1869, Dept. South, 243, RG98, NA; Terry to Sherman, Dec. 23, and reply, Dec. 24, file 1156S1869, AGO, RG94, NA. Some telegraphic exchanges between Washington and Atlanta during December and January are printed as *Sen. Exec. Docs.*, 41st Cong., 2nd Sess., No. 41, which will be cited in preference to the National Archives files when possible. In the case of Terry to Sherman, Dec. 23, the printed version is incomplete, omitting the phrase "till I can be heard," and his politically revealing wire to Bullock of Dec. 24 is omitted entirely.

trict commanders by the Reconstruction Acts.[34] Thus the remanding of Georgia to full military control was a purely executive action with no specific authorization from Congress.

The problem which took up most of Terry's attention during January, 1870, was that of the organization of the legislature and the disputed eligibility of various members. The question was really a twofold one. First, who was the ultimate judge of eligibility—the member, the house to which he was elected, or the commanding general? And second, could the commanding general replace those found ineligible with the candidates who had received the second highest number of votes in the election? On January 11 Terry wired Sherman for instructions, asking if he were authorized to investigate the question of eligibility. Sherman's reply was not as helpful as Terry would have liked: "Your dispatch of this morning shown to the President and Secretary of War, and the result is in these words: Exercise your own discretion. If a flagrant case arises, where a disqualified person proposes to take oath, investigate the question of eligibility and determine for the time being his right." Terry then reported that the code of Georgia allowed the second highest candidate to assume an office if the winner were constitutionally ineligible, and he asked if he could declare such persons elected. Sherman said he saw no objection, "if it will stand the test of law." [35]

Terry thought about the whole business. On the thirteenth he appointed a three-man board of Army officers, one of whom was his judge-advocate, to investigate the cases of six representatives, and two days later he gave them fifteen more.[36] For two weeks there was a lull in affairs as Governor Bullock conveniently arranged for the legislature to adjourn each day while the board conducted its investigations. Terry utilized this breathing spell to give Sherman a personal evaluation of the difficulty. He viewed it as arising from a struggle for political control of the Georgia House of Representatives, with one side attempting to install members whom Congress meant to keep out "and thus retain that majority which was responsible for the acts which led to the recent Congressional action." In such circumstances Terry naturally found himself in the midst of an uncomfortable cross fire; as he told his friend, "The pressure upon me from the contending parties, is very great and I

---

[34]GO 83, AGO, Dec. 24, 1869; Terry to Sherman, Jan. 2, 1870; GO 1, AGO, Jan. 4, in *Sen. Exec. Docs.*, 41st Cong., 2nd Sess., No. 41, pp. 3–4.

[35]Telegraphic exchange, Jan. 11–13, 1870, in *Sen. Exec. Docs.*, 41st Cong., 2nd Sess., No. 41, pp. 4–7.

[36]GO 3, Dist. Ga., Jan. 13, 1870, and GO 4, Jan. 15, Orders, 599, RG94, NA.

would not again go through with a job of this kind even if it would make me a Marshal of France." [37]

To accompany this private letter Terry also wrote an official one asking for legal advice. Bullock continued to urge him to declare the second highest candidates entitled to the seats of those found ineligible, but Terry was hesitant. He wanted an opinion from the Attorney General and also to be "instructed to act upon the conclusions to which he may arrive." He received an opinion presently, and he must surely have sworn. Now even the Attorney General was telling him to use his own judgment, as Sherman had told him before. Ebenezer R. Hoar, the nation's chief legal officer, said he thought the second highest candidate should receive the seat only where the winner had been clearly and absolutely ineligible at the time of the election. But he hedged exasperatingly on the whole question, really: "The questions are very difficult, and some of them hardly admit of a solution that can be pronounced certainly correct. I can only say that I have not been able to conclude that any other course is more probably the right one than that which General Terry indicates as the tendency of his own opinion." Southern commanders received some obscure communications from Washington between 1865 and 1877, but this one has to be the ultimate. The last sentence was even more indeterminate than it appeared on its face because it was not really clear what was the "tendency" of Terry's own opinion. [38]

Just after Terry received this unhelpful message, his board of officers gave him their report: three ineligible, eleven eligible, and the sixteen who had refused to take the oath and had applied to Congress for removal of their disabilities, ipso facto ineligible. In announcing the findings Terry thus prevented nineteen members-elect from taking their seats, but he did not replace them with the runners-up because he finally decided he was not authorized to do so by the act of December 22. [39]

[37]Terry to Sherman, Jan. 19, 1870, file 1155S1869, AGO, RG94, NA. There are two copies: the original, in Terry's fine distinctive script and violet ink, and one made apparently in the AGO. In the margin of the latter appears this notation in Sherman's equally distinctive scribble: "P.S. Feb. 9, 1870. This letter was purely private. Never designed for publication, and had probably better be withdrawn from this series; but it supplies a link in the chain of official letters and is therefore submitted to the Secretary of War." A second marginal note in an unknown hand: "(Sec'y of War decides not to send to congress)."

[38]Terry to Sherman, Jan. 19, 1870, and reply, Jan. 22, in Sen. Exec. Docs., 41st Cong., 2nd Sess., No. 41, pp. 13–14, 27–28.

[39]House Exec. Docs., 41st Cong., 2nd Sess., No. 288, pp. 124–207; GO 9, Dist. Ga., Jan. 25, 1870, Orders, 599, RG94, NA; Terry to Sherman, Jan. 26, in Sen. Exec. Docs., 41st Cong., 2nd Sess., No. 41, p. 28.

The Georgia House of Representatives which consequently met and elected a speaker on January 26 was not a complete body. Not everyone was fully satisfied that Terry's actions had been legal, and the Senate Judiciary Committee conducted its own investigation. It reported in March, 1870, that Terry's action was not warranted because the legislature was not a "provisional" one within the meaning of the Reconstruction Act and was thus not subject to military authority. As evidence, the committee pointed out that Grant himself had expressed this view in instructing Meade in the spring of 1868 and also that the Senate in debating the 1869 act had rejected a provision specifically calling the legislature "provisional." The committee thus made a very strong legal case against Terry's course, but it also recognized his honesty of purpose and commended him for his calm handling of such a delicate question even if he was technically wrong. The question then became, what should Congress do, if anything? Since the lower house would be completely re-elected in November anyhow, and since none of the nineteen Terry excluded was really eligible, the committee recommended that Congress not interfere with the legislature as it then existed.[40]

Following the organization of the legislature Georgia became quieter and conditions improved. There were still outrages against Negroes from time to time; and in October, 1870, Terry reported that seventeen places in the state had been occupied temporarily by troops upon request of the civil authorities, either state or federal, to protect them in enforcing the laws. The mere presence of Terry with a federal military force, however, induced people to approach him with many problems. An attempt to have him dictate with respect to Negroes serving on juries particularly irritated him and he used a favorite means of unburdening himself: a personal letter to his friend Sherman. An inequity definitely existed, and Terry readily recognized it. No racial distinction was inherent in the Georgia law on juries, but at each term of the county courts the jurors were drawn by lot from a pool of names assembled by the county jury commissioners, and very seldom were Negroes' names placed in these pools. Even if a Negro were drawn for a particular jury he could be rejected easily because of the liberal grounds of challenge.

Without much question this loophole worked injustice, and Terry observed that in most cases "Sambo generally goes to the wall." But he was not in sympathy with the proposed remedy: a positive military order requiring that in all civil cases between parties of opposite color, all cases of crimes by whites against Negroes, and all criminal prosecutions

[40]*Sen. Reports,* 41st Cong., 2nd Sess., No. 58.

of Negroes, the jury must contain at least three Negroes. What aggravated Terry most was the attitude of those who approached him on the subject. He had understandably inquired why the legislature could not pass the required law and was told in reply, " 'We fear that we cannot bring our people up to the point of passing such a law. . . . ' " Thus Terry's order was to be an " 'entering wedge' " to get the people used to having Negroes on juries (apparently General Pope's 1867 order had not been a large enough "wedge"). "I confess," he wrote Sherman, "that I am a little sick of being applied to to remedy every fault in the laws of this State. I don't like to be always a sort of wet-nurse to the Negroes. I think that they should depend somewhat on themselves and if with a majority in each branch of the Legislature favorable to them, they cannot pass measures necessary to their protection they had better suffer for a time. The State of Georgia has got to govern itself ultimately and in such matters I think it had better begin now." The real question in Terry's mind was whether it would be judicious to interfere militarily. Since Georgia would probably soon be readmitted and the order would thus have a legal effect only for a short while, it seemed senseless to incur the bitterness that such an order would provoke. Sherman gave Terry an answer; its contents are not known but it was doubtless more negative than positive, judging from Sherman's general views and the fact that the order never appeared.[41]

The Georgia tangle remained before Congress during the spring and summer of 1870, the principal problem being whether new elections for the legislature should be held in the fall. Governor Bullock and his extreme Radical followers wanted the election postponed so as to continue their own political control for two more years following readmission; the more conservative elements hoped for a new canvass. Again Terry became concerned about the Army's role and wrote another worried personal letter to Sherman. He could find some comfort in the bill that soon passed on July 15, 1870, which declared Georgia entitled to representation in Congress and added that nothing should deprive Georgians of the right to elect members of the General Assembly, as provided for in the state constitution. The legislature then ordered an election for the fall, defeating a stalling attempt by the Bullock faction.[42]

Terry was thus saved from the necessity of making any more politically charged decisions, but the mere fact that an election was to be held

---

[41]Terry to Sherman, June 20, 1870, in Sherman Papers, LC. Sherman scrawled "Answered" on the back, but the reply could not be found.

[42]Terry to Sherman, July 3, 1870, in Sherman Papers, LC; 16 U.S. Statutes at Large 363; Thompson, *Georgia,* 267–69.

meant delicate duties for the Army. He drew up careful instructions for his troops and sent them to Washington, where both Sherman and War Secretary William Belknap approved them. In truth Sherman disliked the idea of troops performing such duty and feared that "we subject our soldiers to danger worse than an ordinary battle." He understood that Grant had personally ordered this use of troops, however, and thus he grudingly reconciled himself to it, hoping that the troops would not be stationed too near the polls and would not have to use armed force. It was the law prohibiting military interference at elections passed in February, 1865, that worried him; but if as the Radicals insisted, Georgia was still out of the Union—even though by now declared entitled to be back in it—that law probably did not apply.[43]

Terry himself was out of Georgia for several weeks at the end of 1870, serving on a board to determine the fitness of officers for promotion. That duty he found the most disagreeable he had ever had, and he happily informed another of his Army friends, "Tomorrow, I suppose that it will end and I shall be heartily glad to exchange back to the work of reconstruction. I hardly supposed that I should ever be glad to go back to Atlanta from Washington but anything is better than being a member of a 'Benzine Board.' "[44] Elections were held, the Georgia delegates were seated in Congress, and in early 1871 Terry's special control over Georgia came to an end. The Union was whole again.

The years under the Reconstruction Acts were trying ones for both the Army and the Southern populace. As a method of government, military rule seemed harsh because it was not in accord with American principles. In practice it was as harsh as the individual commander chose to make it. It is true that the number of troops in the South during these years was comparatively small—scarcely 18,000 (one third of the Army) for all commands in the autumn of 1868. [45] Some extremists would doubtless have liked more—a company of bluecoats in every county seat in the South, perhaps. Under that plan, however, the three states of Virginia, Georgia, and Arkansas alone would have used up half the total number of regiments existing in 1868—29 out of 56. Since the bulk of the Army was needed for the Plains, any more thorough blanketing of the South than was in fact carried out would have required an increase in the size of the Army. Congress, however, was bent on a

---

[43]File 1260S1870, AGO, and Sherman to Terry, Dec. 6, 1870, AGO, 53, RG94, NA.
[44]Terry to C. B. Comstock, Dec. 30, 1870, in Comstock Papers, LC.
[45]*Report of the Sec. of War, 1867–68*, pp. 755–67.

decrease rather than an increase. In the debate over the act of March 3, 1869, which reduced the Army's size, only one or two members referred to Southern affairs at all. Everyone was far more concerned about financial details and the best method of trimming the officer corps. Congressman Benjamin Butler offered a particularly singular opinion: "We will want no army in the South after the 4th day of March next. An event will then happen [Grant's inauguration] which will be more potent for peace than soldiers in every village and hamlet. It will then be understood that all disorder and riot and murder must cease." [46]

The financial anthem of a penny-pinching Congress and the country at large was "Retrenchment!" Military reconstruction was costly enough as it was. Sickles estimated in July, 1867, that he would need $431,000 for conducting the registration of voters in the two Carolinas, plus another $100,000 for administering justice where civil authorities failed. In September of the same year Schofield told Washington he would need $40,000 just to revise the registration in Virginia, plus another $45,000 to get the convention delegates elected. [47]

One crucial reason for not scattering troops about in small semipermanent detachments throughout the South was the deterioration of morale and discipline resulting from the fragmentation of commands. Southern duty, although not as potentially fatal as service on the Plains, was disagreeable in other ways, and during 1866 and 1867 many of the regiments which had experienced large numbers of desertions were stationed in the South. General Pope had a particularly difficult time with desertions in the fall of 1867, and he wrote to Grant complaining that enlistment-and-desertion was becoming almost a game. Men who disliked the "pinching cold and want of a Northern city" enlisted in the Army in the autumn and had themselves assigned to a regiment on occupation duty. While wintering in the South they made just enough minor trouble to keep themselves in the guardhouse, so they would be clothed and fed with no work to do. Then in the spring they deserted, returned North, and if times again became hard, went through the process again by merely enlisting under a different name. As a means of curbing this game, deserters who were caught and court-martialed often were branded on the hip with a small letter "D" so that if they tried to re-enlist it would be discovered at the physical examination. The Judge Advocate General frowned on this practice, however, and it had to be discontinued. [48]

[46]*Cong. Globe.*, 40th Cong., 3rd Sess., appendix, 183.
[47]Sickles to AG USA, July 6, 1867, 2MD, 1; Schofield to AG USA, Sept. 20, 1867, 1MD, 1, RG98, NA.
[48]Pope to Grant, Nov. 28, 1867, 3MD, 1, RG98, NA.

But the fact that the number of troops in the South was comparatively small did not mean that their legal power and influence were small.[49] The generals had the legal authority to control many aspects of the lives of the inhabitants, and they exercised their power in numerous ways. Their potential influence over Southern politics was enormous, and they wielded it at times—in one case to the extent of the Florida commander becoming temporary presiding officer of the constitutional convention to facilitate its organization. Certainly the course of political events in Arkansas turned on the action of General Gillem, and in Georgia on the actions of Pope and Terry.

Even a very small detachment, just to "show the flag," was often sufficient to keep a community quiet. Perhaps the most striking illustration occurred in Mississippi in October, 1869. When the little town of Clinton experienced some lawlessness and disorder, the commanding general sent a lone sergeant there to preserve the peace and arrest offenders. Sometimes it sufficed for the Army merely to pretend it was sending a force to a particular area. In March, 1868, the Louisiana commander sent a company of the 20th Infantry en route from Baton Rouge to Pointe Coupee, a short distance up the Mississippi River. The troops were to halt at a point across the river from the troubled area, make ostensible preparations to cross, and then return to Baton Rouge when the commotion died down. In both instances it was the tremendous psychological effect of the blue and gold uniform that solved the problem.[50] As one officer reminisced, Southerners "don't care a fig for law, sheriffs, or marshals, but they would rather see the devil than the Federal uniform." [51]

In two respects military rule worked to the disadvantage of the inhabitants for whose benefit it was imposed. In the first place it sometimes encouraged them to look too much to the Army for support rather than to depend upon themselves. Without question there were many cases of manifest injustice or brutality to freedmen and white Unionists which were proper subjects for military interposition and without which interposition the plight of loyalists would have been unbearable. But the Army—quite apart from the times it did so on its own initiative—was *asked* to interfere in other instances where there was no real ground for doing so. Perhaps the ultimate example of this, if the story as reported is true, occurred in June, 1867. A young lad living near Rome,

[49]Among other historians, Franklin, *Reconstruction,* 119–20, makes this erroneous assumption.

[50]AAAG to CO Jackson, Oct. 23, 1869, 4MD, 27; AAAG to CO 20th Inf., March 24, 1868, Dept. Gulf, 274, RG98, NA.

[51]Charles King, *Kitty's Conquest* (Philadelphia, 1888), 42.

Georgia, allegedly of Union sentiments, was desperately in love with a young lady whose father was a staunch Rebel. The father would not hear of marriage, whereupon the youth pleaded with the nearest post commander to send a squad of men to liberate the young lady. It may have been difficult for the officer to refuse, but he properly did so, and told the young man that any redress to which he was entitled would have to come from the civil courts.[52]

In addition to encouraging people to ask for military interference where such action was improper, the Army's presence also lulled Union men into a false sense of security. When the bluecoats were nearby, loyalists were often as fierce in their denunciation of their opponents as the "unreconstructed" were when troops were not at hand. The result was that the loyalists clearly marked themselves and became easy prey for retaliation any time an opportunity presented itself. Thus in some respects it can be argued that the longer the Army exercised full control, the longer it became necessary to exercise full control—and that would have required keeping the states unrepresented for some years to come.

In December, 1865, the South might with good reason have been readmitted, but for a mixture of reasons including some political ones, it was kept out. By 1868, when certain aspects of Southern conditions dictated a continuance of military rule, most of the states had been taken back into the fold for reasons which were largely political. It was a curious reversal of circumstances. In the intervening years the Army, with certain clear exceptions, had done well considering that it had been called upon to enforce policies over which the politicians had fought bitterly. Political battles continued during the seventies, though the scene now shifted from Washington to Southern capitals. By its practical and legal position from Appomattox to Readmission the Army had been unavoidably in the thick of the political fighting; by its legal position after Readmission it was theoretically removed from politics. But during the seventies Southern commanders were to find, alas, that theory and practice did not always coincide.

[52]Galveston *Daily News,* June 6, 1867, reprinting an article from the Rome *Courier.*

PART III

AFTER READMISSION

Once the states were readmitted, direct military supervision over civil affairs ceased, and the Army's functions were reduced. The "national policy" was now directed towards a new goal—preservation of the Republican governments in Southern capitals. This goal required continued protection of the Negroes and their white allies upon whom these Republican governments rested. Through the use of the Army to police elections, help apprehend criminals, and keep the peace in conflicts between rival state officials, this goal was pursued until by 1877 the country had tired of "reconstruction."

10

Moonshiners, Klansmen, and Voters

DURING the years following readmission of the states, the Army's civil duties were greatly diminished. No longer did citizens face military commissions for their wrongdoings; no longer did general or special orders direct judges to halt their proceedings in particular cases or to close down their court for disobeying a military edict. The Army's reduced activities after readmission fell within three general areas. First, the Army continued to receive requests for aid in enforcing civil law, both state and federal. Second, bluecoats still visited remote parts of the countryside on election day to prevent disorder and violence. And third, when these elections resulted in more than one person claiming to be the duly elected governor of a state, or produced rival bodies claiming to be the state legislature, it was the Army which prevented bloodshed while the political questions were decided. These were delicate duties, which frequently subjected the Army to criticism from all sides no matter what course it followed. The situation was essentially one of a military establishment with limited legal power desiring to keep out of political disagreements in circumstances which actually forced the Army into the conflicts.

Since readmission marked an obvious change in the nature of the Southern problem, the Army understandably wanted new instructions from Washington. These were not long in coming. General Buchanan was wondering how he should proceed in Louisiana; and in August, 1868, the War Department offered some enlightenment—but not very much. The instructions recited the parts of the Constitution and laws concerning federal suppression of domestic violence. Article IV, Section

4 of the Constitution, in guaranteeing each state a republican form of gov-

213

ernment, requires federal protection against disorder "on application of the legislature, or of the executive (when the legislature cannot be convened. . . ." A 1795 statute authorized the President to call out the militia in such circumstances. An 1807 law authorized the President to use the regular military forces whenever it was lawful for him to use the militia. So the legal background was meager to begin with, and on the crucial question of the procedures by which these provisions of law were to be applied, the instructions from Washington were vague. Buchanan was expected to keep himself informed of conditions in his territory and promptly telegraph to the War Department "any facts which may make it the duty of the President, under the constitution and laws, to employ the Military force of the United States." He was also to dispose of his troops strategically by moving them around from place to place "where you may have reason to apprehend a necessity for their use." [1]

From these instructions it was still not fully clear what procedures would make legal the use of troops. It appeared that final authorization had to come from the President, but the method of routing requests for help from the civil authorities to him was left vague. Presently a situation arose in Tennessee which afforded an opportunity for clarification. The state legislature asked Thomas to put a military force at the governor's disposal to suppress lawlessness, and Thomas asked Washington what to do. In reply he received a copy of the earlier letter to Buchanan and also one from Attorney General William Evarts to a United States marshal in Florida concerning military aid to federal law enforcement officers. Evarts said that federal marshals could call on the Army for help in executing court processes, and that in such cases the soldiers had to act in obedience to the marshal. He differentiated between these cases and the protection of the states against domestic violence, which he said was strictly the duty of the President until that official delegated the power to subordinates. [2]

In transmitting Evarts' letter to Thomas, and also to Meade and Buchanan, Army Headquarters took care to add a cautionary message. Even though an officer might be called upon by a civil agent for aid, he still had to judge for himself whether the task requested of him was a lawful one, and "compatible with the proper discharge of his ordinary military duties. . . ." Thus the Army did not have to do everything a

[1]Townsend to Buchanan, Aug. 10, 1868, *Report of the Sec. of War, 1867–68,* xx–xxi.

[2]Thomas to AG USA, Aug. 11, 1868, and Evarts to A.B. Magruder, Aug. 20, *ibid.,* xxii–xxiv.

civil officer might demand. The procedures to be followed also became a bit clearer. "If time will permit, every demand from a civil officer for military aid, whether it be for the execution of a civil process or to suppress insurrection, should be forwarded to the President with all the material facts of the case, for his orders; and in all cases the highest commander whose orders can be given in time to meet the emergency will alone assume the responsibility of action." Hopefully the "timely disposition of troops" previously recommended, plus their "passive interposition between hostile parties," would go far to preclude troublesome situations. In any case, this latest message concluded, the main goal was to preserve the peace.[3]

Clearly, trouble would arise over the "discretion" of the commanding general and how much latitude each could safely be allowed. Test cases soon began to arise. In September, 1868, Thomas was asked for help by a federal marshal in Kentucky. He turned to Washington, whence he received a confusing message from War Secretary Schofield. That gentlemen first repeated the necessity of the President's having a full report in each case so that "in so delicate a matter" he would not have to act solely on the civil official's version. Then Schofield added, "In all ordinary cases the request for the President's order is only a formality required by the law." After remarking that if the President actually *did* give any orders they would have to rest largely on the Army's recommendation, Schofield continued his cryptic dispatch: "In all plain cases, unless there is ample time to send here for instructions, the President's orders may very well be anticipated by the department commander. And, in doubtful cases, the President ought to have the opinion and advice of that commander before giving his orders." By themselves these general instructions were hardly lucid, and they could even be regarded as conflicting with the earlier August directions. On the specific Kentucky problem, Washington threw the burden of decision back to Thomas. Meade and Buchanan also received September messages conveying the President's wish that they exercise full discretion within the limits of their "lawful authority" to preserve the peace.[4]

"To help or not to help" was a hard enough question when there was only one set of officials involved; imagine the added difficulty if rival groups of law enforcement personnel each expected military aid. Such a situation faced General Rousseau in New Orleans shortly after he suc-

---

[3]Gen. J. C. Kelton, AAG USA, to Thomas, Meade, and Buchanan, Aug. 25, 1868, *ibid.*, xxii–xxvi.
[4]Schofield to Thomas, Sept. 12, 1868, to Buchanan, Sept. 14, and Townsend to Meade, Sept. 29, *ibid.*, xxxi–xxxiii.

ceeded Buchanan in September, 1868. The issue was control over the
New Orleans police force. The police were originally under the jurisdiction of the mayor, but a recent act of the state legislature had vested
control in a Metropolitan Police Board of three whites and three Negroes. The board organized a police force of 243 Negroes and 130 whites,
a wholly unnecessary racial imbalance which the generally low caliber
of all personnel involved further aggravated. Considering the new law
invalid, the populace refused to recognize the Metropolitan police, and
the mayor insisted on his own prerogatives. The danger thus impended
of a collision between rival police forces. Rousseau prevailed on the
Metropolitan board to appoint as chief of police former General Steedman, the collector of internal revenue in New Orleans; this appointment
had a salutary effect.

But there still remained the question of which police force was the
legal one and therefore entitled to military support. After the governor
requested his intercession, Rousseau wired Schofield for instructions,
saying that he did not want to decide the question of legality. Schofield
told Rousseau to preserve the peace and that he had ample authority
to do whatever was necessary. The War Secretary followed this up
with an "unofficial" communique telling the general he could not escape
determining the question of legality since the only police force he could
support was the legal one. The Secretary added as an afterthought that
perhaps Rousseau's troops would make a good temporary substitute for
both police forces, but that Rousseau would have to decide the propriety
of such a course. Rousseau succeeded in convincing the opposing parties
to have the matter settled in court but once more he asked for guidance—what if there were a collision before the court decided? This time
the reply came from Johnson—Schofield, unlike his predecessor in 1866,
had kept the President closely informed—Rousseau should do whatever
he lawfully could to preserve the peace and let the courts settle questions of the "civil polity" of the state.[5] Once the question came to the
courts the crisis lessened, since both sides thought a legal settlement
safer than risking direct interference by the Army.

This particular incident did not result in very serious trouble, but
such handling of affairs by Washington caused uneasiness on the part
of field commanders. Always the bothersome question was discretion. The
officer on the scene wanted guidance, which higher echelons seemed
reluctant to provide. Actually, both sides had understandable points
of view. Given the delicacy of such situations, the general in command

[5]Telegraphic exchanges, Oct. 26–Nov. 4, 1868, and Rousseau's report, *ibid.*,
xxxv–xxxix, 305–306.

desired to have as much specific advice as possible on which to base his actions. But as the Washington high command thought, the man on the spot was clearly the best informed on local conditions and therefore the best judge of circumstances. The problem was basically insoluble, and throughout the seventies many of the exchanges between Washington and Southern command posts were variations on the theme, " 'What shall I do?' 'Use your own judgment.' "

Sometimes the Army did not approve a request for troops. In October, 1869, a northern Louisiana sheriff informed the governor that he feared an attempt on his jail for the purpose of releasing some murder suspects. He asked for troops to prevent it. The governor transmitted the request to General Mower who refused to supply them. Mower then referred the case to Halleck, the division commander, who approved his subordinate's action with the crotchety remark that the Army should not become another police force. Halleck then sent the papers up another level to Sherman, who added his approving endorsement to the effect that the state authorities should exhaust their own power first and that the final decision was properly Mower's.[6]

On occasion a request to send troops was sidetracked by turning it over to the state authorities. In 1869 a resident of Fountain Hills, Arkansas, complained to the military authorities about depredations on his property by the state's militia; a group of merchants also had complained earlier that, by occupying plantations, the Arkansas Militia was interfering with agricultural production. The Army referred both matters to the governor and heard nothing more about either.[7]

Another instance of refusal occurred in Texas in October, 1871. Governor E. J. Davis asked Secretary Belknap to lend the state 1,000 breech-loading rifles plus ammunition, and also to put 100 troops at his disposal, to cope with outlawry in Limestone County, near Waco. The telegraph wires carried this message from Washington to San Antonio: "You have authority to use your discretion in the matter, and will, of course, act with caution." Reynolds, the district commander, did act with caution. Rather than accept the governor's statement at face value, he went to the neighborhood himself and concluded that there was no need for help to execute the state or federal laws. Doubtless it was the thought of turning federal troops over to the governor which made Reynolds hesitant.[8]

[6]File 1450S1869, AGO, RG94, NA.
[7]Townsend to Buchanan, Feb. 18, 1869, and to Mower, June 21, 1869, AGO, 49, RG94, NA.
[8]File 3478 of 1871, AGO, RG94, NA.

Sometimes the civil powers appealed to Washington when the local commander refused to provide troops. In September, 1870, trouble occurred in the little northeastern Alabama town of Stevenson, described as "a one-horse concern, and not able to protect *any man,* when a dozen or more disguised men come to do anything with him." Huntsville was the nearest post, whose commanding officer sent the mayor's request for troops on to Atlanta, the next higher headquarters. The mayor's letter came back to Huntsville with this endorsement: "The time has arrived when Alabama should be able to enforce her own laws, and protect her citizens without reference to the military power of the United States. The troops applied for will not be furnished. By order of Brig. Gen. Terry. J. H. Taylor, A.A.G." This peevish reply annoyed the mayor, who sent the letter to Governor W. H. Smith. He was peeved too, and scratched on it, "Respectfully referred to the President of the United States through the Hon. Secretary of War. The indorsement [*sic*] on this paper assumes to decide a question that does not belong to the commanding General." [9] Again the vexing question of discretion. Who were the better judges of need—the Army or the civil officials? In this case, as in most, the field commanders found support in Washington, but that support did not eliminate the problem. Commanders certainly did not like to antagonize their civil counterparts, but in exercising their discretion they could hardly escape doing so upon occasion. Dispatching troops every time on the slightest pretext might have instilled in the civil governments an unhealthy disposition to rely entirely on military aid, and it would have imposed a burden which the "best interests of the service" would scarcely bear.

One can readily imagine the serious problems that would arise if a soldier, while assisting a sheriff, committed some negligent or criminal act. In Alabama in October, 1870, four soldiers who were on guard when a prisoner escaped were turned over to the civil authorities on a criminal warrant. After surrendering them, their commanding officer requested instructions from department headquarters and was informed, "In theory the men on guard were sheriff's men, part of a posse, and stood in the same relation as citizens would." All the commanding general could suggest was that the officer attend the trial and be very observant, so that if the trial were unfair, he could "make such representations to the

[9] S. Crawford to Gen. S. Crawford, Sept. 2, 1870, file 661A1870, AGO, RG94, NA. Gov. Smith thought the endorsement purporting to be by Terry's authority had been made while Terry was absent and that he never saw it. Whatever the case, it is not in Terry's handwriting.

Governor of Alabama, as will lead his Excellency to exert his preroga-
tive and grant a pardon." [10] Apparently this was an isolated instance,
which in view of the frequent aid given to civil officers was both remarkable and fortunate.

The Army also furnished aid to federal law enforcement officers, often a less difficult procedure than furnishing aid to state officials. Since
United States marshals and district attorneys, unlike the state officers, all
had a common superior in Washington—the Attorney General—requests for aid usually went to Washington first unless the case required
immediate action. A successful request originating, say, in the office of
the United States Marshal for Georgia might pursue this typical journey:
Attorney General's Office—War Department—White House—War Department—Headquarters of the Army—Adjutant General's Office—
Headquarters, Department of the South—Headquarters, Post of Atlanta.
Depending upon what the Secretary of War thought when he first received the request, the detour via the White House might be eliminated,
or sometimes in an urgent case Sherman might be bypassed. If all the
long-distance transmitting were done by telegraph, and if the troops did
not have far to go, the marshal might have his escort two or three days
after he had asked for it. On July 18, 1871, a federal district attorney
telegraphed Attorney General A. T. Ackerman requesting that cavalry
be sent to Meridian, Mississippi, to help round up some lawless individuals. The next day Adjutant General Townsend sent a wire to Atlanta
telling Terry, the department commander, to send the help by order of
the President. The nearest available unit was Company F of the 7th
Cavalry at Louisville, Kentucky, about 500 miles away, and on the
twentieth Terry sent out the order. On the twenty-fifth Captain George
F. Yates reported that he had arrived in Meridian and would com-
municate with the federal officials. About a week later the district attorney grumbled to Ackerman that things were not going well. He said
he had ordered some arrests made in Winston County, sixty miles from
Meridian, but because the orders of the cavalry officers restricted the
men to traveling only twenty miles a day, news of the expedition's approach got to the area the day before the troops did, "and the parties
were *non est.*" Company F stayed at Meridian until November when the
United States marshal wired Terry that they were no longer needed,
adding, "I have the honor to say that Captain Yates and his troop have

[10]AAG to Capt. William Mills, Oct. 29, 1870, Dept. South, 243, RG98, NA. The
records do not indicate the outcome.

acquitted themselves with ability, fidelity, and entire acceptability [;] he is at your disposal." Terry sent them back to Louisville since mounted troops were much needed in Kentucky for the same purpose.[11]

In July of 1869 the collector of internal revenue in Florida requested military surveillance of some St. Augustine property that had been sold for nonpayment of taxes. His request went to the Secretary of the Treasury, whose War Department colleague ordered the Army to secure the premises until an agent designated by the Treasury could take charge of it.[12]

In addition to helping arrest criminals, the Army also assisted federal revenue agents in breaking up illicit distilleries run by individuals who did not bother to pay the federal tax. The commissioner for North Carolina asked General McDowell in April, 1873, to station a company at Asheville permanently for his assistance. McDowell, with Sherman's concurrence, refused to send troops there permanently but allowed the Raleigh commander to send an officer and a few men to Asheville for up to thirty days. The commissioner was advised, "It might be well to have the whole subject so far in hand that the arrests shall commence on the arrival of the troops." [13] In an 1875 case, a Mississippi commissioner complained that armed men were chasing one of his deputies from county to county in the southwest portion of the state. Up through channels to the President went the complaint; down through channels came the order to send the agent some help. It later turned out that the deputy, in addition to being disliked as a "revenooer," was also a former Confederate who had turned Republican partisan after the war. It is hard to determine which factor was the greater cause of his difficulties. One is led to wonder if the troops ever appropriated some of the leftover contents of the stills to their own use following a raid, but reports on their conduct seemed regularly to resemble that of the Louisiana agent who called his mission a "grand success" thanks to military aid.[14] Of course, they could all have refreshed themselves together.

Many of the joint operations between the Army and the federal civil authorities had for their object the suppression of the Ku Klux Klan. Originally formed as a small organization in Tennessee in 1865, the Klan spread rapidly throughout the South and achieved its greatest membership in 1870–71.[15] Its goal was the deliverance of the South from Negro-

[11]Files 2464 of 1871 and 3949 of 1871, AGO, RG94, NA.
[12]Townsend to CG Dept. South, July 21, 1869, AGO, 49, RG94, NA.
[13]AAG to P. W. Perry, April 21, 1873, Dept. South, 246, RG94, NA.
[14]Files 6467 of 1875 and 1393 of 1874, AGO, RG94, NA.
[15]James G. Randall and David Donald, *The Civil War and Reconstruction* (Boston, 1961), 682–83.

Radical rule; its methods were terror, intimidation, violence, and the use of weird disguises to prey upon the superstitions of the Negro. Although the Klan had distinctly political motives, there were doubtless members who joined as a means of wreaking vengeance on their personal enemies; and although most Northerners regarded it as a single unified conspiracy, there were doubtless nonmembers who appropriated Klan methods to gain the advantage of secrecy for their crimes. The Army was naturally a repository of complaints, affidavits, and testimony about the Klan, and many of the accounts were almost identical in their general pattern. It was not uncommon for a victim to report having been taken out into the woods and having been "Ku-Kluxed." The verb was newly-coined and covered a multitude of unpleasant details.[16]

The Army's general duties in the suppression of crime naturally made the Klan an object of special concern. In his October, 1868, report on affairs in his Kentucky-Tennessee command, General Thomas included much documentary evidence on the Klan's doings; General Reynolds blamed the turbulence in northeastern Texas in 1868 and 1869 on the hooded nightriders. Other officers were more skeptical. In November of 1869 General Halleck, whose Division of the South lacked only Texas and Virginia, reported, "Although there may be special organizations of outlaws in particular localities under the name of Ku-Klux, I am of the opinion that no such general organization now exists in the southern States. It is probable, however, that outlaws not unfrequently [*sic*] assume this name in order to intimidate the weak and credulous, especially when calculated to increase their own importance." [17] But an ex-chaplain of the 8th Indiana Cavalry who had served under Sherman and was now a minister in Alabama wrote to his wartime leader, "They are now in full blast in North Alabama." The courts either could not or would not do anything, he said; "indeed, there is as much Ku-Kluxing in the courts, as by disguised men in the streets." He had read Halleck's report, which he thought "grates harshly on the nerves of loyal men, worse, the people are indignant, and clamor, another Andy Johnson." [18]

The Klan fast became a problem that only the federal government could handle because the state authorities were in many places either timid or in collusion with the outlaws. As one federal official in Mississippi remarked after describing a visit by the nightriders, "They think

[16]In the summer of 1871 a congressional committee toured the South investigating the Klan. The result was a thirteen-volume production of testimony, *House Reports,* 42nd Cong., 2nd Sess., No. 22.

[17]*Report of the Sec. of War, 1867–68,* pp. 142–202; file 1434M1868, with 311869, AGO, RG94, NA; *Report of the Sec. of War, 1868–69,* p. 78.

[18]A. S. Lakin to Sherman, Jan. 15, 1870, in Sherman Papers, LC.

the Government is playing with them. The story goes now that the Federal Court is about to fail, and so they will be tried in the State Courts which they do not regard more than a game of base ball." [19]

In June, 1871, General Terry sent in a general report on the Klan. He began with the pessimistic but correct observation that the entire United States Army would be insufficient to give protection throughout the South to everyone in possible danger from the Klan. Since the organization was so large that it could not be broken in all states simultaneously, Terry advised that it be severely dealt with in one area as an example, to make suppression easier elsewhere. After emphasizing that military force alone was not enough and that joint civil-military efforts would be necessary, Terry again became pessimistic. The state authorities "at the best are imbecile," he opined, and the federal officials too few and too scattered. He also stressed the need of overcoming the fear of testifying which seemed to possess many Klan victims. Terry recommended that vigorous action be taken against the Klan and suggested South Carolina as the best theater of operations. As matters turned out, it was essentially Terry's philosophy that the government employed. [20]

Congressional legislation designed to break the Klan began in May, 1870, with an act that provided heavy penalties for intimidating or hindering persons seeking to vote. The law also made it a crime for two or more persons to "band or conspire together, or go in disguise upon the public highway, or upon the premises of another" in order to carry out such intimidation. Federal courts received exclusive jurisdiction over offenses against the act; the federal marshals and commissioners who executed court processes under the law were empowered to call upon the Army for aid; and the President had the power to use any needful military force. [21]

A new act of February, 1871, which Grant himself had asked for, did not specify any further duties for the Army but did provide for more direct federal supervision of congressional elections. [22] In April the last of three laws appeared. Intimidation designed to discourage voting was already a federal crime, but now intimidation designed to discourage numerous other actions—holding office, testifying in court, serving on juries—was also forbidden. When conspiracies were so powerful that enforcement of federal laws was obstructed and nonmilitary means were

[19] J. D. Barton to G. W. Wells, Apr. 11, 1872, file 116 of 1872, AGO, RG94, NA.
[20] Terry to AAG Div. South, June 11, 1871, Dept. South, 244, RG98, NA.
[21] 16 U.S. Statutes at Large 140.
[22] 16 U.S. Statutes at Large 433.

unequal to the task of halting the trouble, the President could employ whatever military force he deemed necessary, and he could also suspend the habeas corpus privilege in the affected districts.[23]

While Congress battled the Klan in the legislative halls the Army battled it on the Southern countryside. The most common procedure was for a federal court to issue warrants to its marshal for the arrest of several suspected Klansmen; the marshal would then ask the nearest post commander for an escort, and the little expedition would sally forth on its errand of justice. Sometimes these detachments had ludicrous if dangerous experiences, such as in a Mississippi incident of September, 1871. Having been ordered to arrest James J. Bell, a deputy marshal at Aberdeen requisitioned an escort of fifteen men from Company H of the 6th Cavalry, recently arrived from Fort Hays, Kansas, and set out for Starkville in the next county. The troops surrounded Bell's house and searched it, but Bell had fled, and two soldiers went off in pursuit without catching him. The party was about to leave Starkville when a "special deputy" appeared with warrants issued by the local United States commissioner to arrest the marshal and his fifteen troopers. The charge was violation of one of the recent federal anti-Klan laws in that the marshal and his escort "had conspired to intimidate, molest and make afraid the ladies of the household of said James J. Bell" and had actually done so. The marshal protected the troops, they protected him, and the "special deputy" was sent scurrying away. He attempted the arrests again later, with no greater success, and for a time it appeared as though some of Bell's friends in Starkville might follow and ambush the marshal's party, but since only ten volunteers could be found that plan fell through. The marshal returned to Aberdeen and got a larger escort so he could return to Starkville and take Bell by surprise at night; whether he succeeded was not reported. As for the United States commissioner's legally preposterous action, it had a very understandable personal basis: the commissioner's own son had been indicted as a Klansman and was a bit further down on the marshal's "wanted" list.[24]

The stronger and more efficient the organization of the Klan and Klan-like groups, the harder the problem of apprehension. One young lieutenant of the 16th Infantry, sent with a detachment to the brushy, rolling country around Philadelphia, Mississippi, complained: "The services of my Detachment have not been called upon since my arrival and if they were—I would respectfully suggest it would be worse than

---

[23]17 U.S. Statutes at Large 13.

[24]Allen Huggins to Col. Sheldon Sturgeon, CO Aberdeen, Sept. 18, 1871, file 2527 of 1871, AGO, RG94, NA.

useless. Every man in the country has a horse or mule—or in lieu of them a Canebrake wherein to conceal himself at the briefest warning— Infantry could not move two miles before the cry "Yankees are coming" would be spread over a circuit of six—giving of course ample time for the wicked to flee—The sheriff has told me he could not possibly mount even a part of the Detachment." Only cavalry was of any use in such circumstances, but cavalry was scarce. Indian depredations on the Plains created a pressing need for it there, and poor Sherman had a difficult time shuttling cavalry commands from department to department. No sooner did Sheridan lend two companies to Mississippi than he wanted them back to escort Northern Pacific surveying parties from Fort Rice to the Yellowstone, but the Justice Department pleaded to keep them, and so they stayed. The other alternative was to hire horses locally for the use of infantry detachments, but the War Department never liked this practice.[25]

The rural character of the South was an advantage to the Klan and all criminals of such magnitude that even the presence of a squad of men in every village could not have overcome it. The melancholy fact was that no amount of troops could have prevented assaults on Negroes when the crimes took place on remote stretches of country roads by disguised men. Concealment of identity partially counteracted the troops' psychological impact, at least so long as the criminals remained unknown. It also made victims unwilling to testify for fear of retribution without warning and, therefore, made it difficult for the Army to protect those who did agree to testify.

The most intense military activity against the Klan took place in South Carolina during 1870–72. Charleston and Columbia were the two principal posts in the state. As conditions worsened General Terry concentrated some additional infantry there, obtained from Kentucky, Tennessee, and Georgia, and established several new posts. Since mounted troops were in special demand, in March of 1871 Washington sent Terry the 7th Cavalry from the Department of the Missouri. Part of it had to stay in Kentucky for similar anti-guerrilla activities; the rest was scattered in various parts of South Carolina. At their greatest extent the troops in the state numbered about 1,000 men, with garrisons of one or more companies at nine locations. In May, 1871, President Grant ordered the troops to help make whatever arrests the federal courts might desire, "and in all cases to arrest disguised night marauders and break up their bands." In October he suspended the habeas

[25]Lt. W. H. Vinal to AAAG Dept. Gulf, March 1, 1872, file 116 of 1872, AGO; file 2484 of 1872, AGO; Terry to AG USA, Oct. 31, 1870, file 1156S1870, AGO, RG94, NA.

corpus privilege in nine counties. The only civil duty of the troops was to serve as escorts for the federal marshals; no military commissions were employed since the law gave jurisdiction to the federal civil courts. Armed resistance to escorted marshals was the exception rather than the rule, and there was apparently no instance of a pitched battle between Army and Klan. Colonel Lewis Merrill, who commanded the post of Yorkville, preferred to have troops go along on all occasions to stave off the possibility of resistance, remarking that the presence of the blue uniform had a beneficial psychological effect.[26]

The performance of this kind of duty made discipline and control over the troops difficult. It was harder, though perhaps more necessary, to maintain close watch on troops stationed in towns and villages than on those in camps and forts, and close contact with civilians was sometimes detrimental. Merrill, who reported that desertions from his three companies were "unduly frequent," was certain that the Klan encouraged and protected deserters in an effort to undermine morale.[27] One of Merrill's units was Company K of the 7th Cavalry, and if the diary kept by a blacksmith of that troop is any indication, garrison duty at Yorkville was a rather humdrum affair. On June 11, 1871, he recorded that the Klan was reportedly massing for an assault on the troops that night. Next day he wrote disappointedly, "The K.K.K. did not come as reported. Our Troop laid on their arms ready to receive them but they are too big of a coward [*sic*] to come and let us see them." Even the Fourth of July was not too eventful: "The morning was opened with cheers and shouts for the old Flag of ninety-five years. The citizens of this town are opposed to the keeping of the 4th of July. They are a very angry set of people [,] or some few of them. Our Troop again played a game of ball with Co. C. of the 18th U.S. Infantry and Co. C. beat. Some of our boys are on a drunk. Plenty to do in my shop. No further news." The diarist was mustered out of service at Yorkville in September, 1871, which event occasioned his final entry: "I now close my soldiering for the present by bringing my history to a close. Everything in good condition and hope never to enlist again. No further news. All is well."[28]

---

[26]*Report of the Sec. of War, 1870–71*, pp. 59–64; Townsend to Terry, May 13, 1871, file 1670 of 1871, AGO, RG94, NA; *Messages and Papers*, VII, 138–39, 150–51; *Report of the Sec. of War, 1871–72*, pp. 88–91.

[27]*Report of the Sec. of War, 1871–72*, p. 86.

[28]Typescript of Winfield S. Harvey's notes, in Edward S. Godfrey Papers, LC. The typescript begins in September, 1868, when the 7th was on the Plains; the ms does not appear. Godfrey was a lieutenant in Co. K. in 1871; he was in command of the company at the Battle of the Little Big Horn in 1876 but survived, Co. K being with Capt. Frederick Benteen's battalion instead of Custer's.

The application of military force broke the Klan in South Carolina, and eighty-two convictions resulted from a large number of indictments. Sometimes Klansmen resorted to legal retribution against military officers who had helped arrest them. One brought a civil suit for false arrest against Colonel Merrill, and the government had to undertake Merrill's defense. But there were compensations. The South Carolina state government provided funds for rewards to be given to anyone, civilian or military, who aided in the arrest of offenders, and a special $10,000 gratuity for Merrill. This led Democratic Senator James A. Bayard to introduce a resolution calling for an investigation. Merrill, when asked for a report, furnished a rather vitriolic one denying any agency in the state's action and concluding, "If therefore I have exceeded the coldness of diction which is becoming to an Official paper, I hope it will be credited to no intention to be disrespectful, but to the fact that I am put on my defense against a stab in the back." [29]

Early in 1873 Merrill and the 7th Cavalry returned to the Plains, but before long they were back in the South. This time they supplied the great need for mounted troops in the Shreveport area of northwestern Louisiana, which along with South Carolina was one of the most lawless parts of Secessia in the 1870's. Their duties here were similar to those in South Carolina—aiding law officers to enforce court orders. But in Louisiana the offenders, members of the White League rather than the Klan, were a little bolder; and when the state officials were in sympathy with them, as was often the case, the Army sometimes had unpleasant experiences. Such was the case of Lieutenant B. H. Hodgson, one of Merrill's officers. Hodgson and a twelve-man detachment were helping a federal marshal when a backwoods sheriff appeared with a posse of two hundred men, arrested the lieutenant and marshal on the unusual charge of cutting telegraph wires, and took them to the little village of Vienna. It was characteristic that the citizens offered no violence to the soldiers; to have massacred a command of federal troops would have had serious repercussions.

In trying to direct things from Shreveport, Merrill in the space of six days added eighty-eight telegrams to the government's bill and kept the Vienna operator busy day and night. He ordered reinforcements to Vienna for Hodgson's protection, but he gave strict orders not to forcibly release the lieutenant or interfere with any legal processes. Merrill desired to let the civil authorities proceed so that he could have the case trans-

[29]Files 3622 of 1871 and 840 of 1873, AGO, RG94, NA. One sometimes regrets that writers of "official papers" did not "exceed the coldness of diction" more often.

ferred to federal court and then presumably prosecute the state authorities for interfering with a federal officer in the discharge of his duties. A civilian attorney was hired to defend Hodgson, but Merrill could not make him handle the case the way he wanted it handled, and the wires became hot with mutual recrimination. The colonel called the lawyer an "obstinate ignoramus" who could not follow a course "so plain and simple that a student would understand it"; the lawyer retorted, "There is a wide difference between a gentleman and a blackguard; you furnish an illustration." The civil authorities foiled Merrill's scheme, however. Apparently the culprits had intended simply to hinder and embarrass the federal government at least expense to themselves, and so they released Hodgson before the case could be transferred to federal court.[30]

Sometimes there were conflicts between the detachment commanders and the federal officials over the extent of the latter's power. These disagreements arose because of the frequent practice of including in the detachment commander's instructions the statement that he was to "obey all lawful orders of the marshal" or some equally unhelpful variant thereof. When Lieutenant Donald McIntosh took Company G of the 7th Cavalry on a mission to help a marshal make arrests in the Natchitoches and Coushatta area, he encountered precisely this difficulty. The expedition made twenty-five arrests, but McIntosh thought several more could have been made except for "want of energy" by the marshal. He was more annoyed over an incident at Natchitoches in which "the course of the marshal placed the troops in a false position." The marshal stated that he had the power to oust the sheriff, parish judge, and other local officials if he pleased and that McIntosh would back him up in doing so. The mayor inquired of McIntosh if this were true, and McIntosh answered that he was there to help the marshal serve legal processes. "Had I concurred with him [the marshal] . . . and used the force under my command accordingly, instead of being here, the chances are I would now be swinging from a tree with a rope round my neck, or be a prisoner in one of the parish jails of Northern Louisiana."[31]

In sending McIntosh's report up to higher headquarters, Merrill commended his subordinate and said that when talking to the marshal afterwards, he discovered that the marshal had been entrusted with making "certain investigations" and that he had not deemed it prudent to tell anyone about it, even McIntosh. Knowledge of these facts, Merrill thought, would have "materially modified" the lieutenant's views of the

[30]Telegraphic exchanges, Nov. 6–13, 1874, in *Sen Exec. Docs.*, 43rd Cong., 2nd Sess., No. 17, pp. 32–50.
[31]McIntosh to AAG Dept. Gulf, Nov. 14, 1874, *ibid.*, 12–15.

marshal's conduct.[32] That being the case, McIntosh's remark that the marshal had put his troops in a "false position" seems more apt than he realized. It was potentially dangerous for a law officer to keep secrets from the only supporting force he had.

The newspapers naturally blasted the Army on every occasion possible and Merrill expressed what many soldiers must have thought: "So long as freedom of the press means license to lie and slander at pleasure every officer whose discharge of duty offends one, or frequently both political parties, there would seem to be no remedy for the officer, and nothing for him to do but possess his soul in patience, and wait for a change of station to some frontier post, where the savages, whose feelings he must hurt, have no newspapers through which to assail him."[33] The Indians did not have newspapers, but they did have rifles; and in direct contrast to Southern terrorists, they did not hesitate to use them against the Army. The 7th Cavalry soon got its "change of station" to the Dakotas, and eighteen months after Merrill wrote, the Custer massacre took place. Both McIntosh and "Benny" Hodgson died that afternoon.

Quantitatively, the furnishing of details to apprehend criminals formed an important part of the Army's work. In the fall of 1871 General Terry reported that more than 200 expeditions had been sent out at the request of civil authorities, both state and federal, during the preceding year. His command embraced the seaboard states from South Carolina to Mississippi, plus Kentucky and Tennessee. A year later he reported more than 160 such operations, not including the ones made in South Carolina to suppress the Klan. Gradually the number seems to have decreased; in the autumn of 1874 General McDowell reported 42 special detachments, all to aid federal marshals and revenue officers, and in 1876 General Ruger reported 71.[34]

Even though small, these temporary detachments were useful, as practically all shades of political opinion testified. But the desirability of these sorties was questioned because of the attitude toward law enforcement which the Army's presence sometimes instilled. In August, 1868, Sherman and Halleck took up the matter of establishing permanent garrisons in the South. Both agreed that the best plan was to keep the troops concentrated in several carefully chosen locations, from which detachments could be sent out. Sherman remarked at this time, "Already people in the South begin to see the profit and advantage of hav-

[32]Merrill to AAG Dept. Gulf, Nov. 18, 1874, *ibid.*, 17–19.
[33]*Ibid.*, 17–19.
[34]*Report of the Sec. of War, 1870–71*, p. 63; *ibid., 1871–72*, p. 84; *ibid., 1873–74*, p. 51; *ibid., 1875–76*, p. 83.

a garrison in their town and village and in some instances have produced a cause, and then alleged it as a reason for stationing troops at the point." After some experience with the problems involved in furnishing aid to the civil authorities, Halleck reported that federal officials "assured" him the use of troops "seemed" to increase rather than decrease the necessity of resorting to military force. "The ill disposed become more and more exasperated at being coerced by a force which they think has been unconstitutionally employed against them, and the better disposed relax their efforts to punish local crimes on the plea that this duty now devolves on the military." [35] No matter what course the Army followed with respect to crime, it seems, there would be fault-finding of some kind.

Another of the Army's principal duties after the states rejoined the Union was the preservation of peace and order at elections. This was no new task for the men in blue, who had acquired practice while the Reconstruction Acts were operating. But there was now a difference in the Army's legal position. The generals no longer established detailed procedures for the mechanics of elections—this was the duty of the civil power. All the soldiers could do was to see that events transpired peacefully. Tennessee was the first state readmitted, and it was there, in September, 1867, that the Army received its baptism of fire in the art of preventing election disorders in a state over which it had no civil jurisdiction. The difficulty arose over a municipal election in Nashville. "Parson" Brownlow, the Radical governor, insisted that it be conducted according to a newly-passed franchise law; the mayor believed the law invalid and was determined to hold the election under previous rules. The underlying issue was that more Negroes would apparently be able to vote under Brownlow's method. There was danger of a conflict between the city police acting to support the mayor and the state guards acting to uphold Brownlow.

The numerous ensuing telegraphic dispatches can be reduced to this paraphrased substance:

THOMAS: Under existing instructions I feel compelled to support Brownlow and will do so unless you order differently.
GRANT: The Army can't decide which election procedure is legal. All you can do is preserve the peace.
THOMAS: Am I to sustain the governor or the mayor?
GRANT: I'm not telling you to sustain either the governor or the mayor, just

[35]Sherman to Halleck, Aug. 11, 1869, AGO, 49, RG94, NA; *Report of the Sec. of War, 1869–70*, p. 38.

preserve the peace. Only the governor can legally call for military aid, and must do so by reporting the state authorities powerless to keep the peace.

THOMAS: I can't preserve the peace without interfering in case of a collision, and if I do that, it may be a practical decision against state authority and the new franchise law. Please tell me what to do.

GRANT: You are to prevent conflict. You can't employ military force to defeat the executive of a state in carrying out a state law.

Thomas' predicament was plain, and it was also plain that Grant was saying, "stay politically neutral, and don't defeat the governor in the process." Thomas' orders to his subordinates finally appeared: guard the polls, keep the peace, and support the governor's election officials.[36]

It was usually the Republicans who requested troops for election day, and often the request went direct from party leaders to the President. On November 4, 1871, the Arkansas governor wired Grant that the Democrats and "a few disafected [sic] Republicans . . . threaten violent proceedings" at the forthcoming Little Rock city election. He hoped the post commander would be ordered to help maintain the peace. The President scribbled a memo in pencil on a scrap of paper and pinned it to the telegram: "Please acknowledge receipt of dispatch but give no order to Military, at least not further than to exercise a proper discretion in quelling any disturbances should the necessity arise. U. S. Grant." Adjutant General Townsend made the presidential memo into a wire for the post commander, that officer replied that the message was "understood," and nothing happened on election day.[37]

What made election duty delicate was the dilemma of how to make the voters behave peacefully without influencing them politically or predetermining the result of the election. The summer of 1868 saw the readmission of several more states, and Johnson, looking ahead to the November presidential canvass, gave the Army a warning. He directed Grant to republish for the soldiers' guidance the 1865 law prohibiting military interference with elections in any of the states. The generals heeded the reminder and cautioned their troops; in North Carolina General Nelson Miles advised them not to "fraternize with political parties" or interfere with citizens' expressing their views.[38] The method most commonly adopted for successfully preserving the peace and warding off charges of improper political influence was to determine in advance

[36]Telegraphic exchanges in *Report of the Sec. of War, 1866–67*, pp. 186–94.
[37]File 3858 of 1871, AGO, RG94, NA.
[38]GO 82, AGO, Oct. 10, 1868, RG94, NA; *Army and Navy Journal*, VI (Nov. 7, 1868), 178.

where disturbances would be most likely, send a small detachment to each place a day or so before the election, have it stay within sight of the polls but at a discreet distance, and prohibit it from handling any records or ballots. With precautions such as these the presidential election of 1868 took place in an atmosphere of comparative quiet.

One point that caused some uncertainty in policing elections was who among the civil officers had the legal authority to call for military aid and who did not. In the Tennessee case Grant had thought only the governor did, and in most instances after 1868 any formal request did come through the governor. But there never was any clear statement on the point. In the fall of 1870 several detachment commanders were told, "You will respond to officers who have the right to call out a posse comitatus and to no others." On one occasion in 1875 War Secretary Belknap told General C. C. Augur to have troops ready to suppress disorder in a Mississippi election "on receiving a proper call for such assistance." Augur wired back asking whose call he should regard as proper. At least Belknap showed the general's telegram to the President and Attorney General, but the answer was yet another manifestation of Washington's reluctance to give detailed instructions: "I am directed to say that further instructions are not deemed necessary. You are expected to be vigilant and to do your duty discreetly. Order must be preserved and bloodshed prevented if possible." [39]

Sometimes a disagreement over the necessity for troops at elections was resolved by not sending any at all. In July, 1874, acting Mississippi Governor A. K. Davis asked General William H. Emory to have troops at hand for elections in Vicksburg. The municipal authorities asked him not to. The staff officer Emory sent to appraise conditions concluded that a riot was not likely. This report ultimately found its way to Long Branch, New Jersey, where President Grant was vacationing, and he decided not to send troops. The election went off quietly. [40]

Sometimes political feelings ran so high that troops were requested to protect meetings and conventions before an election. In August, 1871, a Republican convention was to meet in the New Orleans Customs House, and a federal marshal asked for troops to protect the government's property because "much fear is anticipated of a disturbance from Thugs and Bruisers." Colonel Alfred Sully, who received the resulting order, wired his commanding general that it would be obeyed but added, "The trouble is between two factions of the republican party and is not the

[39] AAG to Lt. A. W. Corliss and others, Oct. 15, 1870, Dept. South, 243, RG98, NA; file 5569 of 1875, AGO, RG94, NA.
[40] File 1495 of 1874, AGO, RG94, NA.

act of persons enemies [*sic*] of the government but of those who profess to be its friends. It is entirely a political row among the republican politicians." [41]

If elections had been confined to a presidential canvass every four years, the Army's problem would have been considerably simplified. But during the Civil War era elections were poorly synchronized in the several states, and the constant holding of elections resulted in an almost permanent state of political campaigning and agitation. The state and congressional elections of 1870 particularly threatened trouble. In Alabama Republican leaders feared they might lose control of the state and wanted military aid. From Patona, Senator Willard Warner received the opinion, "To say there is no danger with the facts that have been developed here and which almost every breeze brings to our ears, would be to talk like simpletons." Warner urged the War Department to send more troops to his adopted state. He made a special point of asking that all of them be placed under the command of General S. W. Crawford, already in Alabama, and that Crawford be authorized to move the troops from place to place. Since Alabama was part of Terry's command, the War Office asked for his opinion. He replied that in addition to the 2nd Infantry, already in the state, he could gather up some scattered companies of the 16th from various places, thus making an aggregate of about 1,000 men. As for Crawford, there were "certain reasons," not explained, why Terry would prefer to control things himself rather than let Crawford do it; but he concluded, "Of course, if the Secretary thinks it best to put him in command I shall have no objection to offer." [42]

Someone apparently thought it best, for Crawford received the command and exercised it from mid-October until mid-November. He scattered the troops to ten key locations, from which details went out to thirty additional points, selected in consultation with the governor and United States marshal. He cautioned the troops, "The duties devolving upon you are delicate and important, and will require the exercise of

[41]File 2747 of 1871, AGO, RG94, NA.

[42]T. M. Peters to Warner, Sept. 25, 1870; Townsend to Terry, Sept. 30, and reply, Oct. 3, file 661A1870, AGO, RG94, NA. In the 1870's the AGO made increasing use of the "consolidation file," in which papers on the same general topic, though receiving individual file numbers, were all grouped together under one master number. Before 1870 such papers more often remained separate. 661A1870 is an example—a compilation of papers on the Alabama elections with some on Georgia thrown in too. Such files are a blessing in that related papers are together but a curse in that the larger they are the more poorly they are organized.

the utmost discretion and prudence; but I look to you to establish the fact to the people of Alabama, that the United States troops in their midst are not partisans, but in the highest degree conservators of the peace and the supporters of law and order." After the elections he reported that no serious disturbances had taken place and that most of the troops could be safely returned to their proper stations. He did think it prudent, however, on the basis of his own travels in the western part of the state, to keep some mounted detachments there for a while. He closed by commending the troops and declining to offer any opinion concerning the "very great political change in the State." [43]

The "political change" referred to was the election of the Democratic candidate for governor. The legislature was split between the parties, and the congressional delegation was similarly mixed. No apparent correlation existed between the location of troops and the results of the election. Out of eleven counties with Negro majorities where troops were stationed, the Republicans maintained control of six and lost four; the other was very closely divided. The Republicans kept control of four Black Belt counties where there were no troops. In nine counties where troops were present, a white majority resulted in Democratic victory. The same result occurred in a like number of counties where there were no troops. [44]

Indeed, for the period after readmission it would be difficult to generalize about the presence or absence of troops leading to a particular political result. Soldiers had much more extensive election duty in Alabama than in Arkansas, yet the "Redeemers" in both states required until 1874 to establish a conservative government. Louisiana saw much greater military activity than Florida, yet Republican regimes lasted in both until 1877. Virginia fell into conservative hands even before military control was relinquished and the state readmitted. Before elections local Republicans claimed that with military force they could win (an implied confession that without it they could not); after they lost an election it was easy for them to complain about inadequate protection. One instance was the 1870 Florida election, which also displays other characteristics of the entire election-policing problem. In October Governor Harrison Reed began getting letters from various parts of the state expressing fear that Negroes would be intimidated on election day.

[43]Crawford's instructions, Oct. 31, 1868, and report, Nov. 18, file 661A1870, AGO, RG94, NA.

[44]Fleming, *Alabama*, 750, gives the political results by county. He attempts to show that the troops had some responsibility for the 1872 and 1874 results, but the case does not seem convincing. *Ibid.*, 755, 795.

"I think," said one office-holder, "the plan will be to crowd the polls and jostle them away and then get up so much of a row that there will be a chance to shoot and stab without being identified." The informant wanted a company of troops in his little town before the election and added, "I think great care should be exercised in sending discreet officers—If this is done I am sure that troops will not only be an advantage to all here, but that it will not be an unpopular movement." Reed promptly wrote Grant, lamenting about "political demagogues" and "organized bands of enemies of the government"; at least five companies should be put at his disposal, he claimed.[45]

Grant was slow to act, however, and a week before the election he received another request for troops, this time from Senator Thomas W. Osborne. Grant and his advisors studied the current deployment of Southern forces and pondered the Florida request. Alabama was about to have her elections, and some were pending in Georgia too. The high command thought some more. Finally Grant decided that none could be spared; Florida would have to make do without additional forces. The wires informed the Florida leaders on November 2 and then fell silent. On the fourth came this terse message: "If we can have the support we expected we shall carry the state [;] if not the probabilities are decidedly against us and many assassinations will be committed." That intelligence set Grant thinking again. He certainly did not like the thought of violence, and he doubtless did not like the prospect of Florida being lost to the Republicans. Grant finally turned the problem over to the Army high command with instructions to send the aid if they thought it could be spared; otherwise they need not bother answering the last telegram. On November 5 scribbled memos circulated among Belknap, Sherman, and Adjutant General Townsend. Sherman finally suggested that a couple of companies could go from New Orleans to Tallahassee; Belknap approved, and the order went out to Halleck the same day. On the seventh Townsend received this reply: "Lt. Col. Ayres telegraphs from New Orleans that there is no steamer swift enough to take troops to Tallahassee before midnight on Tuesday which will be too late for the election." One wonders whose opinion was reflected in the cryptic notation this wire received by the Adjutant General's pen: "Reply—Despatch received and is satisfactory. EDT Novr 7/70." [46]

Election day in Florida came and went, and on the face of the returns it appeared the Republicans had lost. Before long Grant received

---

[45]J. Q. Dickinson to Reed, Oct. 1, 1870, and Reed to Grant, Oct. 5, file 12401870, AGO, RG94, NA.
[46]Telegraphic exchanges, file 12401870, AGO, RG94, NA.

this evidence of mixed indignation and panic on the part of Governor Reed:

Through treachery and intimidation a republican majority of over 10,000 [registered voters] has been overcome and the Democrats or rebels now proclaim their purpose to seize the government by violence, depose the Executive, by assassination if necessary, and drive from the state all leading republicans. Two companies of infantry sent us to secure the execution of the Enforcement law would have saved us. I now most respectfully ask that you order a full regiment of U.S. Troops to remain here until the Legislature adjourns in February. The capitol is liable at any time to be seized by armed hords [*sic*] of outlaws and unless you extend immediate assistance we cannot sustain Republican government in Florida.

A postscript urged secrecy until the troops actually arrived. On the twenty-second Washington sent two companies, which were all that could be spared.[47] The Republicans controlled the state returning board, however, and manipulation of the returns by that group saved them. Reed may have been right that the presence of more troops would have saved him though it seems a moot point. Perhaps the Republican regime in Florida was really too distasteful for the voters.

In editorializing about the Army's political duties the Atlanta *Constitution,* a Democratic paper, observed: "The generally prevailing idea that because one political party happens to be always calling for troops, with a view to benefiting its cause, the soldiers are partisans of that party, is a gross error. Federal troops are not bugbears to our people." [48] It was a true enough statement, but it did not elaborate on the crux of the Army's problem. Republicans were constantly clamoring for troops because they were afraid of being turned out of office; and because the desire to turn them out was so great, the results of elections were often contested by one or both parties. Political turmoil in the South, therefore, did not always end on election day, and so neither did the Army's political duties.

[47]Reed to Grant, Nov. 17, 1870, and reply, Nov. 22, file 12401870, AGO, RG94, NA.
[48]Quoted in *Army and Navy Journal,* XIV (Oct. 28, 1876), 184.

11

1877—The Only Possible Ending

O F all the duties the Army performed during the seventies, the most delicate was that of maintaining peace in times of post-election conflict between rival claimants for state governorships, or between rival legislatures. The federal government preferred such quarrels to be settled by legal action, but in the meantime someone had to keep the opponents from assaulting each other's supporters, and the Army was the only trustworthy power available. The state governments had their own militia forces, but these were worse than useless in such circumstances because they were clearly partisan units. The factionalizing of the Republican party which proceeded rapidly in many Southern states after 1868 often figured prominently in the causation of these brawls and created situations made to order for the political opposition. Since the initiative in requesting federal aid was legally supposed to be taken by the state authorities, the troops were thus put in the position of responding to the call of one or the other of the conflicting parties even though the avowed purpose of the intervention was preservation of the peace rather than preservation of a political faction.

Arkansas, quiet in comparison to some of its neighbors during the seventies, was the scene of one such affair, usually called the "Brooks-Baxter War." This imbroglio began with the gubernatorial election of 1872 in which Joseph Brooks opposed Elisha Baxter. Both were nominally Republicans, but the state's politics at that time were complicated in the extreme. Although the election was close, it appeared Baxter had won and he took office amidst a storm of charges of fraud. In the ensuing months Brooks and Baxter waged an intermittent battle in the courts, with Baxter holding the office, *de facto* at least, all the while.

236

In April, 1874, the Brooks cabal made its most active bid for victory. A state judge decreed Brooks entitled to the office, and the Brooks supporters ejected Baxter from the statehouse without too much difficulty. The deposed governor gathered his friends and set up a command post at a hotel not far from the capitol, which the usurpers prepared to defend as their own fortress. Each side began recruiting forces, and partisans converged on Little Rock from all directions.

The two companies of infantry at Little Rock had not taken much notice of the contest until the April coup. Then the telegraph keys began clicking furiously. They brought the local commander instructions from General W. H. Emory at New Orleans: until the wishes of the government are known, observe the strictest neutrality—and from Washington: the President says to take no part in any political controversy unless necessary to prevent bloodshed or conflict between armed gangs.[1]

Some potential embarrassment for the government arose over the command of the troops at Little Rock. Captain W. H. Bartholomew, the post commander, was under arrest and awaiting the result of his trial for being drunk on duty; the command thus devolved on the senior officer present, Captain Thomas E. Rose—the same one who had gotten into trouble during the 1867 Virginia elections. Rose had absented himself from the sessions of the court martial which tried Bartholomew, and this "erratic conduct" induced Emory to send another officer from New Orleans to take temporary command. During the tense April days Rose became involved in a newspaper controversy over his conduct. On April 21 danger of an armed clash occurred, and Rose's troops had to act to prevent it. An article in the next morning's paper cast aspersions on Rose's personal bravery; Rose retorted in print that the author was "a liar and a coward; a low hind, probably born in a hovel where the swine made his parents take a back seat." Rose's retort, when sent to the Secretary of War, brought the captain a rebuke for the article and commendation for the rest of his conduct. The court martial had meanwhile found Bartholomew guilty and sentenced him to be cashiered, but upon review early in May a legal technicality in the proceedings caused their disapproval and Bartholomew ultimately resumed command.[2]

Meanwhile the fever in Little Rock spread to other parts of the state,

[1]The political details can be followed in Staples, *Arkansas,* 402–24. The telegraphic exchanges are in file 1491 of 1874, AGO, RG94, NA; some are printed in *House Exec. Docs.,* 43rd Cong., 1st Sess., No. 229.

[2]Papers in file 1491 of 1874, AGO, RG94, NA. The papers dealing with Bartholomew are endorsed, "copy not furnished under House resolution. . . ." Thus they do not appear in *House Exec. Docs.,* 43rd Cong., 1st Sess., No. 229.

and some lives were lost in rural skirmishes between adherents of the two factions. From Marianna, in the eastern part of the state, a sheriff pleaded with Grant:

For the sake of law and order take some steps to suppress the riot in Arkansas. . . . The general impression is that you will not interfere thus they keep up the fight. Will you save us? We are in a pitiable condition—for God's sake help us. Our whole salvation depends upon our crops. If this matter continues much longer we are ruined. . . . President Grant you can stop this muddle if you will and if you do not you are responsible for our ruin. Know from whence this comes. We do not care—and I speak the sentiments of the people of Arkansas without egotism—who is Governor? [sic] All we want is peace. The people will obey. Answer.[3]

But for the moment Grant did nothing, and partisans continued to congregate in Little Rock. Captain Rose became more and more concerned, and on May 11 he telegraphed the War Department asking for some cavalry to have on hand in case of need. Townsend turned the telegram over to Sherman "for remark." After five years of reading dispatches on Southern turbulence Sherman was weary. At 4 P.M. he sat at his desk and scribbled with imaginable vexation, "Returned with the remark that this whole business has been managed so that I cannot understand it." Sherman thought Rose should have called on Emory, his superior, for reinforcements before pestering the War Office. "I have seen no orders of any kind relieving him [Rose] from the supervision of his Department Commander and until he recognizes him I have not one word to say, Except [sic] that in my judgment it is time for General Emory to go in person to Little Rock and exercise command in his own Department, or be relieved." [4]

At that same moment Baxter was making preparations to regain his office. He had already called on Grant for aid, and on May 11 he assembled a special session of the state legislature, which by joint resolution also asked Grant for assistance. On the fifteenth Grant issued a proclamation recognizing Baxter as the legitimate governor and commanding "all turbulent and disorderly persons" to go home peacefully within ten days. The armed partisans obeyed the President, Little Rock became quiet, and the Army's direct role in the Brooks-Baxter War ended, although the legal wrangling continued into 1875.[5]

Far more involved and troublesome than the Arkansas conflict was the

---

[3]W. H. Forbish to Grant, April 21, 1874, file 1491 of 1874, AGO, RG94, NA.
[4]Rose to Townsend, May 11, 1874, file 1491 of 1874, AGO, RG94, NA. This paper was withheld from the House, too.
[5]*Messages and Papers*, VII, 272–73; Gen. W. D. Whipple, AAG USA, to Emory, May 16, 1874, file 1491 of 1874, AGO, RG94, NA.

bitter feuding over the state government of Louisiana which continued incessantly, but with variable intensity, from 1872 to 1877. During those five years Louisiana was unquestionably the most turbulent state in the whole South—much more so, for example, than Virginia, Georgia, North Carolina, Texas, or Arkansas. The political alignments, shifts, and fusions of this five-year period in Louisiana almost defy comprehension and were complicated, as were all Southern politics, by the race issue. The animosities of previous years reached a peak in the 1872 gubernatorial election between Republican William P. Kellogg and Democrat John McEnery. Intimidation and fraud marked the contest, and it is impossible to tell now, as it was then, who really won. Kellogg promptly brought suit in federal court to obtain possession of the election returns, and when the process of the court met with resistance, Grant authorized the federal marshals to call on the Army for assistance. The result was that in January, 1873, the Kellogg government was inaugurated in New Orleans, while a few blocks away McEnery also took the oath of office. There being two rival bodies claiming to be the state legislature, the state witnessed the spectacle of dual governments, and all the while federal troops stood ready to act in case of a riot. For a time the two rival factions coexisted peacefully, but in March, 1873, the McEnery group sought to assemble a militia force in New Orleans. This resulted in the city police dispersing the McEnery legislature, an action which General Emory did not attempt to prevent since he regarded it as the authorized act of the Kellogg government.[6]

During the remainder of 1873 and early 1874 the Kellogg group remained the *de facto* government of the state, and while the atmosphere in New Orleans was tense, there was no necessity for interference by federal troops. In other parts of the state, however, political animosity led to loss of life, as in the disturbances at Colfax and Coushatta. Louisiana skies grew dark again in September, 1874, as the fall elections approached. On the fourteenth D. P. Penn, claiming to have been elected lieutenant-governor in 1872, issued a proclamation calling on the militia to arm itself and drive Kellogg from the statehouse. Kellogg applied to Grant for aid, and on the fifteenth the President issued a proclamation commanding the attackers to disperse. Before the proclamation became public in New Orleans, however, armed men had taken the statehouse by surprise, and Kellogg sought refuge in the federal customs house. Under instructions from Washington the troops, which had earlier been

[6]This account is based in part on a special message to Congress by Grant on Jan. 13, 1875, giving the history of the problem, in *Messages and Papers*, VII, 305–308. Also of use is Ella Lonn, *Reconstruction in Louisiana After 1868* (New York, 1918), 166–229.

reduced in numbers and relocated, were brought in immediately; the trespassers surrendered to them, and Kellogg's men resumed possession.[7]

Thus the troops effected another uneasy truce, but it was less than two months until the November elections, and passions were not cooled. The canvass was for members of the legislature and lesser state offices, and the usual charges of fraud and coercion raged on both sides. Although the returns gave the Democrats a majority, the state returning board finally decided that fifty-three Republicans and fifty-three Democrats were legally elected to the legislature, with five additional cases left for that body itself to determine. As if that decision was not a sufficient cause for trouble, a Democratic group declared seventy-one of its candidates elected, as opposed to thirty-seven Republicans. The stage was set for more tumult when the legislature met in January of 1875. Newspapers indulged in outright advocacy of assassination: "If George L. Smith is counted in over W. M. Levy, or if Twitchell is counted in over Elam, let Smith and Twitchell be killed." [8]

In this crisis Grant arrived at a hardly surprising solution: Sheridan must go back to New Orleans. On Christmas Eve Secretary Belknap wired "confidential" instructions to Sheridan at Chicago. He was to visit Mississippi and Louisiana, "especially New Orleans," and find out for Grant's information "the general condition of matters in those localities." He could go anywhere else in the South he thought proper. "What the President desires," Belknap said, "is to ascertain the true condition of affairs, and to receive such suggestions from you as you may deem advisable and judicious." Sheridan also had the specific authority to assume command of the Division of the South, or any part of it, if he thought proper to do so. He could take this step without even bothering to tell General McDowell in Louisville, the division commander, about it or even what he was doing in the South. The day after Christmas Sheridan wired back, "Your letter received. All right. Kind regards to madam and baby." [9]

The legislature was scheduled to convene on the fourth of January, and Sheridan arrived in New Orleans several days previously. Emory's troops were in command of the city as they had been ever since the

[7]*Messages and Papers,* VII, 276–77, 309–10; Lonn, *Louisiana,* 268–91. The telegraphic exchanges between Washington and Louisiana commanders are in file 3579 of 1874, AGO, RG94, NA. A few messages between the civil authorities are printed in *Sen. Exec. Docs.,* 43rd Cong., 2nd Sess., No. 13, pp. 13–15.

[8]Lonn, *Louisiana,* 289–93; Shreveport *Times,* Nov. 15, 1874.

[9]Belknap to Sheridan, Dec. 24, 1874, and reply, Dec. 26, file 3579 of 1874, AGO, RG94, NA. Both are printed in *Sen. Exec. Docs.,* 43rd Cong., 2nd Sess., No. 17, pp. 19–20, but the last sentence of Sheridan's reply is omitted and the rest mispunctuated.

September proceedings. Nearly a regiment of infantry was scattered along the riverbank, cavalry was further inland, artillery was at hand, and naval power lay at anchor in the river. More troops were in reserve at Jackson Barracks, and on December 13 Emory gave orders to the commander there to keep the men ready to move into the city at any time upon receiving orders from him or upon hearing three signal guns fired by the warships in the harbor at any hour of the day or night. These orders were "confidential," but the substance of them appeared in the New Orleans papers immediately thereafter; this was apparently a deliberate "leak" on Emory's part to let the city know that he meant business.[10]

Before the legislature met, Emory stationed troops near the state-house—some had been there previously but they had been removed in November—at the request of Governor Kellogg. The legislature convened at noon. The former clerk called the roll; fifty-two Republicans and fifty Democrats answered. But before the result was announced a Democratic member nominated Louis A. Wiltz, previously chosen by a Democratic caucus, for temporary speaker. The clerk ruled it out of order but Wiltz rushed to the stand and declared himself speaker. In accordance with an obviously prearranged plan, the Democratic members began nominating people for clerk and sergeant-at-arms; Wiltz declared them elected; numbers of men in various parts of the hall then turned down their lapels to display badges marked "assistant sergeant-at-arms." Thus the hall was in possession of the minority, and the former clerk and the Republicans withdrew. One of the Democratic members then moved that the Army be asked to clear the lobbies; this was done, and presently Colonel P. Regis deTrobriand, commanding the troops at the statehouse, appeared with his staff. Wiltz said he could not keep order without military aid, so deTrobriand went out to the lobby, induced the crowd to disperse, was thanked by the Democrats, and left. While the Democrats went about seating their five colleagues whom the returning board had not declared elected, the Republicans protested to Governor Kellogg, who asked the Army to restore the status quo by ejecting "those persons who had been illegally seated and who had no legal right to be there." The Army did so forcibly, the Democrats got up and walked out, and the hall became the possession of the Republicans.[11]

Sheridan claimed that the Army's action had been politically neutral

---

[10]Emory to AG USA, Oct. 28 and Dec. 19, 1874, in *Sen. Exec. Docs.,* 43rd Cong., 2nd Sess., No. 17, pp. 62–67.

[11]Sheridan to Belknap, Jan. 8, 1875, in *Sen. Exec. Docs.,* 43rd Cong., 2nd Sess., No. 13, pp. 27–29; Lonn, *Louisiana,* 292–98.

and preservative of the peace, since the first visit to the legislature came at the instance of the Democrats, the second at the instance of the Republicans, and there had been no bloodshed. That analysis was rather shallow, however, because the result of the whole affair obviously put the Republicans in control. The Republicans, having a quorum present, were able to effect a permanent organization, and nothing was left for the opposition but to protest or make another ludicrous attempt at dual governments.

Sheridan's function was to tell Washington what was really happening in New Orleans and make "advisable and judicious" suggestions. He lost no time in doing so, and a constant stream of typically-phrased telegrams came in from the troubled city. He began by describing a "spirit of defiance to all lawful authority" in the state and supplemented this with a characterization of the White Leagues and other organizations as "banditti." If Congress would declare them such, he boasted, "I will relieve it from the necessity of any special legislation for the preservation of peace and equality of rights in the States of Louisiana, Mississippi [and] Arkansas, and the Executive from much of the trouble heretofore had in this section of the country." Sheridan was thinking of trial by military commission, of course.[12]

The messages continued. "Some of the banditti made idle threats last night that they would assassinate me because I dared to tell the truth. I am not afraid, and will not be stopped from informing the government that there are localities in this department where the very air has been impregnated with assassination for several years." Then this smugness: "The dog is dead. White leagues here are trying to make arrangements to surrender to civil authorities[,] fearing to come under my jurisdiction." He followed this up with the announcement that his previous messages were "so truthful of the condition of affairs in this section and strike so near the water line that ministers of the gospel and others are appealed to to keep the ship from sinking. Human life has been held too cheaply in this state for many years." The return messages from Belknap congratulated him and assured him that the President and Cabinet had confidence in his wisdom and judiciousness.[13]

Sheridan's habitual rashness of judgment manifested itself in his relations with General William H. Emory, who commanded the Department

[12]Sheridan to Belknap, Jan. 4, 5, and 8, 1875, in *Sen. Exec. Docs.*, 43rd Cong., 2nd Sess., No. 13, pp. 21–27.

[13]Of the three telegrams quoted, only the first (Jan. 6, 1875) appears *ibid.*, 25. The other two (Jan. 6 and Jan. 8) are in file 3400 of 1874, filed with 3579 of 1874, AGO, RG94, NA.

of the Gulf during the trying times of 1874. Emory, a Marylander, was sixty-three years old and had graduated from West Point in the year Sheridan was born. During Sheridan's 1864 Shenandoah Valley campaign he had commanded a corps of infantry. He assumed the Gulf command in November, 1871. Grant's permission for Sheridan to supplant Emory or even McDowell may perhaps have been motivated by some distrust of Emory; but on the other hand, considering Grant's regard for Sheridan, the permission would not have been too remarkable whoever commanded at New Orleans. Sheridan could hardly have been in New Orleans more than a couple of days when on January 2, 1875, he dashed off a wire to Belknap: "Affairs here still quite feverish, but I scarcely believe there will be any serious trouble. On Monday the 4th instant I think it would be very well to annex this Department to my military Division and eventually change the Department commanding officer as I doubt his ability to keep things steady and inspire confidence. I would recommend R. S. Mackenzie in such case." [14]

Sheridan did in fact assume control of Emory's department on the fourth, though not until 9 P.M., after the day's excitement was over. On the eighth he sent Belknap a detailed report of what had transpired four days earlier, which diverged on several points from his message of the second. In the first dispatch he said he did not expect trouble, but on the eighth he said he had repeatedly heard threats of assassination of Kellogg and the Republican legislators. On the second he doubted Emory's ability, but on the eighth he said Emory had stationed troops at the statehouse at Kellogg's request and that "Owing to these precautions the legislature assembled in the statehouse without any disturbance of the public peace."

There were additional points of interest. In his report of January 8 Sheridan said, "I was not in command of this military department until 9 o'clock at night on the 4th instant, but I fully endorse and am willing to be held responsible for the acts of the military as conservators of the public peace upon that day." [15] The last clause of this statement was hardly a commendable one, and it was in addition totally useless, whether Sheridan meant official or public accountability. He certainly knew he had the official support of Washington—this from Belknap's two bolstering telegrams of January 6. As for public reaction, Sheridan's very presence in New Orleans would automatically give him responsibility in

[14]Sheridan to Belknap, Jan. 2, 1875, file 3400 of 1874, filed with 3579 of 1874, AGO, RG94, NA.
[15]Sheridan to Belknap, Jan. 8, 1875, in *Sen. Exec. Docs.*, 43rd Cong., 2nd Sess., No. 13, p. 27.

the public's eyes for what transpired there. Sheridan was not a man to evoke moderate reaction; on the basis of his earlier sojourn in New Orleans people either idolized him or damned him. His current role would gain him praise in some quarters, which he would naturally enjoy, and denunciation in others, which he had scorned before and would again.

Perhaps the most noteworthy point of all was the inconsistency in Sheridan's message of the second. He doubted there would be any serious trouble, but wanted to assume command anyhow. If no trouble were likely it must have been because Emory's troops controlled the city, which fact would reflect credit on him and thus reduce the necessity for his relief. Had Emory's troops been badly disposed Sheridan would presumably have changed them, yet there is no evidence that he did so. Again, why assume command at 9 P.M. of the fourth after peace had been maintained with Emory in charge? Lack of evidence of change in troop displacements that evening reduced the likelihood that serious troubles were feared.

A partial explanation of Sheridan's attitude may be his recommendation of Mackenzie for Emory's post. Without doubt Mackenzie was a brilliant officer. When the shooting began in 1861 he was still reading his engineering manuals at West Point; when it was over he was in command of a brigade. In 1873 Sheridan sent him on a raid into Mexico to destroy villages where Indians who raided across the border into Texas took refuge. He performed this feat by covering about 160 miles in thirty-two hours.[16] Sheridan may have been simply trying to push Mackenzie, though the latter was by no means a senior officer in 1874. The best explanation of Sheridan's attitude and conduct would seem to be that he made a very hasty and insupportable appraisal of Emory's abilities in the first place and then attempted to achieve additional credit for actions which he admitted were not his own. Emory had in any case maintained the peace in New Orleans since the September rebellion, and that was no mean task.

Sheridan's mere presence in Louisiana was enough to antagonize people, and his blustering missives about assassins, banditti, and military commissions brought him additional derision. The Democratic press raved and shouted; and in Washington the gentlemen on Capitol Hill denounced him as a tyrant, a Stuart despot and a disgrace to the Irish.[17] Grant came in for his share of the abuse as well, and on January 13, 1875, he sent Congress a special message on Louisiana affairs. The first he knew of the events of the fourth, he said, was when he read of them

---

[16]Boatner, *Civil War Dictionary,* 499.
[17]*Cong. Record,* 43rd Cong., 2nd Sess., 287–90, 1143.

in his newspaper the next morning. He agreed that military interference with the civil authorities was "repugnant" to American principles, but he absolved the Army from any "intentional wrong." He also absolved Sheridan of partisan feelings or prejudices, and said the "banditti" messages stemmed from an honest concern with the facts of the situation rather than an intention to propose something illegal.

As his summary showed, Grant was well aware of the problems facing troops in the South, their attitude, and the factors which made the command relationship between Washington and Southern headquarters very difficult: "I repeat that the task assumed by the troops is not a pleasant one to them; that the Army is not composed of lawyers capable of judging at a moment's notice just how far they can go in the maintenance of law and order, and that it was impossible to give specific instructions providing for all possible contingencies that might arise. The troops were bound to act upon the judgment of the commanding officer upon each sudden contingency that arose, or wait instructions which could only reach them after the threatened wrongs had been committed which they were called on to prevent." [18] Grant's words were just as applicable to many a situation the Army had found itself in since 1865 as to the Louisiana proceedings of 1875.

Sherman was principally a spectator to the troublous Louisiana winter of 1874–75, though his position as General-in-Chief ought to have given him a vital role. The reason for his detachment was that Sherman became so aggravated with the political machinations around Washington that in October, 1874, he moved to St. Louis and took the Headquarters of the Army with him, consciously following the precedent set by Winfield Scott after the Mexican War. Scott had quarreled with War Secretary Jefferson Davis and had moved to New York; Sherman's relations with Belknap were not particularly cordial and so he went "home," though he was forced to return in March, 1875, when the scandal over Belknap's dishonest contracts broke. Because many of the Southern disturbances of the seventies involved federal law officers, the Attorney General figured prominently in the decision-making process at Washington. Military questions gradually came to be decided by Grant, Belknap, and Williams (or whoever the incumbent Attorney General happened to be) with Sherman reduced to the function of a clerk. An example occurred in September, 1874. Sherman dutifully transmitted to McDowell a letter from the Attorney General to the Secretary of War, with the explanation that Belknap wished McDowell to distribute his

[18]*Messages and Papers,* VII, 305–14.

troops in accordance with the desires of the Attorney General as much as possible. All Sherman added on his own accord was the request that McDowell please try not to need any reinforcements.[19]

But it was more than just the question of lines of command that bothered Sherman; it was the whole policy. As he wrote to deTrobriand several weeks before that officer became famous at the New Orleans statehouse, the troops scattered around in the South for election day were deployed "at the instance of the [sic] Attorney Genl. Williams, who doubtless supposed them necessary to prevent conflict and even bloodshed. He may have been right, but politically he has brought on a catastrophe which will give infinite trouble. The late elections show how common people regard these things. . . . I confess I looked on increased military display in New Orleans as wrong, and the people generally have jumped clean across the chasm, and we find North and South united against the doctrine of military compulsion, even to secure what we all aim at, the protection of the weak. . . . What the future has in store I don't know, but in my opinion we will have lively times for some years." [20]

The "lively times" went on, built up to a tremendous climax, and died away in a little more than two years after Sherman had written. The North was rapidly becoming disenchanted with the whole idea of reconstruction and found economic expansion, the Indian problem, and agricultural difficulties more interesting subjects. The Louisiana muddle still remained. Grant realized the sentiments of the country, and for some time he had been trying to get Congress to take some action, not only to pacify Louisiana but also in order that the burden of national policy would be shared by both ends of Pennsylvania Avenue. Congress investigated, talked, and proposed regulations; but the only definite action was the Senate's refusal to seat the mulatto Pinckney B. S. Pinchback—and Pinchback represented the Kellogg government, which the Army with Grant's approval had been supporting.

The year 1875 was not as vexing for the Army in Louisiana as 1874 had been. Everyone realized that the Army would prevent a forceful overthrow of the Kellogg regime and that consequently the next opportunity to get rid of the Republicans for good was the 1876 election, when the governorship would again be at stake. Intimidation of Negroes

[19]Sherman to Comstock, May 18, 1874, in Comstock Papers, LC; Lloyd Lewis, *Sherman: Fighting Prophet* (New York, 1932), 615–22; Sherman to McDowell, Sept. 5, 1874, HQA, 24, RG108, NA.
[20]Sherman to deTrobriand, Nov. 13, 1874, in Post, *Trobriand*, 442–43.

and white Unionists by the White League and other organizations continued in Louisiana in preparation for the campaign, as they did in other parts of the South. The Army shifted troops from place to place to aid law officers, depending on which section was most lawless at a particular moment.

The nation was accustomed to autumnal anarchy in the South, but the excitement surrounding the election of 1876 and its succeeding events was more than anyone had expected. The reason, of course, was the long weeks of uncertainty over whether Samuel Tilden or Rutherford B. Hayes would occupy the Executive Mansion. The election season began with the Army taking the now standard precautions at such times. In August orders came down from Washington to hold all available force in readiness to protect everyone in his right to vote, and to help visit "certain, condign, and effectual punishment" on persons who might attempt to infringe voting rights by terror or intimidation. The principal trouble spots were South Carolina and Louisiana, which along with Florida were the only states whose governments were still Republican-controlled. In October General Thomas H. Ruger issued corresponding orders to the troops in South Carolina: detachments were to remain close enough to the polls to afford assistance, but not to approach the polls except on the request of federal officers.[21]

In the Gulf department General Christopher C. Augur had troops at sixty-two locations on voting day; in South Carolina practically every place on the map received a visit from five or ten bluecoats.[22] From that state came a report of how the troops were received at Edgefield Court House on October 21. When they came into view, marching on foot by fours, two or three hundred people rushed to greet them, "rending the air with shouts and hurrahings," swinging their caps over the soldiers' heads, and carrying on with great enthusiam. "I scanned the soldiers' faces narrowly," wrote the observer, "to discover the effect upon them. It is impossible to describe it. They were very much embarrassed; that much was plain. A fixed grin had set upon their faces as though they had been simultaneously smitten with lock-jaw at the reception of that expression. They stared hopelessly and aimlessly at the crowd on either hand, and smiled the same sardonic smile as long as I could see them." [23]

Election day itself passed without disturbance at most locations, though in some cases only because troops were present. Several officers

---

[21]GO 85, AGO, Aug. 17, 1876; Circ., Dept. South, Oct. 28, 1876, file 25 of 1877, filed with 4788 of 1876, AGO, RG94, NA.

[22]*Report of the Sec. of War, 1876–77*, pp. 99–105.

[23]Quoted in *Army and Navy Journal*, XIV (Nov. 4, 1876), 200.

in South Carolina reported that the greatest danger was from Republican Negroes who tried to intimidate other Negroes who desired to vote Democratic. Post-election disturbances in Charleston stemmed from efforts of Republicans to prevent Negro defections. For weeks before the election Republicans had been telling Negroes that if Wade Hampton, the Democratic gubernatorial candidate, were elected, it would mean a return to slavery. When incoming returns showed Hampton winning, panic-stricken Charleston Negroes rioted. Only the presence of troops prevented a more serious outbreak.[24]

The almost inevitable quarrels over who had been elected to state offices prevented passions from subsiding and created more chores for the Army. Louisiana was the most crucial state because of the long-standing tension there. After the election Augur decided to bring scattered detachments in from outlying districts and concentrate his forces in New Orleans where the state returning board was to meet to examine the returns and "count in" the winning candidates. He thus had the better part of three infantry regiments in the city, and he also had naval support in case of need, for U.S.S. *Ossipee* and later U.S.S. *Plymouth* were out in the river.[25]

The returning board announced its decisions in December—Hayes for President along with the Republican S. B. Packard for governor and a Republican majority in the legislature. Kellogg issued the certificates of election, and the legislature prepared to convene in January. But the Democrats felt the returns had really favored their side; and so McEnery, still claiming to have been the legally elected governor in 1872, laid plans for the inauguration of Francis T. Nicholls and a Democratic legislature. On December 30 Augur wired for instructions—what should he do if there were trouble when the legislature organized? Sherman replied that he was to keep the peace in case of riot. The assembling of the legislature began, and at 11:15 A.M. of January 9 Attorney General Alfonso Taft received a frantic message from the federal marshal: armed whites were massing, stores were closing, and bloodshed was imminent within an hour. This brought from War Secretary J. D. Cameron the order for Augur to tell the mobs to "desist on pain of coming in conflict with United States authority sustained by the military power of the Government." The Secretary wanted Augur to report what was going on, "keeping in mind the fact that this order has no reference to

[24]Report of Col. Henry J. Hunt, Nov. 27, 1876, *ibid.*, XIV (Jan. 20, 1877), 373–74.
[25]*Report of the Sec. of War, 1876–77*, pp. 99–105.

a recognition of either of the claimants for the Governorship or either Legislature."

All day the War Department wondered what was happening. At 4:20 P.M. Augur's message relieved the anxiety. The "armed bodies" were a new police force acting under Nicholls' orders. They had possession of the city except for the statehouse, where Packard and his friends were barricaded. "I have declined to interfere on either side until there was a violent breach of the peace," the general reported. "My orders simply authorize me to prevent bloodshed. None has yet occurred." At 10 o'clock the next morning Cameron received more news from a civilian informant: the statehouse was under siege and in one more day Packard's government would disappear because the people would support Nicholls in order to avoid loss of life. The state supreme court appointed by Kellogg had been forcibly ejected, too. Thus another frantic wire to Augur: Grant does not want the legislature molested; "when he has full knowledge of all the facts in the premises he will decide which should be recognized." In late afternoon came Augur's reply that the city was rather quiet now and that everyone had free access to the statehouse. Packard had asked for troops to liberate the supreme court chamber, but Augur refused to furnish them.[26]

There was a lull in events in New Orleans for a few days. In the meantime Congress had met, and the winner of the presidency being now in doubt, some action was imperative. The electoral returns from South Carolina, Louisiana, and Florida were challenged; and Congress finally decided to send investigatory commissions to those states to ascertain which candidate was entitled to their electoral votes. These commissions had to be safeguarded in their work and as much protection as possible furnished to witnesses who testified before them. The bitterness and malice of the 1876–77 winter may perhaps best be measured by the report of one officer on such duty at Monroe, Louisiana. He claimed that "much vaporing is indulged in, and many idle threats are made," but he nevertheless did think there was a possibility of violence. He also reported that the moral influence of the troops, "of which so much has been said and written," was dissipating—this opinion in contrast to what civilians and soldiers had previously been reporting.[27]

[26]A detailed treatment of the political events is in Lonn, *Louisiana*, 442–94. The telegraphic exchanges are in file 4788 of 1876, AGO, RG94, NA.

[27]Cameron to Sherman, Dec. 13, 1876, file 7325 of 1876; report of Capt. Clayton Hale, Dec. 15, and Augur to AAG Div. Missouri, Dec. 18, file 7179 of 1876, all filed with 4788 of 1876, AGO, RG94, NA. Hale's report on moral influence is the only negative one found for the whole twelve-year period.

It was too much to expect affairs in New Orleans to remain quiet for long, however, and on January 14, 1877, Washington warned Augur of reports that Nicholls was despairing of victory without using force and hence to be prepared for any assault on "Fort Packard," as the Democrats called the statehouse. Grant himself sent Augur a message. The administration was reluctant to interfere at the moment, "but it is not proper to sit quietly by and see the State government gradually taken possession of by one of the claimants for gubernatorial honors, by illegal means." He added at least moral support for Packard, however, by the remark that on the basis of the returning board's action, "should there be a necessity for the recognition of either, it must be Mr. Packard." This dispatch got into the papers, where it ought never to have appeared, and of course the city jumped to the conclusion that the Army was to support Packard. Augur was understandably hasty to ask if the dispatch changed his orders, and he received a negative reply: Grant wanted the status quo maintained, at least for the time being. Another message from Augur on the seventeenth said the city was quiet but that there were still fears that the government would recognize Packard. If Washington intended to do so, Augur requested, would it please send him a battery of light artillery first.[28]

The uneasy truce continued, and on the first of March Grant's position finally became clear. He informed both Augur and Packard that public opinion would no longer support the military maintenance of the Louisiana government. Troops would continue to prevent mob violence, "but under the remaining days of his [Grant's] official life they will not be used to establish or to pull down either claimant for control of the state. It is not his purpose to recognize either claimant." Thus Grant was announcing that for three more days he would take no action, and then the problem would become his successor's. That man was Rutherford B. Hayes, and part of the complicated political compromise whereby he came to office was an agreement to withdraw any objection to the inauguration of Democratic governments in Louisiana and South Carolina. In April the resulting orders formally passed down the chain of command—Hayes to War Minister G. W. McCrary, McCrary to Sherman, Sherman to Augur. On the twenty-fourth, "at 12 o'clock meridian," the troops left the Orleans Hotel near the statehouse (they had not actually been in the latter) and went back to camp outside the city. A similar scene had taken place in Columbia, South Carolina, two weeks earlier

[28]Telegraphic exchanges in file 4788 of 1876, AGO, RG94, NA.

where fear of violence had brought troops into the statehouse.[29] Strictly speaking troops were never entirely "removed from the South" because there were always small garrisons at various points—Atlanta, Little Rock, New Orleans, Raleigh—and in the seacoast fortifications. But they were not subsequently called upon for civil duty. The South had been reconstructed as much as it was going to be for the present.

[29]Telegraphic exchanges in file 4788 of 1876, AGO, RG94, NA. For a study of the political details of the 1876–77 winter see C. Vann Woodward, *Reunion and Reaction* (Boston, 1951).

Retrospect

IN historical perspective the role of the Army in the South from 1865 to 1877 was unique. There were no precedents for the task the soldiers faced, and the experience they gained was largely unneeded in the years following Reconstruction. This is not to say that the Army was never again called upon to quell domestic violence or to enforce civil policy of the federal government; the Pullman Strike of 1894 and the relocation of West Coast Japanese during World War II are examples. But in comparison with Reconstruction these and other episodes seem pale. Also, the Army would again undertake military government of conquered territory in the Philippines at the turn of the century and in Germany and Japan following World War II. But the same factors which made Mexico in 1847 a poor precedent for Reconstruction made 1900 and 1945 poor sequels.

The uniqueness of Reconstruction in American history ought not to detract from the lessons it offers concerning the military implementation of civil policy. With the end of the war in 1865 Northern political leaders had to decide the future of the vanquished South. Some felt that complete military domination was the answer. Others disagreed. After a few weeks of uncertainty President Johnson announced his policy in May, 1865, and for the remainder of that year the Army administered "Presidential Reconstruction." Because disagreement among politicians over the South's future increased during 1866, the Army was obliged to administer Southern affairs without benefit of a clear policy to follow. In 1867 Congress succeeded in wresting leadership away from Johnson; from then until the states were readmitted, the Army administered Congress' plan of reconstruction. After readmission the nature of the federal policy again changed. There was no longer a set of steps and procedures for the states to follow; instead the goal was preservation of Republican state governments from violence and protection of the Negro and his white allies, on whose votes the Republican regimes rested.

Because of these frequent changes in federal policy, the legal power and functions of the Army also changed, and one of the most noteworthy aspects of the Army's activity in the South was its ability as an institution to adjust to these changes in policy. It was able to adjust largely because the officers recognized themselves as administering and executing policy rather than originating it or even greatly influencing it. Whatever they might have thought privately of the federal policy, they enforced it, as was their duty. This aloofness was part of the tradition of the regular Army officer, and regulars rather than wartime volunteers (whose appointments were often determined by politics) held most of the Southern commands after 1865.

On the whole military administration of federal policy was creditable to the Army as an institution. This is not to deny that soldiers made avoidable mistakes at times. They antagonized the populace on occasion with interference in situations where such action was unwarranted. Some commanders involved themselves unnecessarily in detailed matters of state and local law. Others were not able to exercise wisely the discretion they possessed, especially with respect to internal Southern politics. The fact that such discretion existed complicates the evaluation of the Army's performance but facilitates the study of comparative statesmanship. On such a scale men like Meade and Schofield must certainly rate higher than Sheridan and Pope.

Many aspects of the Army's role render fruitless an effort to describe military administration of federal policy as a success or a failure. Certainly there was no uniformity of opinion on this point at the time: those who thought federal policy too harsh complained of allegedly extreme enforcement of it; those who thought it too lenient would have preferred more trials by military commission and more removals of civil officials. Protection of Negroes from outrages by Southerners was one of the chief objects of Reconstruction, and there can be little doubt that some form of protection was needed. On this count Reconstruction was a failure, as the dismal history of Southern race relations has demonstrated. Yet it would seem that the failures of Reconstruction are not so much failures on the part of the military administrators as they are failures of the policy itself. During the first years many people in the North looked upon the presence of troops in the South as the means whereby that section would undergo tremendous political, social, and psychological transformations. But as General Sherman wrote to his brother in September, 1865: "No matter what change we may desire in the feelings and thoughts of people South, we cannot accomplish it by force. Nor can we afford to maintain there an army large enough to hold them in subjugation. All we can, or should attempt is to give them rope, to develop in an honest way if possible, preserving in reserve enough military power to check any excesses if they attempt any." [1] During the 1870's people gradually came to realize that the application of military force was a doubtful method of working transformations in a people, no matter how desirable the changes might have been. In the end Sherman proved a bit more astute than the politicians. He and some of his Army colleagues had realized it all along.

[1]Sherman to John, Sept. 21, 1865, in Thorndike (ed.), *Sherman Letters*, 256.

Appendix A

The Structure of Army Commands

The table below indicates, in as concise a compass as possible, the principal changes in Southern commands during Reconstruction. In the interest of clarity, generals who exercised commands for a period of one or two weeks in the temporary absence of the regular commander are omitted. For the same reason no attempt has been made to trace the period before June 27, 1865, when individual states were often split among several commands, or to trace "districts" and "subdistricts" embracing less than a single state, or to trace the commands subsidiary to the five districts established by the Reconstruction Act. The dates indicated at the left-hand margin are those when significant rearrangements occurred; changes at other times are indicated at the appropriate point in the table. In cases where the title of a command does not readily indicate the states involved, this information is given in brackets. All commands not involving a Southern state are omitted.

27 June 1865

Div. of the Atlantic—MEADE
    Dept. of North Carolina—RUGER
    Dept. of South Carolina—GILLMORE (SICKLES after Nov.)
    Dept. of Virginia—TERRY

Div. of the Gulf—SHERIDAN
    Dept. of Florida—FOSTER
    Dept. of Louisiana—CANBY
    Dept. of Mississippi (till 7 Oct.)—SLOCUM (OSTERHAUS, Sept.–Nov.), then WOOD
    Dept. of Texas—WRIGHT

Div. of the Mississippi—SHERMAN
    Dept. of Arkansas—REYNOLDS

Div. of the Tennessee—THOMAS
    Dept. of Alabama—WOODS
    Dept of Georgia—STEEDMAN (BRANNAN after Dec.)

Dept. of the Tennessee—STONEMAN
Dept. of Mississippi (after 7 Oct.)—OSTERHAUS (WOOD after Nov.)

19 May 1866

Div. of the Atlantic—MEADE
　　Dept. of the Carolinas—SICKLES
　　Dept. of Virginia—TERRY

Div. of the Gulf—SHERIDAN
　　Dept. of Florida—FOSTER
　　Dept. of Louisiana—CANBY (BAIRD after 28 May)
　　Dept. of Texas—WRIGHT

Div. of the Mississippi—SHERMAN
　　Dept. of Arkansas—REYNOLDS

Div. of the Tennessee—THOMAS
　　Dept. of the South [Ga., Ala.]—WOODS
　　Dept. of Tennessee (Dept. of the Cumberland after 5 June)—STONEMAN
　　Dept. of Mississippi—WOOD

6 August 1866

Div. of the Missouri—SHERMAN
　　Dept. of Arkansas—ORD

Dept. of the Gulf [Fla., La., Tex.]—SHERIDAN
Dept. of the Potomac [Va.]—SCHOFIELD
Dept. of the South [N.C., S.C]—SICKLES (ROBINSON after 12 Nov.)
Dept. of the Tennessee [Tenn., Ga., Ala., Miss.]—THOMAS

12 March 1867

Dept. of the Cumberland [Tenn.]—THOMAS
First Military District [Va.]—SCHOFIELD (STONEMAN after June 1868)
Second Military District [N.C., S.C.]—SICKLES (CANBY after 5 Sept. 1867)
Third Military District [Ga., Ala., Fla.]—POPE (MEADE after 28 Dec. 1867)
Fourth Military District [Ark., Miss.]—ORD (GILLEM, Dec. 1867-June 1868;
　　MCDOWELL, June-July 1868)
Fifth Military District [La., Tex.]—SHERIDAN (MOWER, Sept.-Nov. 1867;
　　HANCOCK, Nov. 1867-Mar. 1868; then BUCHANAN)

28 July 1868

Dept. of the Cumberland [Tenn.]—THOMAS
Dept. of the South [Ga., Ala., Fla., S.C., N.C.]—MEADE (RUGER after 5
　　Mar. 1869)
Dept. of Louisiana [Ark., La.]—BUCHANAN (ROUSSEAU, Sept. 1868-Jan.
　　1869, then BUCHANAN)
First Military District [Va.]—STONEMAN
Fourth Military District [Miss.]—GILLEM
Fifth Military District [Tex.]—REYNOLDS (CANBY, Dec. 1868-Apr. 1869,
　　then REYNOLDS)

16 March 1869

Div. of the Atlantic—MEADE
  First Military District [Va.]—STONEMAN (WEBB in Apr. 1869, then
  CANBY)

Div. of the South—HALLECK
  Dept. of the Cumberland [Tenn.]—THOMAS (COOKE after 15 May)
  Dept. of Louisiana [Ark., La.]—MOWER
  Dept. of the South [Ga., Ala., Fla., S.C., N.C.]—RUGER (TERRY after 31
  May 1869)
  Fourth Military District [Miss.]—AMES

Fifth Military District [Tex.]—REYNOLDS

24 December 1869

Div. of the Atlantic—MEADE
  First Military District (Dept. of Virginia after 29 Jan. 1870)—CANBY

Div. of the South—HALLECK
  Dept. of the Cumberland [Tenn.]—COOKE
  Dept. of Louisiana [Ark., La.]—MOWER (SMITH after Jan. 1870)
  Dept. of the South [Ala., Fla., S.C., N.C. (till Jan. 1870)]—TERRY
  Fourth Military District [Miss.]—AMES

Fifth Military District [Tex.]—REYNOLDS
District of Georgia—TERRY

26 February 1870

Div. of the Atlantic—MEADE
  Dept. of Virginia [Va.; and N.C. after Jan. 1870]—CANBY

Div. of the South—HALLECK
  Dept. of the Cumberland [Tenn., Miss.]—COOKE
  Dept. of Louisiana [Ark., La.]—MOWER
  Dept. of the South [Ala., Fla., S.C.]—TERRY

Fifth Military District [Tex.]—REYNOLDS
District of Georgia—TERRY

31 March 1870

Div. of the Atlantic—MEADE
  Dept. of Virginia (merged into Dept. of the East after 30 Apr.) [Va.,
  N.C.]—CANBY

Div. of the South—HALLECK
  Dept. of the Cumberland [Tenn., Miss.]—COOKE
  Dept. of the South [Ala., Fla., S.C.]—TERRY
  Dept. of Texas [La., Tex.]—REYNOLDS

Div. of the Missouri—SHERIDAN
  Dept. of the Missouri [Ark.]—SCHOFIELD (POPE after 15 Apr.)

District of Georgia—TERRY

4 May 1870

Div. of the Atlantic—MEADE
Dept. of the East [Va., N.C.]—MCDOWELL

Div. of the South—HALLECK
Dept. of the South [Tenn., Miss., S.C., Ala., Fla.; Ga. (after May
1871)]—TERRY
Dept. of Texas [La., Tex.]—REYNOLDS

Div. of the Missouri—SHERIDAN
Dept. of the Missouri [Ark.]—POPE

District of Georgia (till May 1871)—TERRY

1 November 1871

Div. of the Atlantic—MEADE
Dept. of the East [Va.]—MCDOWELL

Div. of the South—HALLECK
Dept. of the Gulf [Ark., La., Miss.]—EMORY
Dept. of the South [Tenn., Ga., Ala., Fla., S.C., N.C.]—TERRY

Div. of the Missouri—SHERIDAN
Dept. of Texas—AUGUR

15 January 1872

Div. of the Atlantic—MEADE
Dept. of the East [Va.]—MCDOWELL

Div. of the Missouri—SHERIDAN
Dept. of Texas—AUGUR

Dept. of the Gulf [Ark., La., Miss.]—EMORY
Dept. of the South [Tenn., Ga., Ala., Fla., S.C., N.C.]—TERRY

25 November 1872

Div. of the Atlantic (subsidiary depts. abolished 31 Oct. 1873)—HANCOCK
Dept. of the East [Va.]—HANCOCK

Div. of the Missouri—SHERIDAN
Dept. of Texas—AUGUR

Div. of the South—MCDOWELL
Dept. of the South [Tenn., Ga., Ala., Fla., S.C., N.C.]—MCDOWELL
Dept. of the Gulf [Ark., La., Miss.]—EMORY

4 January 1875

Div. of the Atlantic [Va.]—HANCOCK

Div. of the Missouri—SHERIDAN
Dept. of the Gulf [Ark., La., Miss.]—EMORY (AUGUR after Mar. 1875)
Dept. of Texas—AUGUR (ORD after Apr. 1875)

Div. of the South—MCDOWELL
Dept. of the South [Tenn., Ga., Ala., Fla., S.C., N.C.]—MCDOWELL

26 June 1876

Div. of the Atlantic [Va.]—HANCOCK
    Dept. of the South [N.C., S.C., Ga., Fla., and part of Tenn.]—PENNY-PACKER (RUGER after Sept.)

Div. of the Missouri—SHERIDAN
    Dept. of the Gulf [Ark., La., Miss., Ala., and part of Tenn.]—AUGUR
    Dept. of Texas—ORD

Appendix B

Numbers and Locations of Troops

It is difficult to obtain exact and sufficiently detailed information on the number and location of troops in the South during Reconstruction because the sources from which the data must be compiled are not always complete or consistent in the information they offer. In 1867 the Adjutant General began including in his annual reports detailed charts showing exact figures and locations. Before that time the manuscript departmental returns must be used, some of which are incomplete and others in poor physical condition. These returns did not always state the precise locations of troops (although the form used called for that information), and the figures for Mississippi, Tennessee, and Texas in June, 1865, and for Texas in October, 1866, could not be ascertained. In the accompanying table three types of information are given. First, the total number of troops in each state at the time indicated. Second, in parentheses following the quantity, the number of posts or garrisons in the state, where this information is known. And third, the ratio of colored regiments to white, the first figure shown being the number of colored, the second the number of white regiments. Beginning with 1870 this data is omitted because after that time the only colored troops in the South were in the Texas frontier posts.

State	June 1865	Sept. 1865	Jan. 1866	Apr. 1866	Oct. 1866	Oct. 1867
Ala.	35,100 8/39	18,057 7/13	7,832 6/6	1,086 ?	863 1/1½	1,022 (6) —
Ark.	26,376 6/24	11,139 9/11	9,280 6/5	4,082 3/2	1,398 0/2	1,548 (11) —
Fla.	3,235 2/4	8,703 6/4	2,813 3/1½	1,524 1/1½	1,279 0/1½	1,067 (9) —
Ga.	9,256 1/15	15,779 4/21	2,764 1/3½	520 0/1	850 0/1	1,185 (6) —
La.	25,012 15/17	23,747 16/8	9,772 9/5	5,483 5/3	5,124 8/2	1,958 (4) 1/2
Miss.	?	13,873 10/5	9,119 11/1	3,352 3/1	570 1/1½	2,073 (15) —
N.C.	43,948 10/48	8,788 6/5	2,209 1/2	2,020 1/2	1,226 ½/1½	1,203 (11) ½/½
S.C.	14,038 7/12	9,603 5/8	7,408 ?	4,580 1/5	1,506 ½/1½	1,508 (12) ½/1½
Tenn.	?	16,065 15/2	7,345 6/1	1,070 0/1½	1,837 1½/1½	998 (7) —
Tex.	?	45,424 29/37	25,085 17/17	12,105 9/10	?	5,033 (37) 2/5
Va.	45,312 0/56	15,610 0/22	3,923 0/4	2,921 0/3	3,026 0/3	2,522 (12) —
TOTAL	202,277	186,788	87,550	38,743	17,679	20,117

State	Oct. 1868	Oct. 1869	Oct. 1870	Oct. 1871	Oct. 1872	Oct. 1874	Oct. 1876
Ala.	588 (3)	798 (5)	631 (5)	205 (2)	246 (3)	430 (8)	202 (4)
Ark.	1,562 (9)	605 (2)	124 (2)	64 (1)	59 (1)	126 (1)	102 (1)
Fla.	1,131 (6)	354 (3)	317 (3)	453 (4)	—	187 (3)	300 (3)
Ga.	983 (3)	755 (5)	875 (5)	580 (2)	360 (2)	98 (2)	296 (2)
La.	1,944 (12) 1/2	953 (6) 1/1	598 (5)	612 (2)	427 (2)	1,164 (8)	529 (9)
Miss.	1,851 (9)	978 (7)	198 (1)	275 (3)	345 (5)	46 (1)	308 (5)
N.C.	939 (3) 1/0	366 (4)	277 (3)	313 (5)	395 (6)	142 (3)	115 (2)
S.C.	881 (3)	417 (2)	427 (2)	1,030 (8)	965 (8)	649 (10)	683 (10)
Tenn.	370 (5)	311 (3)	430 (3)	338 (3)	321 (3)	197 (3)	47 (1)
Tex.	5,675 (31) 2/6	4,612 (27) 2/5	4,740 (17) 3/4	3,853 (15)	3,944 (15)	4,271 (14)	3,042 (14)
Va.	1,733 (12)	1,088 (7)	433 (1)	315 (1)	306 (1)	391 (1)	387 (1)
TOTAL	17,657	11,237	9,050	8,038	7,368	7,701	6,011

List of References

I. MANUSCRIPT COLLECTIONS

Records of the Headquarters of the Army, Record Group 108, National Archives

Records of the Office of the Adjutant General, Record Group 94, National Archives

Records of the Office of the Secretary of War, Record Group 107, National Archives

Records of United States Army Commands, Record Group 98, National Archives

Orville E. Babcock MSS, Newberry Library

Salmon P. Chase MSS, Historical Society of Pennsylvania

Cyrus B. Comstock MSS, Library of Congress

Daniel O. Drennan MSS, Library of Congress

Edward S. Godfrey MSS, Library of Congress

Ulysses S. Grant MSS, Library of Congress

Joseph R. Hawley MSS, Library of Congress

Samuel P. Heintzelman MSS, Library of Congress

Andrew Johnson MSS, Library of Congress (microfilm)

George G. Meade MSS, Historical Society of Pennsylvania

Horace Porter MSS, Library of Congress

John M. Schofield MSS, Library of Congress

Philip H. Sheridan MSS, Library of Congress

William T. Sherman MSS, Library of Congress

Daniel E. Sickles MSS, Library of Congress

Edwin M. Stanton MSS, Library of Congress

Lyman Trumbull MSS, Library of Congress

Henry Wilson MSS, Library of Congress

II. PRINTED OFFICIAL MATERIALS

Eifort, et al. vs. Bevins, 1 Bush (Ky.) 460 (1867)

In re Egan, Fed. Cas. No. 4303 (1866)

Georgia vs. Stanton, 6 Wallace 50 (1866)

Jones vs. Commonwealth of Kentucky, 1 Bush (Ky.) 34 (1866)

Ex Parte McCardle, 7 Wallace 506 (1868)

Ex Parte Milligan, 4 Wallace 2 (1866)

Mississippi vs. Johnson, 4 Wallace 475 (1867)

Missouri vs. Rogers, 37 Missouri 367 (1867)

Mitchell vs. Harmony, 13 Howard 428 (1852)

Riggs vs. State of Tennessee, 3 Coldwell (Tenn.) 85 (1866)

Taylor vs. Jenkins, 24 Arkansas 337 (1866)

U.S. vs. Commandant of Fort Delaware, Fed. Cas. No. 14842 (1866)

Walker vs. Crane, Fed. Cas. No. 17067 (1865)

Opinions of the Attorneys General. Vols. XI–XII, Washington, 1865–68.

United States Statutes at Large. Vols. XII–XX, Boston and Washington, 1863–79.

Congressional Globe. 39th–42nd Congresses, 36 vols., Washington, 1866–73.

Congressional Record. 43rd–44th Congresses, 5 vols., Washington, 1873–77.

39 Cong., 1 Sess.

> *House Exec. Doc. 70* (circulars of Freedmen's Bureau).
>
> *House Report 30* (Joint Committee on Reconstruction).
>
> *Sen. Exec. Doc. 2* (documents on condition of the South, 1865).
>
> *Sen. Exec. Doc. 26* (correspondence with provisional governors, 1865).

39 Cong., 2 Sess.

> *House Exec. Doc. 68* (correspondence on New Orleans Riot and military investigation).
>
> *House Report 16* (investigation of New Orleans Riot).
>
> *House Report 23* (Keyes murder trial).
>
> *Sen. Exec. Doc. 6* (Black Codes; reports by Freedmen's Bureau).

40 Cong., 1 Sess.

> *Sen. Exec. Doc. 14* (correspondence with district commanders, 1867).

40 Cong., 2 Sess.

> *House Exec. Doc. 57* (removal of Stanton and Sheridan).
>
> *House Exec. Doc. 149* (Johnson-Grant correspondence, 1868).
>
> *House Exec. Doc. 342* (orders and correspondence of district commanders, 1867–68).

40 Cong., 3 Sess.

> *House Misc. Doc. 52* (testimony on Georgia, 1868–69).
>
> *House Misc. Doc. 53* (testimony on Mississippi, 1868).

41 Cong., 2 Sess.

> *House Exec. Doc. 288* (testimony on Georgia, 1869).
>
> *Sen. Exec. Doc. 13* (elections in Texas, Mississippi, and Virginia, 1869–70).
>
> *Sen. Exec. Doc. 41* (military correspondence on Georgia, 1869–70).
>
> *Sen. Report 58* (organization of Georgia legislature, 1869–70).

42 Cong., 2 Sess.

> *House Report 22* (Ku-Klux Klan).

43 Cong., 1 Sess.

> *House Exec. Doc. 229* (Brooks-Baxter War, 1874).

43 Cong., 2 Sess.

> *Sen. Exec. Doc. 13* (correspondence on Louisiana, 1874).
>
> *Sen. Exec. Doc. 17* (correspondence on Louisiana, 1874).
>
> *Sen. Exec. Doc. 23* (statistics on cotton seizures).

Eleventh Legislature of Texas, 1866, *Journal of the House of Representatives.*

Richardson, James D. (comp.). *A Compilation of the Messages and Papers of the Presidents, 1789–1897.* 11 vols. Washington, 1896–1901.

U.S. War Dept. *Report of the Secretary of War.* Washington, annually, 1865–77.

The War of the Rebellion: A Compilation of the Official Records of the Union and Confederate Armies. 73 vols., 128 parts. Washington, 1880–1901.

III. NEWSPAPERS AND JOURNALS

Army and Navy Journal
Atlanta *Constitution*
Batesville *North Arkansas Times*
Early County (Ga.) *News*
Eufaula (Ala.) *News*
Galveston *Daily News*
Huntsville (Ala.) *Advocate*
Lynchburg *Daily Virginian*
Macon (Ga.) *Daily Telegraph*
Meridian (Miss.) *Chronicle*
Milledgeville (Ga.) *Federal Union*
Montgomery (Ala.) *Daily Mail*
Nashville *Daily Dispatch*
Nashville *Republican Banner*
Natchez *Daily Democrat*
The Nation
New York *Times*
New York *Tribune*
Richmond *Daily Dispatch*
Shreveport *Times*

IV. OTHER MATERIAL

Andrews, Sidney. *The South Since the War.* Boston, 1866.

Avary, Myrta L. *Dixie After the War.* New York, 1906.

Badeau, Adam. *Grant in Peace from Appomattox to Mount Macgregor.* Hartford, 1887.

Beale, Howard K. *The Critical Year.* 2nd ed. New York, 1958.

———— (ed.). *The Diary of Gideon Welles.* 3 vols. New York, 1960.

Bentley, George. *A History of the Freedmen's Bureau.* Philadelphia, 1955.

Blaine, James G. *Twenty Years of Congress.* 2 vols. Norwich, 1886.

Boatner, Mark Mayo. *The Civil War Dictionary.* New York, 1959.

The Civil Record of Major General Winfield Scott Hancock During His Administration in Louisiana and Texas. N.p., 1880.

Coleman, Charles H. *The Election of 1868.* New York, 1933.

Davis, William Watson. *The Civil War and Reconstruction in Florida.* New York, 1913.

Dawson, George F. *The Life and Services of General John A. Logan as Soldier and Statesman.* Chicago, 1887.

Dunning, William A. *Essays on the Civil War and Reconstruction and Related Topics.* New York, 1898.

————. *Reconstruction, Political and Economic, 1865–1877.* New York, 1907.

Eckenrode, Hamilton James. *The Political History of Virginia During the Reconstruction.* Baltimore, 1904.

Elliott, Claude. *Leathercoat: The Life History of a Texas Patriot.* San Antonio, 1938.

Fairman, Charles. *The Law of Martial Rule.* Chicago, 1930.

Ficklen, John R. *History of Reconstruction in Louisiana Through 1868.* Baltimore, 1910.

Fleming, Walter L. *The Civil War and Reconstruction in Alabama.* New York, 1905.

———— (ed.). *Documentary History of Reconstruction.* 2 vols. Cleveland, 1906.

Franklin, John Hope. *Reconstruction: After the Civil War.* Chicago, 1961.

Garner, James W. *Reconstruction in Mississippi.* New York, 1901.

Gorham, Edwin C. *Life and Public Services of Edwin M. Stanton.* 2 vols. New York, 1899.

Hamilton, John G. deRoulhac. *Reconstruction in North Carolina.* New York, 1914.

Hancock, Cornelia. *Reminiscences of Winfield Scott Hancock.* New York, 1887.

Heitman, Francis B. *Historical Register and Dictionary of the United States Army.* 2 vols. Washington, 1903.

Hesseltine, William B. *Ulysses S. Grant, Politician.* New York, 1935.

Heyman, Max. *Prudent Soldier: A Biography of Major General E. R. S. Canby, 1817–1873.* Glendale, 1959.

Howe, Mark A. DeWolfe (ed.). *Home Letters of General Sherman.* New York, 1909.

Hunt, Gaillard. "The President's Defense," *Century Magazine,* LXXXV (January, 1913), 422–34.

Hyman, Harold M. "Johnson, Stanton, and Grant: A Reconsideration of the Army's Role in the Events Leading to Impeachment," *American Historical Review,* LXVI (October, 1960), 85–100.

Johnson, Allen, *et al.* (eds.). *Dictionary of American Biography.* 22 vols. New York, 1928–1958.

Kendrick, Benjamin B. *The Journal of the Joint Committee of Fifteen on Reconstruction.* New York, 1914.

Lewis, Lloyd. *Sherman: Fighting Prophet.* New York, 1932.

Lonn, Ella. *Reconstruction in Louisiana After 1868.* New York, 1918.

McKitrick, Eric L. *Andrew Johnson and Reconstruction.* Chicago, 1960.

Merington, Marguerite (ed.). *The Custer Story.* New York, 1950.

Monaghan, Jay. *Custer: The Life of General George Armstrong Custer.* Boston, 1959.

The National Cyclopaedia of American Biography. 55 vols. New York, 1898–1960.

O'Connor, Richard. *Sheridan the Inevitable.* Indianapolis, 1953.

"Original Letters of General Grant," *Colorado Magazine,* XIV (March, 1937), 66–67.

Patton, James W. *Unionism and Reconstruction in Tennessee, 1860–69.* Chapel Hill, 1934.

Post, Marie C. *Memoirs of Count Regis deTrobriand.* New York, 1906.

Pratt, Fletcher. *Stanton, Lincoln's Secretary of War.* New York, 1953.

Ramsdell, Charles W. *Reconstruction in Texas.* New York, 1910.

Randall, James G. *Constitutional Problems Under Lincoln.* Urbana, 1951.

Rankin, Robert S. *When Civil Law Fails.* Durham, 1939.

Reynolds, John S. *Reconstruction in South Carolina.* Columbia, 1905.

Russ, William A. "Was There Danger of a Second Civil War During Reconstruction?" *Mississippi Valley Historical Review,* XXV (June, 1938), 39–58.

Schofield, John M. *Forty-Six Years in the Army.* New York, 1897.

Shanks, William F. G. *Personal Recollections of Distinguished Generals.* New York, 1866.

Sheridan, Philip H. *Personal Memoirs of Philip H. Sheridan.* 2 vols. New York, 1888.

Sherman, William T. *Memoirs of General William T. Sherman.* 2 vols. 2nd ed. New York, 1887.

Simkins, Francis B. and Robert H. Woody. *South Carolina During Reconstruction.* Chapel Hill, 1932.

Singletary, Otis A. *The Negro Militia During Reconstruction.* Austin, 1957.

Sioussat, St. George L. (ed.). "Notes of Col. W. G. Moore, Private Secretary to President Johnson, 1865–68," *American Historical Review,* XIX (October, 1913), 98–132.

Staples, Thomas S. *Reconstruction in Arkansas, 1862–1874.* New York, 1923.

Thian, Raphael P. (comp.). *Notes Illustrating the Military Geography of the United States.* Washington, 1881.

Thomas, Benjamin P. and Harold M. Hyman. *Stanton: The Life and Times of Lincoln's Secretary of War.* New York, 1962.

Thompson, C. Mildred. *Reconstruction in Georgia.* New York, 1915.

Thorndike, Rachel S. (ed.). *The Sherman Letters.* New York, 1894.

Townsend, Edward D. *Anecdotes of the Civil War in the United States.* New York, 1884.

Truman, Benjamin C. "Anecdotes of Andrew Johnson," *Century Magazine,* LXXXV (January, 1913), 435–40.

Woodward, C. Vann. *Reunion and Reaction.* Boston, 1951.

Index

Ableman vs. Booth, 79, 99

Ackerman, A. T., 219. *See also* Attorney General

Alabama: rebel government of, 12; military commissions in, 35, 39, 40; cotton collection in, 39–41; conduct of troops in, 49; colored troops in, 52; churches in, 57–59; Pope and election districts in, 166–67; 1867 election, 168; constitution of, 184, 185; and Fourth Reconstruction Act, 185; readmitted, 186; aid to civil officials in, 218; Klan in, 221; 1870 elections, 232–33; 1872 and 1874 elections, 233*n*. *See also* Commands; Woods

Aldrich, A. P., 162

Alexandria, Va., 198

Americus, Ga., 55

Ames, Adelbert: assigned to Fourth Military District, 190; appointed Governor of Mississippi, 195; Republican partisanship of, 195–97; and levee commissioners, 196; complaints about, 196–97; makes removals, 196; political aspirations of, 197; own estimate of motives, 197; becomes Senator, 197

Amnesty Proclamation of 1865, p. 33

Anderson, T. M., 194–95

Andrews, C. C., 54

Appointment to office: by provisional governors, 29; under Reconstruction Acts, 118, 138; in Virginia, 197; people reluctant to accept, 197

Arkansas: appointment of civil officials in, 29; fear of Negro violence, 29; military commissions in, 36, 119, 146; Freedmen's Bureau in, 47, 93–94; newspapers in, 55, 151–52 and *n;* conditions in, 61, 91–92, 110; need for troops in, 62; harshness of military rule in, 75; colored troops in, 96; and Fourteenth Amendment, 101–102; horse thieves in, 119; Ord and legislature of, 139, 151; constitution of, 185–86; Gillem in, 185–86, 195, 209; readmitted, 186; misconduct of militia in, 217; election disputes in, 236–38. *See also* Commands; Ord; Reynolds

Armstrong, W. B., 89

Army: reorganization at end of war, 7–8; organization and structure of, 1866, pp. 65–66; alleged "law" on control of, 182*n;* size reduced (1869), 208; general evaluation of role, 252–54. *See also* Commands; Regiments; Troops

Army Appropriations Act of 1867: provisions on high command of Army, 111–12, 111*n*, 134*n*, 164; provisions on militia, 112; Stanton and, 154; Johnson did not violate, 164

Army and Navy Journal: on reorganization of Army, 65; on Johnson and Congress, 73; on Stanton's suspension, 156; on Grant, 157; on removal of civil officers, 176

Articles of War of 1806, p. 7

Ashburn, G. W., 170–72 and *n*

Asheville, N.C., 220

Athens, Ga., 149

Attorney General: and aid to federal officials, 219; role in employment of military force, 245–46. *See also* Ackerman; Hoar; Speed; Stanbery; Williams

Augur, Christopher C.: and 1875 Mississippi election, 231; in Louisiana (1876–77), 247–50 *passim*

Augusta, Ga., 9

Ayres, Romeyn B., 234

Baird, Absalom, 84–88 *passim*

Bartholomew, W. H., 237

Dowell for Fourth District, 174;
and 1868 presidential nominations,
174, 180 and *n,* 188–90; embarrasses Hancock, 177–78; duplicity
of, 178, 180; quarrels with Johnson, 179–80 and *n;* suggests ignoring
Stanton's orders, 179 and *n;* political
ability of, 189–90; inaugurated, 190;
favors Sheridan in promotions, 190;
and Georgia, 200, 202, 205, 207;
effect of inauguration, 208; and
Klan, 222, 224–25; and use of
troops at elections, 229–30, 231,
234–35; and Arkansas violence, 237–
38; and Louisiana government, 239–
50 *passim;* on difficulty of Army's
tasks, 245
Greenville, La., 96
Griffin, Charles: relations with Throckmorton, 90, 140; and funeral controversy, 97–98; on arrest of soldiers,
100; requests opinion on registration, 128; and juries, 147–48; removes mayor of Galveston, 153
Guerrillas: punished by military commission, 35

Habeas corpus: restoration of refused
by Johnson, 38; Army refuses to
recognize, 40–41; privilege restored,
77–78, 81–82; privilege restricted in
First Reconstruction Act, 109; suspended in South Carolina, 222, 224–
25
Habeas Corpus Act of 1863: provisions, 7, 66; damage suits under,
57; amended, 1866, p. 66–67. *See also*
Damage suits
Halleck, Henry W.: regulates marriages, 9; on property disputes, 34;
removes Negro troops, 51; seniority
of, 65; not promoted to lieutenant
general, 190; commands Division of
the South, 190; and aid to civil authorities, 217, 228–29; on Klan, 221
Hampton, Wade, 248
Hancock, Winfield Scott: seniority of,
65; political views of, 116, 157, 177;
suggested for Fifth District, 157;
appointed to Fifth District, 162, 163;
on military government, 163; actions
legal under Reconstruction Acts,
175–76; Congress attacks, 175 and
n; Radicals oppose, 175; removal of,

175, 177–78; and registration, 176;
and removals, 176–78; and New Orleans election, 177; embarrassed by
Grant, 177–78; requests relief, 177–
78; alleged leniency of, 178; commands Division of Atlantic, 181–
82; as presidential candidate, 188–
89
Hatch, John P.: Chase on, 14; accused
of racial prejudice, 46
Haviland, J. E., 153
Hawley, Joseph R., 10, 45
Hayden, Julius, 184
Hayes, Rutherford B., 247, 248, 250
Hazen, William B., 13
Heintzelman, Samuel P., 98–100
Herron, Francis, 42
Hoar, Ebenezer Rockwood, 204. *See
also* Attorney General
Hodgson, Benjamin, 226–27, 228
Holden, William W., 37
Holt, Joseph, 81. *See also* Judge Advocate General
Hooker, Joseph, 65
Hotchkiss, Giles, 110
Howard, Oliver Otis: in property dispute, 33; heads Freedmen's Bureau,
41; seniority of, 65
Humphreys, Benjamin, 195
Hurlbut, Stephen, 29

Impeachment: specific cause of, 164;
power over commanding generals
not involved in, 164; voted, 181;
public reaction to, 181; conviction
fails, 182
In re Egan, 82
Infantry: uselessness of, 191, 223–24

Jackson, Joseph L., 37
Jackson, Miss., 193–94
Jacksonport, Ark., 91–92
Jefferson, Tex., 192
Jenkins, Charles J.: conflict with Pope,
138–39; and newspaper order, 149;
and opposition to military government, 152; removed by Meade, 173;
mentioned, 71
Johnson, Andrew: relations with Congress, 8, 73, 164; supports Thomas,
11–12; and rebel governments, 12;
announces policy, 13, 16, 252; advised by Chase, 14–15; realizes need
for military supervision, 15–16; on